Praise for *Request for Proposal*

Bud Porter-Roth is an expert in the field of preparing RFPs, and we could not completed our project without his skill and knowledge. This book is a clear guide to an otherwise complex and difficult process. If you can't hire Bud Porter-Roth to write your RFP, then you should buy this book.

> **—Lori Deibel,**
> **Manager, Library Services**

This book is priceless. It is a must for a novice writing an RFP.

> **—Doris Lopez,**
> **Senior Systems Engineer, O-Cedar Brands, Inc.**

This book brings a structure to a process that is too often unstructured. There have been no standards (outside of government) that I know of that apply to RFP preparation. I also believe that vendors (sellers) would welcome a more uniform and consistent style of RFP.

> **—Frank Tillman,**
> **API Systems Group**

This book provides overall coverage on a subject that deserves some real guidance. I like very much the sentiment concerning the RFP as the basis for a team and the idea that the RFP is the beginning, not the end. His emphasis on the need for clarity in the RFP and for measurable requirements needs to be heard and understood by many within the target audience. He takes an excellent position on "Why Write an RFP."

> **—Patricia Oberndorf,**
> **SEI**

This book is well written and insightful. It provides good information on what makes a good requirement, how proposals are evaluated, and what precautions to take to prevent early elimination.

> **—Linda Fernandez**

Just a note to tell you thank you for providing some tips on how to structure an RFP. I work for a small company who does not have a specific template for this purpose and found your guidance a very useful starting point.

> **—Dan Salo**

Bud Porter-Roth's book RFP: A Guide to Effective Development *is an invaluable guide to managing the RFP process. As the purpose of the RFP is to satisfy business and organizational requirements through a formal purchase process, Mr. Porter-Roth stresses that a properly formed and managed process will indeed lead to discerning those vendors with approaches that portend business benefit. Mr. Porter-Roth dissects the activities associated with the purchase of complex technical solutions and alerts the reader to potential pitfalls incumbent in the RFP process. Mr. Porter-Roth's book also contains many tips for the reader. He emphasizes "marketing" potential bidders to ensure participation. He clearly explains evaluation and includes many good suggestions for ensuring consistency and minimizing contention. I recommend Mr. Porter-Roth's book for any organization embarking on an RFP.*

—Tom Dale, CDIA, MIT
Dale & Associates

Perhaps the best aspect of this book is that the author breaks the RFP processes down into distinct manageable chapters, each of which are important and complete in their own way, and gives clear descriptions to illustrate how these procedures are to be developed to maximize their impact in an effective procurement process. This book would be a useful guide for both the buyer and the supplier in understanding the entire business process—both preparing the RFP and responding to the RFP.

—Basil Manns,
Senior Physical Scientist, Library of Congress

Request for Proposal

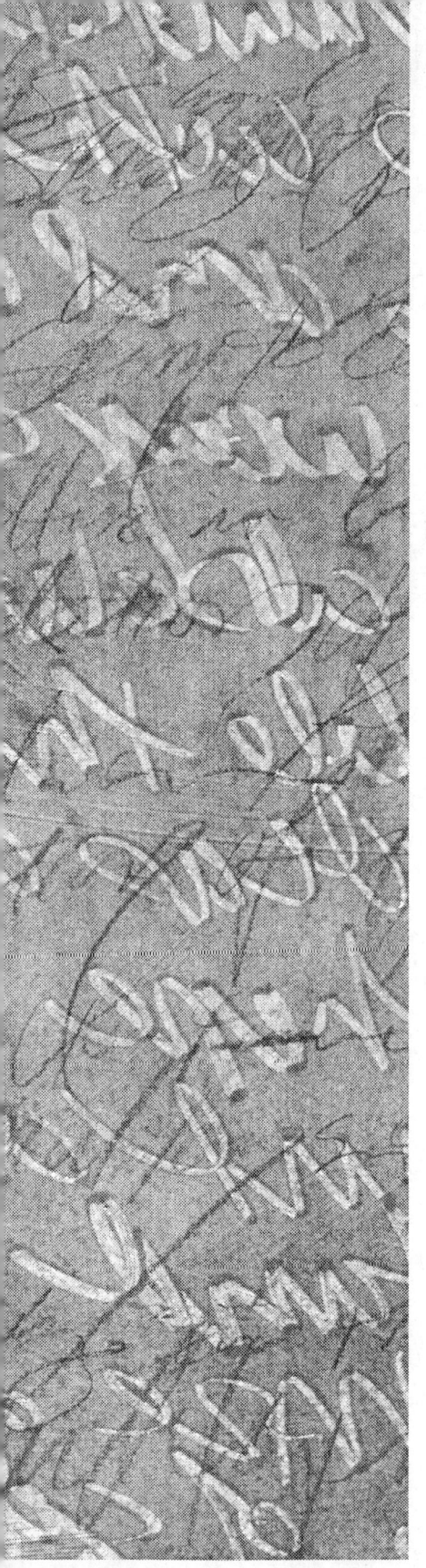

Request for Proposal

A Guide to Effective RFP Development

Bud Porter-Roth

♦♦Addison-Wesley

Boston • San Francisco • New York • Toronto
Montreal • London • Munich • Paris • Madrid
Capetown • Sydney • Tokyo • Singapore • Mexico City

v

Many of the designations used by manufacturers and sellers to distinguish their products are claimed as trademarks. Where those designations appear in this book, and Addison-Wesley was aware of a trademark claim, the designations have been printed with initial capital letters or in all capitals.

The author and publisher have taken care in the preparation of this book, but make no expressed or implied warranty of any kind and assume no responsibility for errors or omissions. No liability is assumed for incidental or consequential damages in connection with or arising out of the use of the information or programs contained herein.

The publisher offers discounts on this book when ordered in quantity for special sales. For more information, please contact:

Pearson Education Corporate Sales Division
201 W. 103rd Street
Indianapolis, IN 46290
(800) 428-5331
corpsales@pearsoned.com

Visit Addison-Wesley on the Web: www.awprofessional.com

Library of Congress Cataloging-in-Publication Data

Porter-Roth, Bud.
    Request for proposal : a guide to effective RFP development / Bud Porter-Roth.
      p. cm. — (Addison-Wesley information technology series)
    ISBN 0-201-77575-1 (alk. paper)
    1. Requests for proposals (Public contracts) I. Title. II. Series.

  HD3860.P67 2002
  325.5'3—dc21

                             2001053526

ISBN 0-201-77575-1

Text printed in the United States at Offset Paperback Manufacturers in Laflin, Pennsylvania.

9th   Printing   May 2010

Contents

1.
Introduction to Writing RFPs

4.

RFP Technical Requirements Section

5.

Management Requirements Section

6.

Pricing

7.
Evaluation Guidelines

Appendices

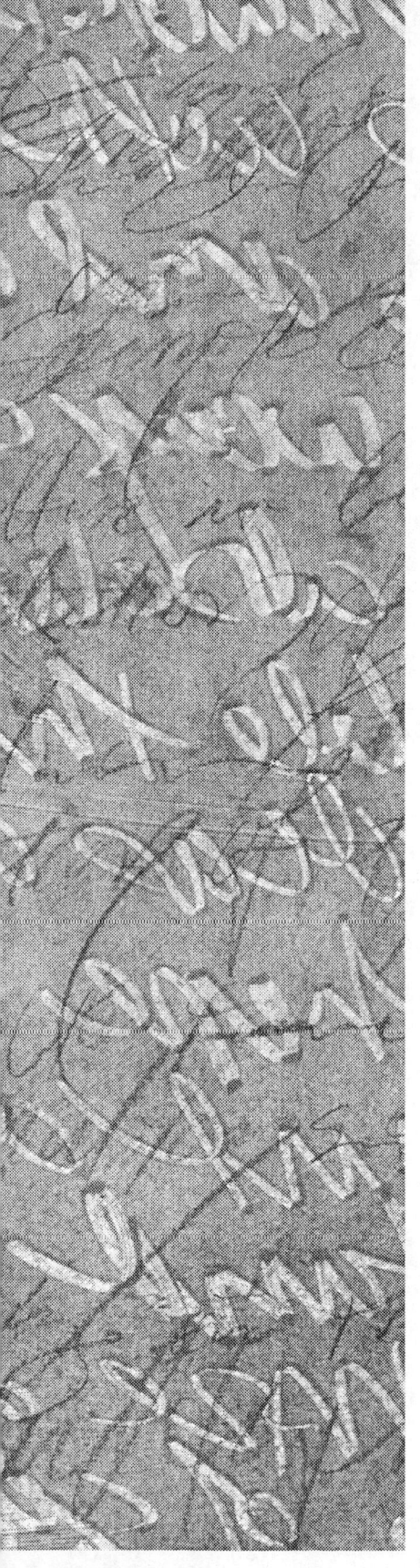

Foreword

It's a disaster we can't afford! Countless hours, time, and money have been spent assembling our Request for Proposals (RFPs), and now the vendors advise us that they can't provide a responsive bid. They say:

- ❑ They don't understand what we need because our requirements aren't clear and may not be achievable.
- ❑ The schedule for the project isn't realistic.
- ❑ They can't propose a technical solution because the technology we've asked for is either unavailable or prohibitive.
- ❑ Our budgets for the needed work are unrealistic.

How could this have happened? Why didn't we "get it together" long before this? Now we are faced with further delays and potential business repercussions, and we *still* don't know how to write an effective RFP!

Sound familiar? Unfortunately, this scenario actually happens far too often. Thanks to Bud Porter-Roth, finally an easily understandable guide is available that should have a major positive impact on industry—if his guidelines are applied.

Bud Porter-Roth has focused his professional life and contributions on end-user applications analysis, cost justification of projects, understanding customer requirements, RFP development, vendor selection, and implementation support. The title of his book is straightforward—and so is his advice! Bud provides the rationale for writing an RFP and describes a structure for a process that is too often unstructured. He provides practical advice and suggestions for each section of the RFP and an extensive set of examples and templates you can use to develop your own RFPs. This book fills the gap between requirements analysis and development and project initiation. Too often, organizations that don't use a formal RFP process have ill-defined requirements and a less rigorous selection process. They are probably spending more than they should on this phase of the project. The result: real customer needs are left unmet, and funds are wasted trying to get the job done.

The RFP constitutes the foundation for a project, enabling the real needs to be clarified before the project starts. It allows organizations to leverage their resources to provide a statement of real requirements. It builds the foundation for clear and accurate communication between the contractor and the customer.

The tone of this book is that of an experienced, knowledgeable industry adviser. The material is easy to read, understand, and apply but does not lapse into technical jargon to make a point. Valuable guidance and suggestions are provided—for example, in regard to how vendors recognize requirements, the qualities of well-written requirements, areas of cost that need to be considered in pricing, and how proposals are evaluated. I know of no other publication that covers the topic as well as this book does.

Bud Porter-Roth has done far more than just share his experience and advice with us. He has provided a guide that will save time, effort, and money throughout industry, wherever it is applied.

Ralph R. Young

Author, *Effective Requirements Practices*

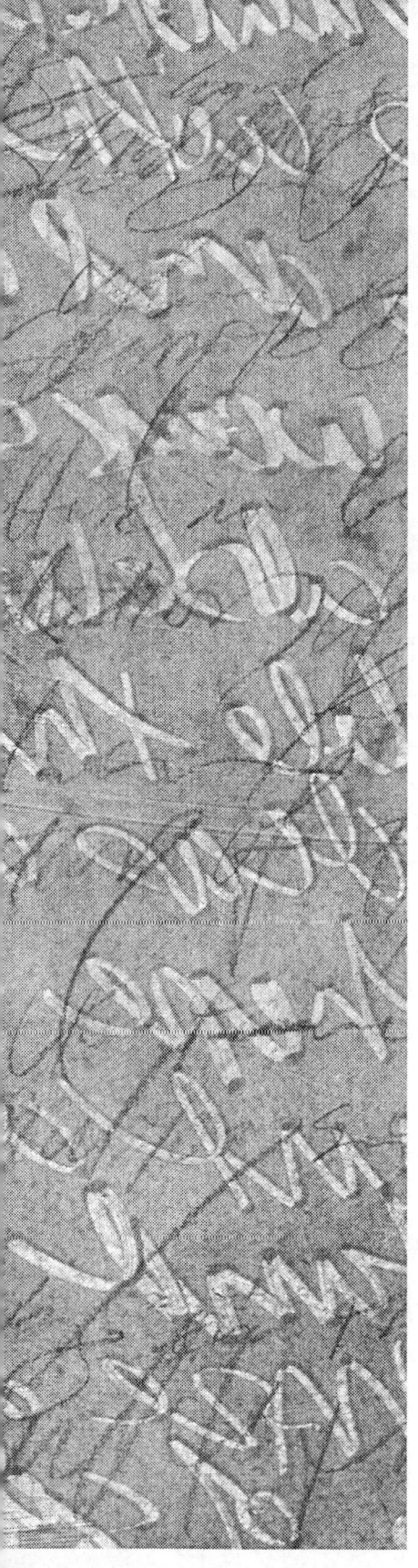

Preface

For many years, I wrote sales proposals in response to a request for proposal (RFP). As a vendor, I responded to both well-written and poorly written RFPs and found that there was no consistency among them either in the structure or the quality of information. Several times I was stumped as to what the subject of the RFP was, and after several rounds of questions and answers, I determined that the company issuing the RFP was also stumped—they had neglected to do their homework properly and could not properly define their requirements.

After becoming a consultant, I began writing RFPs on behalf of my clients. As I wrote them, I tried not to make the same mistakes I had seen as a vendor and began to develop a structure and organization methodology for writing RFPs. I began to write and speak to customers and at conferences about writing RFPs and what makes a good RFP. Time after time I was approached by people in the audience who asked if I had additional material. Frequently, I was asked to recommend a book that would provide some guidance. But the literature is very slim on this subject, and I could find no "general" guide to writing RFPs.

This book aims to fill that gap, bringing order and stability to the process of writing RFPs for those who are new to it, as well as reaffirming effective practices for veterans. I have included ideas from the best RFPs and share what I have learned from poorly written RFPs. Three major themes run through this book:

1. Quality of information is paramount to getting good proposal responses. Only if your requirements are well formed and complete will suppliers have enough information to write quality proposals.

2. Presentation, structure, and organization are all necessary if suppliers are to understand how to read your RFP and respond to it in a productive manner. Without a structured and organized RFP, vendors will find it difficult to write proposals, and you will find it difficult to evaluate them.

3. An RFP is much more than a request to buy a product; it is an offer from the supplier to form a team with you and to jointly solve a problem. As a team, both sides stand to benefit from the relationship, but the project itself is the real winner.

An RFP is not the end of the project, but rather the start of a new phase in the project. While the general requirements for a project have already been defined, quite often the real requirements are not understood until well after the RFP is released, a contract is awarded, and the project development begins. Sometimes it takes two or three iterations of the requirements development process before both companies fully understand the problem they are trying to solve or the products they hope to use to overcome these difficulties:

We can only shape the path as we are cutting its course through the forest. Many requirements of a system become known only as the system develops. This is especially true for a system that makes use of multiple commercial products, since their interactions will have a substantial influence on the system's eventual design. [1]

While this book is directed toward the computer system project, the disciplines of gathering requirements, organizing and writing an RFP, and interacting

---

1. David J. Carney. *Quotations from Chairman David.* Pittsburgh: Carnegie Mellon University, 1998. Sponsored by the U.S. Department of Defense.

with suppliers during and after the RFP has been issued can be applied in many other contexts. The material in this book can therefore be used, with some adjustments, to write RFPs for many industries. However, this book does not cover every type of application for every project; some parts may not apply to your specific needs.

A Word of Encouragement

All of the following material, including the sample RFP paragraphs, should be considered as a starting point and guideline for your own RFP. While the book provides you with a general format and general language, it is up to you to build upon this base of information and these examples. In the commercial world there are no rulebooks or laws that force you to write an RFP in a certain manner, and the federal government's Federal Acquisition Regulations (FARs) still leave room to be creative.

So within reason, be creative and include the requirements in your RFP that will make your project successful for both you and the chosen supplier.

A Word of Caution

Vendors do not have unlimited time and resources. When your RFP is complete, take a moment to look at it from a vendor's point of view and consider whether it is fair or if you are asking for too much. Remember that if you succeed in your bid, the vendor will become your partner. Successful business relationships are built on foundations of fairness and mutual respect. To bully or cajole a vendor into reducing pricing or including free services is to impair your relationship from the beginning. As Andrew Carnegie once said about J. P. Morgan, *"Mr. Morgan buys his partners; I grow my own."* [2]

---

2. *Columbia Dictionary of Quotations.* New York: Columbia University Press, 1995.

Who Should Read This Book?

In my experience writing RFPs, I have worked with all kinds of people from all types of companies and departments. I find that many companies do not have RFP writing guidelines, procedures, or support and rely on company history and previously written RFPs as source materials. If there is no previous history in writing RFPs, a company may turn to consultants for help or ask vendors for copies of RFPs that can be used. I have been asked many times if I could send someone a "good" RFP as an example.

People who have been assigned to write an RFP but have not written one before and, perhaps, have little history and support to draw upon will find this book invaluable. A suggested outline, a wealth of examples, and good solid advice will guide you from starting the project to signing the contract.

People who have previously written RFPs will find that this book adds to their existing knowledge by providing some fresh examples for developing technical and management requirements.

Request for Proposal has been written for people in many different commercial industries as well as federal, state, and local government workers who need guidance, procedures, and direction. People who should read this book include the following:

- information technology (IT) managers asked to write or manage an RFP
- business unit managers who may not have dedicated IT support and find that they need to write an RFP
- purchasing managers who provide RFP oversight for their company
- federal, state, and local government IT and business managers who need to supplement their internal guidelines
- consultants who are responsible for writing RFPs or helping their clients write RFPs
- university and college professors looking for primary or supplemental course material

After reading this book, the reader will be able to do the following:

- ❏ organize the RFP project effort
- ❏ outline each RFP section
- ❏ develop, write, and review requirements—technical, management, and pricing
- ❏ pre-screen a vendor list selecting only the best vendors for the project
- ❏ set up the evaluation criteria for evaluating vendor proposals
- ❏ select the best solution based on objective evaluation criteria
- ❏ prepare for the post-RFP activities such as site visits and reference checks, plan and schedule implementation activities, and put in place project management plans

There is no prerequisite for reading this book—you do not need to be a senior IT manager or a certified purchasing agent. The text provides a standard format for the recommended sections in an RFP and includes examples for each section, as well as examples of how to write the technical and nontechnical requirements for each section.

The text also provides guidelines for evaluating proposals and selecting a winning vendor once proposals have been received. Evaluation guidelines include evaluating technical and management content as well as pricing.

Acknowledgments

As with any endeavor this large, many people have provided help, constructive criticism, encouragement, and support. I would like to thank all of the reviewers who took the time to review and comment on the manuscript. The finished book is much better as a result of their efforts.

Ralph Young has been especially helpful in providing detailed suggestions and encouragement and in graciously agreeing to write the foreword. Thank you, Ralph.

Special thanks go to Addison-Wesley for publishing this book and to my editor, Debbie Lafferty, for her professionalism, great suggestions and attitude, and lots of behind-the-scenes hard work that I will never know about.

Finally, my wife Anne and daughter Lizzie endured many early mornings, late nights, and missed weekends as I toiled away writing and revising the manuscript. Their support helped make this book possible.

Bud Porter-Roth
Mill Valley, California
bud@rfphandbook.com
http://www.rfphandbook.com

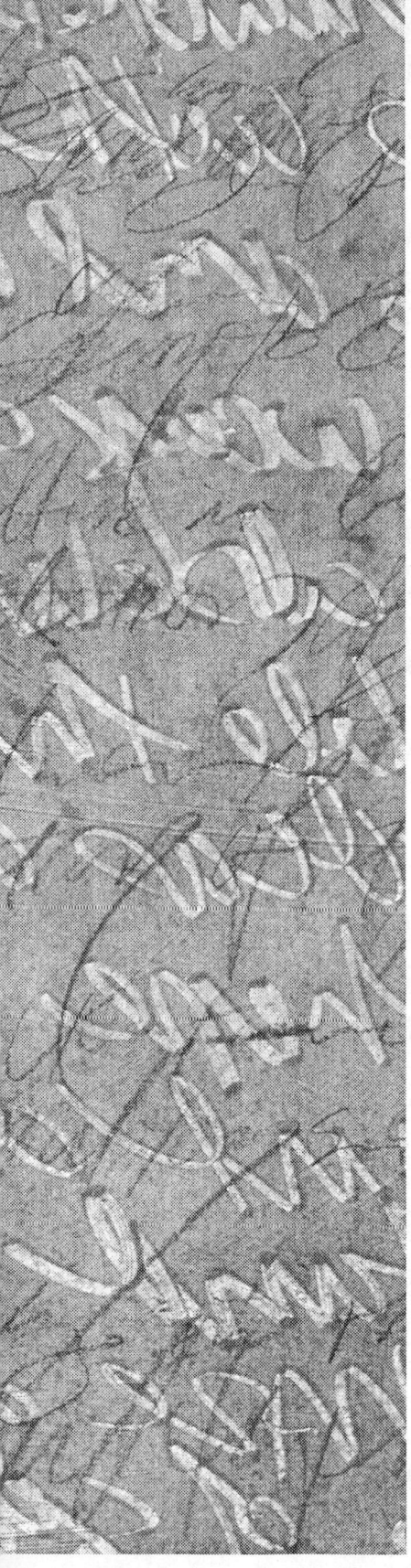

1

Introduction to Writing RFPs

Introduction

This is a guidebook for writing a request for proposal (RFP). An RFP is a standard tool used by governments and businesses to purchase equipment and services by promoting competitive proposals among suppliers.[1] Through this competitive process, suppliers offer a wide array of potential solutions and prices and compete with one another to win the business. Buyers evaluate the many different supplier solutions and pick the one that most closely fits their needs and budgets.

The RFP becomes a vehicle that allows both the buyer and the supplier to establish a dialogue and to work from the same set of rules, requirements, schedules, and information. The opportunity to have this dialogue is an important element in the process, because RFP requirements are often not clear and the supplier, as the expert on the particular product or service, is allowed to question and interpret what is being requested. Conversely, the buyer has the opportunity to clarify issues in supplier proposals.

Proposals, by their very nature, are a supplier's interpretation of an RFP's requirements. RFPs, therefore, promote a diversity of thinking among suppliers and encourage them to provide unique solutions based on their products and services. RFPs are used when the following conditions apply:

---

1. For the sake of establishing a standard terminology, the term "supplier" is used here to mean a vendor of equipment, hardware, software, services, or whatever else is being purchased. A "buyer" is the company or government agency that is writing the RFP.

✎ RFPs encourage creative thinking by suppliers.

❑ Multiple solutions are available that will fit the need.

❑ Multiple suppliers can provide the same solution.

❑ Buyers seek to determine the "best value" of suppliers' solutions.

❑ Products for the project cannot be clearly specified.

❑ The project requires different skills, expertise, and technical capabilities from suppliers.

❑ The problem requires suppliers to combine and subcontract products and services.

❑ Lowest price is not the determining criterion for awarding the contract.

❑ Final pricing is negotiated with the supplier.

When a supplier responds to an RFP, both the RFP and the proposal become the foundation for a working relationship between the two companies. This relationship allows both companies to operate against the same agreed-upon requirements, schedules, and understandings, based on the RFP and the proposal. It also provides both parties with a starting place when the requirements or schedule need to be modified once the contract has started.

The RFP process typically requires that a buyer establish a budget for the project. This budget is based on supplier research, supplier interviews, the requirements for the project, and the RFP team's understanding of the various solutions. (The RFP team and organization are discussed later in the section titled RFP Project Development.) The establishment of the requirements is the primary task that allows a budget to be built and verified. How closely the estimated budget matches proposals that are submitted depends entirely on how much product research has been performed by the RFP team. Figure 1.1 shows the interrelationships necessary for constructing the project budget. The process of establishing the project budget is discussed in more detail in Appendix D, Budget Planning and Investment Analysis.

Internally, RFPs require buyers to examine their needs and translate those needs into measurable requirements. In the process of developing requirements,

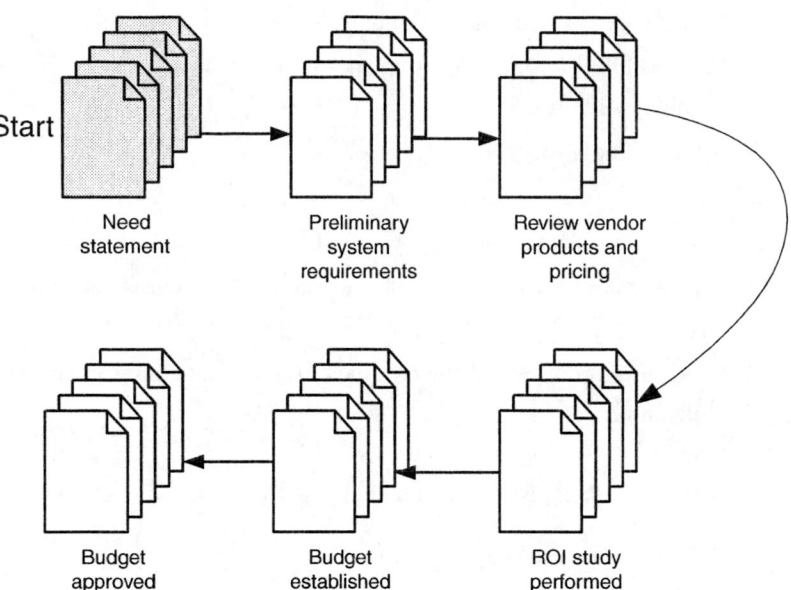

Figure 1.1   Budget
Development
Process

Need
statement

Preliminary
system
requirements

Review vendor
products and
pricing

Budget
approved

Budget
established

ROI study
performed

an RFP team often discovers divergent interests that must be resolved,
so that a requirement actually represents a consensus of opinion, not a single view.

RFP requirements must also take into consideration the technical, implementation, and project management requirements; the project budget; and
company contract provisions. Getting agreement on these requirements
means that those departments within a buyer's organization must work
together, in addition to working with the chosen supplier.

✍ An RFP must
represent all views
of the issue.

Properly developed and written, RFPs are powerful tools for selecting the
most appropriate solution and developing straightforward relationships
with suppliers. A successful RFP process requires us to do the following:

❑ Formally recognize a deficiency or need in current operations that
could be resolved through the purchase of equipment or services.

❑ Develop and implement a plan for understanding the problem.

- ❑ Identify appropriate potential suppliers and solutions.
- ❑ Gain visibility for internal acceptance of the identified need and potential solutions.
- ❑ Establish the project budget.
- ❑ Develop a project schedule.
- ❑ Organize project personnel.
- ❑ Evolve real requirements and ensure that they are clearly stated and measurable.
- ❑ Develop rigorous evaluation criteria, thus ensuring an objective evaluation.

A less successful RFP process may include the following issues:

- ❑ Not enough time has been allocated for the RFP process.
- ❑ Requirements are overly restrictive and limit suppliers to a predetermined solution.
- ❑ Requirements unfairly limit the range of suppliers who may participate.
- ❑ Requirements are either not clear or downright ambiguous.
- ❑ Project deadlines are too short to allow for reasonable project development by suppliers.
- ❑ The project team has not been fully educated about available technologies.
- ❑ A budget has not been established, or has been based on unverified data and is not sufficient for the project.

These issues create the risk of a problem contract or no contract. The risks, if large enough, can be very costly, leading suppliers to refrain from bidding on the project, or to submit proposals that are overly conservative as they add in money or equipment to cover all possible contingencies.

Strong leadership, dedicated resources, and management commitment are critical to a successful RFP and a successful relationship with the chosen supplier.

What Is Presented in *Request for Proposal* Book?

This book was written to help clarify the basic operating principles of an RFP and to provide not only a suggested structure for an RFP but also examples of individual RFP sections. *Therefore, this material provides an RFP framework that you can use to create, strengthen, or improve your company's RFP.* It contains many examples that you can reuse and edit to fit your needs or use as templates to build your own RFP.

The methods and structure suggested here apply to RFPs written for products ranging from computer systems to services such as training, consulting, or outsourcing. This guide stresses the organizational aspects of writing RFPs, the need for a standard organization of the RFP, and the processes that need to be attended to before and after the RFP is produced.

This guide stresses the organizational aspects of an RFP.

For our readers who work for the federal government, this book is not meant to supplant the Federal Acquisition Regulations (FARs), but rather to supplement them in the areas of developing and writing requirements, working with suppliers during the "educational phase" of the project, and beginning the post-RFP work. Indeed, our commercial readers should take note that the FARs are a tremendous resource for ideas and procedures.

Many of the examples used in this book are from the computer technology sector, and many of those examples are based on purchasing computer products, not building systems from the ground up. For example, a typical accounting system example will be based on buying an existing accounting software package rather than designing one from scratch.

While there are considerable differences between building systems from the ground up and buying a ready-made product, in both cases there is the need to develop technical and management requirements, organize the project, and write the RFP.

This book covers a wide variety of RFP types and situations, and not all of the material, tasks, and advice may be applicable to a particular situation.

Readers should not feel compelled to incorporate all of the ideas presented here but rather should feel free to build upon what is presented in the book.

Different Types of RFPs

To enable suppliers to offer their best solutions, an RFP must represent a clear understanding of all the technical issues (technical section), must provide a method for implementing and managing those issues (management section), and must provide the supplier with an acceptable method for doing business (contracts and price section). Many RFPs are not successful because they fail to communicate one or more of the above requirements properly.

✍ The type of RFP used depends on your understanding of the technology.

Buyers often find new products and technologies hard to understand. Typically, the RFP team will read white papers, brochures, and datasheets; attend conferences and demonstrations; and invite the supplier to give a presentation or demonstration. Even with all of this research, the RFP team may *still not fully understand* how the technology will fit and work within their project. When more information is needed than is publicly available, the RFP team may use a "pre-RFP" request for information (RFI).

Request for Information (RFI)

An RFI is a way for buyers to determine what is available from suppliers who respond to its requirements. It is also a way for the buyer to determine whether the requested requirements are reasonable and whether appropriate technology is available. Suppliers are encouraged to respond to the requirements and also to spell out where there may be potential problems, areas in which technology may not exist, or unrealistic project goals and schedules. The information gleaned from proposals may help guide the subsequent RFP or cause it to be canceled if suppliers do not respond.

An RFI is not a mandatory prerequisite to writing an RFP; many companies write RFPs without going through the RFI stage. RFIs may be considered when the goals of the project are in question or when the technology for the project is new to the industry or your company—or when you would like to explore a variety of potential solutions.

Figure 1.2 shows that an RFP is dependent on both the team's education concerning suppliers and on the available products and suppliers' responses to the RFI. Responses to the RFI may show that (1) the technology mandated by the requirements is not available, (2) the technology is available but far more costly than originally anticipated, or (3) suppliers do not understand the RFI requirements. If the suppliers are not responsive, it could mean either going back to the requirements analysis phase or stopping further work on the project.

If suppliers' proposals are responsive to an RFI, the requirements are first reviewed according to the information gained by reading these proposals. These requirements then become part of the RFP, and finally the RFP is developed and released.

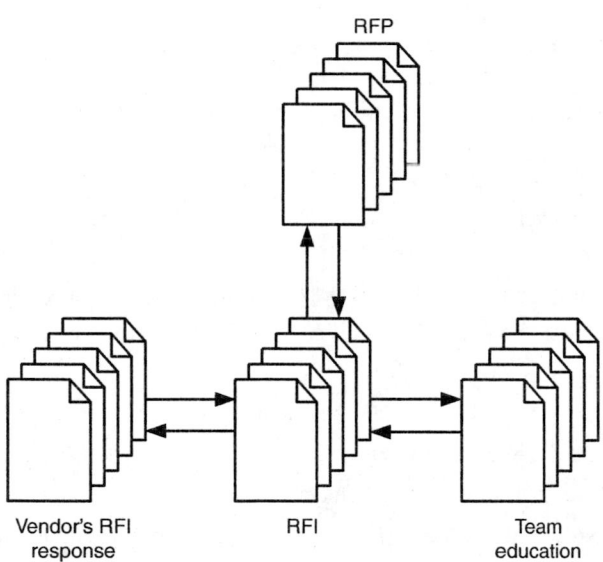

RFP

Vendor's RFI
response

RFI

Team
education

Figure 1.2   RFI/RFP
Development Cycle

✎ Use RFIs when you need to validate technology and requirements.

Typically, an RFI encompasses all of the requirements and is structured just like an RFP. It is important to list not only the technical issues but also the requirements for project management, maintenance, training, and support. Thus, potential suppliers are allowed to comment on all aspects of the procurement and to establish what is possible and not possible—from their point of view. Of course, the RFP team will have to separate the wheat from the chaff—since suppliers may try to say that technology other than their own does not exist. (However, it is important not to combine competing technologies within a single requirement when rewriting requirements based on multiple suppliers' proposals.)

The following paragraphs were taken directly from an RFI:

> *[Our company]* is in the process of researching corporate Intranet technology and systems that will support our internal Intranet, public site, and an extranet for . . . . The objective of this RFI is to obtain information about systems that are available from suppliers.
>
> It must be clearly understood that this RFI is being used as a vehicle to obtain information about Intranet technologies and potential system suppliers. This RFI should not be interpreted as a contract (implicit, explicit, or implied), nor does it imply any form of an agreement to candidate suppliers. In addition, no inference should be made that we will purchase and/or implement in the future any of the technology or systems proposed by the suppliers responding to this RFI.
>
> We will, however, use responses to this RFI to build and fine-tune our RFP.

In this case the buyer is making it very clear that the purpose of the RFI is to gain an understanding of a specific technology and to develop a list of the potential suppliers.

Why would a supplier respond to this type of request when there may be many other RFPs in the hopper? One reason is that an RFI gives them a chance to participate in the early planning stages of a project and to try to influence the RFP's strategy and direction. It allows suppliers to provide information about their products so that the RFP team members are better informed by the time they release an RFP. Also, many companies send the subsequent RFP only to those suppliers who responded to the RFI. Therefore, the RFI becomes an important tool for determining who should be on the bidders' list for the RFP.

A note of caution: If an RFI is poorly put together, has little focus, and demonstrates a fundamentally poor grasp of the technology, many suppliers will respond with datasheets and boilerplate text, or else not at all. Many potential RFPs are not released after an RFI, because the RFP team has severely misjudged the technology, the implementation, and the cost. Suppliers are quick to grasp which projects are likely to move forward and which appear to be misguided "fishing expeditions."

On the other hand, an RFI is the best place for a supplier to try to influence the requirements and therefore have the inside track if and when the RFP is released. As an old supplier proverb goes, "If you didn't help write the RFI, don't bother with the RFP." So, in the spirit of team education, let suppliers provide you with as much information, help, support, and interaction as appropriate to your needs.

Request for Proposal (RFP)

An RFP is a formal request for proposals from suppliers, and such proposals often become part of the resulting contract. An RFP may be the result of an RFI that tested the technical waters, or it may be written based on current knowledge of products and suppliers.

The following is taken from the Proposal Preparation Instructions of an RFP:

> [This company] reserves the right to award the contract according to the evaluation criteria. . . . The supplier chosen for award should be prepared to have the proposal incorporated, along with all other written correspondence concerning this RFP, into the contract. Any false or misleading statements found in the proposal will be grounds for disqualification.

An RFI should not be a fishing expedition.

✎ RFPs becomes the basis for the contract.

Unlike an RFI, in which the RFP team is still fact-finding, the RFP represents a decision to buy technology or services. Proposals submitted in response to an RFP are incorporated into the contract as an addendum or exhibit. This procedure allows the company to obligate the supplier contractually to comply with statements made in the proposal, and to seek legal recourse if the supplier cannot meet the requirements as stated.

An RFP represents a significant opportunity for suppliers to sell their products, systems, or services:

❑ It provides a stable set of specifications and requirements for suppliers to work from.

❑ It provides a platform for describing and promoting products.

❑ It allows suppliers a chance to interact with the buyer organization.

❑ It demonstrates a buyer's commitment to the project and indicates that funding is available.

In summary, we can say that an RFP is a written document that represents a certain amount of time, resources, and money in order to communicate an understanding of the business needs of a company. Resulting proposals represent an interpretation of those needs and involve the expenditure of a commensurate amount of time and resources on the supplier's part.

Why Write an RFP?

An RFP fills an important gap between the initial project definition phase and the implementation phase of the project. The RFP provides the structure that allows you to take the project requirements that have been developed and put them into a form that suppliers can use, understand, and respond to. The RFP also spells out how the project is to be implemented (the next phase), what the first steps will be, and how success will be measured.

The RFP is an intermediate, but important, step in a project. It facilitates someone's wish to buy new technology or replace old technology, but the

RFP is a means to an end, not the end itself. On the other side of the fence, the RFP lays the groundwork for the project but is not the project itself. As with any undertaking, if the foundation is not solid, the project will more than likely not be successful. An RFP allows you to state the project management requirements and to get the supplier's buy-in (in writing) thus ensuring that you will have good project controls when the project begins.

Why write an RFP? It allows you to gather and develop the essential components of a project as shown in Figure 1.3. Each of the four wings in the illustration represents a major concept in an RFP. The RFP itself is the unifying document that will lay the groundwork for how the project will be controlled from the time the contract is awarded to, perhaps, when the contract is finished and the project is no longer operational.

Once a contract has been awarded to a supplier, the agreed-upon project plan and schedule will become the primary method for organizing and controlling the project implementation and, perhaps, the life cycle of the project itself.

As with the saying, "If you don't know where you are going, any road will get you there," the RFP not only tells suppliers where you are going but also selects the road on which they will travel.

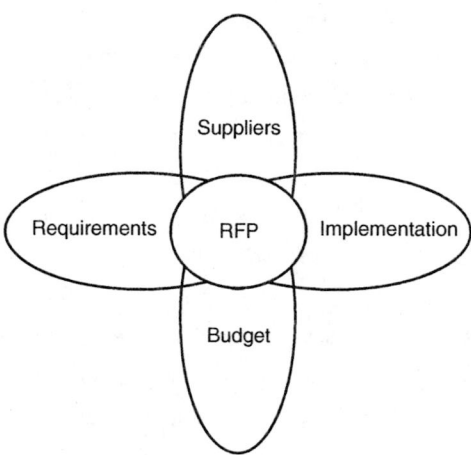

Figure 1.3 Essential components of an RFP

The advantages of using an RFP far outweigh the potential problems of dealing directly with suppliers and of not having a formal set of requirements to work from.

❏ An RFP requires the RFP team to examine the problems and issues concerning the project in greater detail than would normally occur.

❏ An RFP forces suppliers to create competitive solutions that not only respond to the RFP requirements but go beyond them, thus providing additional value for a given price.

❏ An RFP does not favor one supplier over another, but allows all to compete fairly based on the same set of rules and requirements.

❏ Because suppliers are working from the same set of rules and requirements, it will be easier to understand the differences between proposed solutions.

❏ Having similar, but different, proposed solutions facilitates the evaluation.

RFP Development and Preparation

RFP Project Development

The request to buy technology or services can come from almost any department within a company. It may initially come from workers who are unable to keep pace with their work and know that there is technology available to help them. Alternatively, the request may come from the information technology (IT) group, which may want to build a corporate Intranet to share information more easily with employees.

🖎 Users buy tactical; IT buys strategic.

Most often, the "users" in a company are the force behind RFPs that involves buying products to increase or enhance the efficiency of a department or a business process. IT buyers are the drivers for companywide products that add to or enhance existing IT services or provide corporate infrastructure such as a corporate Intranet or Internet site. It is important to have both the users and the IT group participate in an RFP effort when it is appropriate.

The project team should include an equal balance of skills among the following three departments:

Operations, or system users. Users, whether claims adjusters, customer service, or a supporting service such as human resources, perform the work of the business. Users know what they do now, as well as what they want to do but cannot currently do, and they can develop the operational and functional requirements for the system. Users are typically not strong on the underlying technology of systems, such as how a network connects to servers, how to set up and run an acceptance test, or how to pass data through a firewall. They depend on the IT group for those aspects of the technology requirements.

Information technology. IT staff are typically knowledgeable about whether a product will technically fit into existing technical infrastructures and what those requirements will be, what is needed to support the product, and what is needed to support the users when the product is installed. IT staff typically do not know how a department works on a business level or how to specify those business requirements.

Procurement (purchasing office). Procurement personnel understand what type of contract should be provided with the proposal (hardware versus software versus services) and can help in identifying suppliers, requesting D&Bs to ascertain financial stability, and reviewing and negotiating supplier contracts. It is vital to involve procurement personnel early in the RFP process so that they become familiar with the project and can lend their contract expertise to the effort. Procurement personnel typically are familiar neither with underlying technologies nor with project organization requirements and will depend on the RFP team for those decisions.

The planning phase of the RFP should include the following key areas:

1. RFP project personnel and organization.
2. Project schedule.

3. Technology and supplier education.

4. Budget estimation and development.

5. Return on investment (ROI) analysis (if required).

6. RFP development.

7. Proposal evaluation.

8. Contracts and awards.

9. Post-RFP activities.

10. Project personnel and organization for the new product.

Planning should be a team activity and all parties should be part of each planning session. Depending on the company culture, one person should become the project leader and manager. If the project is to purchase a new business application, the project leader may come from the user community, which is the primary driver for the project. Depending on the company culture and history, the project leader may be from the user community or the IT community. In many companies, IT takes the lead on major acquisition projects because IT staff have the knowledge of technology, project management skills, and experience dealing with suppliers. Other companies may not have a strong IT department, in which case the user community becomes the lead, tapping the IT resources when needed.

More detailed information on RFP planning activities and developing project budgets can be found in Chapter 2, "RFP Planning and Preparation," and in Appendix D, "Budget Planning and Investment Analysis."

Evaluation Criteria

✍ Evaluation criteria provide the method for measuring proposals.

As the project requirements are confirmed and agreed upon, the method for evaluating requirements must also be established. Requirements can range from hard technical requirements to more subjective ones such as a supplier's references. Chapter 7, "Evaluation Guidelines" contains more detailed information and examples for the evaluation process.

The following are examples of suitable areas for evaluation:

1. Technical requirements.
2. Management requirements.
3. Price.
4. References.
5. Qualifications/similar projects.
6. Site visits/oral presentations.
7. Product tests or demonstrations.
8. Overall response to the RFP.
9. Ability to work with the supplier's team.

Some requirements will be more difficult to measure than others and will therefore be judged subjectively. Ideally, all requirements should be measured by the same agreed-upon criteria, with subjective requirements being discussed during the evaluation team meetings. Keep in mind that all requirements should have measurable criteria.

 An RFP is, in some sense, a collection of requirements. It must be made clear to the suppliers what are requirements and what is simply information. Requirements may be divided between mandatory and optional requirements. Mandatory requirements are those requirements that are essential to meeting the project's needs, and suppliers that take exception to mandatory requirements may be disqualified. Optional requirements are often termed "nice to have but not essential."

Reviewing the RFP

Before an RFP is sent out, it should be reviewed by people outside the primary RFP team. This review group may look at different aspects of the RFP, for example:

✎ Allow time for an independent review of the RFP.

❑ Are the network structures current and accurate?

❑ Are there any basic system architectural concerns?

❑ Is the current working environment description accurate?

❑ Are the functional requirements stated clearly and accurately?

❑ Does the pricing section meet company standards?

❑ Is the project plan achievable?

This "objective" review will help team members to see their RFP's strengths and weaknesses. Once the review is complete and the review issues responded to, the RFP should be a stronger document.

Anatomy of an RFP

An RFP is a tool a buyer uses to purchase from a supplier many types of products or services, such as software programs; corporate computers systems; administrative, technical, or legal services; machinery; medical supplies; and many other types of products. Each type of purchase requires a different RFP. This guide provides a suggested structure for building your RFP.

Broadly speaking, a basic RFP consists of the following sections:

1. A project overview and administrative information section contains an overview or summary statement of the problem, similar to a proposal's executive summary, as well as the administrative information concerning the management of the RFP.

2. A technical requirements section provides suppliers with technical requirements and enough information to enable them to understand the issues and write a firm proposal.

3. A management requirements section states the conditions for managing and implementing the project.

4. A supplier qualifications and references section asks the supplier to describe qualifications and list references.

5. A suppliers' section allows suppliers to include information they feel is relevant although not required or requested in the RFP.

6. A pricing section specifies how suppliers are to provide pricing information.

7. A contract and license agreement section contains the purchase contract, nondisclosure agreements, and other legal documents.

8. Appendices contain bulky but relevant information such as network diagrams, technical requirements studies, and project plan outlines.

Figure 1.4 provides a "roadmap" to the typical sections of an RFP. This is a suggested roadmap only; you may choose, for example, to fold the supplier's qualifications and references into the management section or not to include a supplier's section. However, Sections 1, 2, 3, and 6 in the figure below should be considered the minimum sections of an RFP. Always consider using appendices when providing additional information that supports the primary sections.

The following paragraphs describe what constitutes an RFP. Subsequent chapters will expand upon the ideas presented below.

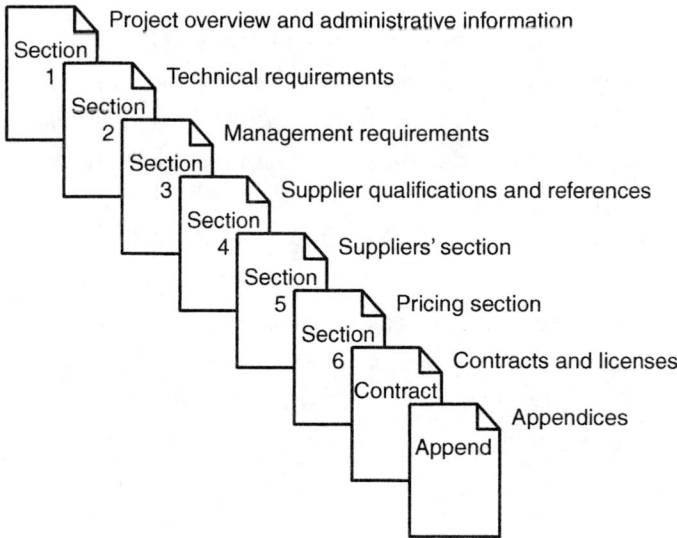

Figure 1.4   RFP Roadmap

Project Overview and Administrative Information

The first part of this section provides suppliers with an overview of your company and a statement of the problem that you hope to resolve through this RFP. The statement of the problem must be detailed enough for suppliers to grasp both the business issues that are driving the RFP and the technical issues that may have precipitated the problem.

✑ The administrative section contains the RFP's rules for the road.

The administrative section contains all of the administrative requirements and information with which a supplier must comply in order to submit an acceptable proposal. The administrative section also provides the ground rules for the procurement, from receiving the RFP to awarding the contract. This section should contain the following types of information:

- ❏ where and when to submit the proposal
- ❏ if and when a bidders' conference will be held
- ❏ relevant dates for the procurement
- ❏ requirements for preparing proposals
- ❏ how proposals will be evaluated
- ❏ RFP contact names and addresses
- ❏ other information that is required for a supplier to be responsive

Administrative requirements are very important to keep suppliers moving forward with their proposals in a timely manner. If the instructions are missing or not clear, suppliers may overlook important meetings or milestones. For perceptive suppliers, lack of instructions may signal a weak RFP team and a confused or conflicted project. This potential weakness may influence whether they decide to continue with their proposal.

On the other hand, failure to comply with the administrative requirements might be cause for rejecting that supplier's proposal. The purpose of this section is to lay down clear rules for responding to the RFP and to ensure that suppliers are aware of the penalties for not following them. If a supplier fails to abide by these rules, it may be a sign of carelessness and lack of attention to detail.

Section 3, RFP Administrative Section, covers this topic and provides examples of typical administrative requirements.

Technical Requirements

This section contains all of the information and requirements needed to enable suppliers to respond to your RFP. It should first summarize the problem or issue that is the basis for the RFP. This overview should address both the current business application and the technical environment (hardware, software, communications).

✎ Requirements are the heart of the technical section.

Following the problem statement, the rest of the section lists the requirements to which a supplier must respond in the proposal, for example:

- ❑ goals and objectives for the project
- ❑ critical success factors
- ❑ functional specifications for the current system
- ❑ functional specifications for the projected system
- ❑ performance specifications
- ❑ hardware requirements (if mandatory)
- ❑ software requirements
- ❑ communications requirements (if mandatory)

This section must be well documented and complete; otherwise, suppliers will have to ask questions in order to clarify statements or requirements.

Management Requirements

This section provides suppliers with the information they need to develop a project plan that will cover the implementation, installation, training, maintenance, and other aspects of the project. The proposed project plan

✎ The project plan is the heart of the management section.

provides the needed assurance that the supplier has the resources required to perform the contract successfully.

The project management plan typically contains the following:

- ❑ Functional project requirements.
- ❑ Staffing requirements.
- ❑ Site preparation responsibilities.
- ❑ Delivery and installation schedule and plan.
- ❑ System acceptance test requirements.
- ❑ System maintenance requirements.
- ❑ System training requirements.
- ❑ Documentation requirements.

Development of this section is essential for ensuring that suppliers can meet the overall project requirements. It is possible that suppliers can meet the technical requirements but cannot meet the management requirements as evidenced in their poor or inadequate responses to the requirements in this section. It is possible that a company has put all of its energy into product development and little or no effort into determining how the product should be installed and maintained, specifying what type of training is needed, and providing good readable documentation. The management section will help you to differentiate the suppliers with good management capabilities from those with little management capability.

Supplier Qualifications and References

✑ Supplier qualifications provide financial data, while references provide the "who," "what," and "where."

The supplier's qualifications and references are as important as the technical and management requirements. This section requires suppliers to provide information about their company and financial status and the customers who will serve as references for their proposal effort.

It is important not to bury this section and to ensure that suppliers do not take it lightly or simply say that the information requested is already provided in their annual report.

The following are examples of what is typically required in this section:

- ❑ A brief history of the supplier's firm.
- ❑ The supplier's installation and maintenance offerings and capabilities.
- ❑ A description of the relationship between the supplier and each manufacturer, and how long this relationship has been in existence.
- ❑ Evidence that the supplier has the necessary technical skills, technical staff, and financial resources to perform the contract.
- ❑ A list of the currently installed systems.
- ❑ Names of customers with similar configurations and/or applications who can provide references, including contact names and telephone numbers.

 It is impossible to say how many times I have had to scramble when asked for information about a particular supplier. Invariably, at least one person will ask for information that was not requseted or was not provided in the proposals—thus forcing me to read annual reports, search Web sites, or call the suppliers to get the information. Therefore, I encourage you to review Appendix B and add it to the list of questions. Ensure that this type of questionnaire is in your RFP. Consider making it a separate section in the RFP so that the information is consolidated into one area.

Suppliers' Section

This section reserves a place in the RFP for suppliers to provide information that they feel is necessary but was not requested. Suppliers can also discuss potential issues that are relevant to the RFP and to their proposal. For example, a supplier may have additional product features to demonstrate that are outside the scope of the RFP. Suppliers may also comment on requirements they feel are missing from the RFP, or present a unique solution that was not anticipated by the buyer.

This section is also an appropriate place for suppliers to discuss issues they believe are relevant to the project that have not been covered in the RFP. The RFP's instructions to suppliers will direct them to use the suppliers' section for any additional information outside the scope of the RFP.

Remember to take notes from ideas provided in this section. A supplier might provide a solution to a problem evident in the RFP that other suppliers did not consider. Even if this particular supplier does not win, the explanation of the problem and the potential solution will still be worth considering for use with the winning vendor.

Pricing Section

≫ The pricing section gives suppliers a format to follow when pricing their proposals.

This section provides a detailed format for suppliers to follow in developing their price proposals. Instructions should be in a clear format to ensure that price proposals from different suppliers can be compared on an equal basis. To facilitate this comparison, you may consider providing a sample spreadsheet that breaks the proposed system into components such as the following:

❑ Hardware.

❑ System software.

❑ Application development software.

❑ Installation.

❑ Maintenance.

❑ Training.

❑ Documentation.

❑ Project management.

❑ Integration of unique hardware or software.

❑ License fees (ongoing).

An area deserving of particular attention involves onetime costs versus recurring costs. The initial price of a software package is a onetime cost;

annual maintenance and software licensing fees are recurring costs. Recurring costs need to be identified if you are developing a life-cycle cost for a project that is expected to have a valid life of ten years.

Pricing is not usually the sole determinant for winning but should be used to break a tie between two suppliers with equally good technical and management proposals.

Contracts and License Agreements Section

This section provides basic guidance to the supplier on how to respond to contracts and agreements. It can either become part of the pricing section or stand alone.

Contracts are provided to suppliers, who can begin to study them along with the RFP requirements. If contract provisions are such that suppliers cannot respond, suppliers may either choose not to bid on the RFP or take exception to the contract provision in their proposal. For example, a contract may state that custom software products must pass a 90-day acceptance test period prior to the first payment. A supplier may agree to only a 30-day test, or may not agree to any acceptance test that is tied to payments.

Identify showstopper issues during the proposal evaluation period because it is possible to select a supplier who will not accept your contract. Do not spend time and resources on an unproductive supplier, as this takes time away from working with the potential winners.

Types of contracts can include the following:

- ❑ purchase agreement
- ❑ maintenance contract
- ❑ warranty period
- ❑ software license agreement
- ❑ performance bonds

✎ Provide contracts in your RFP to get the ball rolling.

❑ payment bonds

❑ nondisclosure agreements

Appendices

 Place detailed information in an appendix.

If the RFP team generates detailed information that is too lengthy for the body of the RFP, place it in an appendix. Examples include the following:

❑ Workflow diagrams and studies.

❑ Spreadsheets with statistical information.

❑ Communications network drawings and plans.

❑ List of current equipment.

❑ Standards used within the company.

❑ Tentative project plan with dates.

The information is then available to the supplier but does not distract from the narrative portion of the RFP. Note: Tell suppliers whether they must use this information when developing their proposals.

> ☑ Consider making information available to suppliers via a Web site established for your RFP. You may be able to supply more examples of documents, workflow diagrams, network diagrams, and other related information that would be costly to reproduce and bind with the RFP.

RFP Activities

Pre-RFP Activities

Who reads an RFP? How do prospective suppliers receive it? And what do they do with it?

An RFP may take a roundabout route through a supplier's organization before it finally lands on the right desk. Unless specifically addressed to an individual, the RFP package will be opened and given to the appropriate sales manager, where it may sit because the manager is traveling or too busy to look at a lengthy RFP. When your RFP is finally and *briefly* reviewed by the manager, it is routed to the correct sales representative, who may be traveling or busy working on a big final contract. As you can see, it is advantageous to find the right person in the supplier's organization to whom to send your RFP; otherwise, it is possible that delays will make it impossible for the supplier to respond in time.

Sales personnel typically read the RFP and decide whether to bid on your project. *Most suppliers do not do this scientifically or methodically!* Most suppliers do not evaluate your RFP in a formal manner to determine whether they have the right product, the time, or the resources—rather, the salesperson decides to bid and then obtains the resources and approvals from management. A salesperson who is too busy may actually *not bid* on your project.

It is important to understand this point because you should not confuse the salesperson with his or her product. If the product is right, you may have to work with the salesperson to get your project recognized and put on the priority list. If the salesperson appears indifferent, contact his or her managers and work with them to get your RFP recognized and on the right track. Remember not to confuse the salesperson with the product, especially when dealing with new sales staff or fairly new companies.

✎ Don't confuse the salesperson with the product.

The pre-RFP activity here is to identify accurately the supplier and the contact within the supplier's organization. Start a list of suppliers and contacts, so that you can establish early contact with suppliers and also send advance messages to them that the RFP will be arriving shortly.

Identifying Suppliers

There are many different ways to gather a list of suppliers for your project. One of the easiest is to work with your procurement or purchasing office, which will either have or be able to get a list of suppliers who work in or have products in the subject area of your RFP.

You may also attend conferences and supplier demonstrations to gather information about suppliers. For example, if you are interested in Customer Relations Management (CRM) products, you might look online for conferences about CRM. Typically, an online brochure will list the conference sponsors (who are typically large suppliers) and also provide a supplier list.

Once you have established a list of suppliers, you may consider sending each one a letter or e-mail that briefly describes your project, indicates when you will be ready to send the RFP, and states when it will be due. This information allows suppliers to start organizing their resources, doing their qualifying work on your project, and determining whether they need to team with other suppliers.

 If you have set up a Web site for the RFP effort, you may be able to post preliminary information about the RFP and its progress on the site. When you initially contact suppliers, you can provide them with the Web site address (and password, if you don't want the whole world to see your RFP effort).

You may also ask potential suppliers to respond to you if they are interested in receiving the RFP. Make sure they include the name and address of a specific person who should receive the RFP; this might differ from your contact information. Be sure to reestablish this contact just before sending the RFP, as salespeople frequently move within a company or move to new companies.

Now the RFP recipient will, of course, have your name and address and will most likely contact you with various questions such as, "What is the budget for your project?" or, "Will you buy within six months?" This is a good time to develop a dialogue with the suppliers and answer as many of their questions as possible, without giving away confidential information. Building a relationship early will help your suppliers better understand your project and your company's needs. This relationship will, in turn, help suppliers write better proposals.

Qualifying Suppliers

Suppliers who receive the RFP should be qualified. First, identify all potential suppliers with the products or services required for the project. Once these suppliers are identified, you should take several steps to ensure that they are qualified:

> ✎ Only qualified suppliers should participate in the RFP.

1. Suppliers must be technically qualified. Do they have the correct products, or will they have to subcontract to other suppliers? If they subcontract portions of work, who are their primary subcontractors?

2. Do they have the resources to manage the project properly?

3. Are they considered a "local" company? If not, how will you work with them? Do they need to travel every time a meeting takes place? How do they handle regular maintenance activities?

4. How many people does the supplier employ at how many locations? Where is the nearest location to your project site? If the project is to take place in many locations, can the supplier support multiple locations? Is there a need for international support?

5. How many projects is the supplier currently managing, and will the supplier be stretched too thin? Is the supplier managing other projects similar in size to yours, or are they typically much smaller or bigger?

6. Suppliers must be financially qualified. Is the supplier in good shape financially and certain to remain in business and continue to support the product?

Suppliers are qualified for obvious reasons, but there are also some not-so-obvious reasons to consider. After you thoroughly review their capabilities and previous projects and resources, you will realize that not all suppliers have the correct product mix and not all will be able to manage a large project.

Some suppliers may be changing their company focus and while they could still bid on your project, would you want to be the last customer to have the last version of a product? In addition, many suppliers may "integrate" the products you need, but do they "own" the primary product being bid? If not, is the supplier who makes the product included in the bidder's list? Finally, why read and evaluate a proposal that is not from a qualified source? This takes valuable time and resources away from the suppliers who have good, responsive proposals.

Here is a checklist of activities that apply to the pre-RFP period:

1. Develop a list of suppliers.
2. Send a brief pre-RFP introduction letter and request information about the supplier and the product.
3. Hold pre-RFP interviews with suppliers, if appropriate, and request a product demonstration or their basic sales presentation.
4. Attend industry conventions and conferences or local supplier sponsored events.
5. Qualify the potential bidders for your project.
6. Consider holding a conference before the RFP is released with all suppliers to present your project and its principal requirements. Request comments and feedback within a specified time from the suppliers in attendance.
7. Develop a final supplier list with the names and addresses of specific people who should receive the RFP. Let suppliers know when the RFP will be sent.

In the spirit of "measure twice, cut once," it is important to identify the right suppliers and not spend time on organizations and proposals that are not right for your project. This approach will not only save you time but will also allow you to spend more time reviewing the right suppliers.

RFP Activities

Once you have identified the suppliers and attended demonstrations and conferences, it is time to write the actual RFP. It is assumed that you have already selected and recruited the core RFP team members and that you are ready to begin work. Below is a recap of the basic RFP writing and releasing activities:

1. Develop a project schedule for the RFP portion of the project (see Appendix K, "RFP Reverse Planning Calendar"). This is a "reverse calendar" in which you start from the date when the project is to be finished and work backward in time. You may be surprised at how long an RFP project will take.

2. Develop a clear and agreed-upon statement of the problem that is causing this RFP to be written. This statement will help everyone on the team not only to grasp the issues but also to agree that the statement accurately reflects the problem. This statement will also be used several times in the RFP itself.

3. Develop a high-level outline of the RFP and have the RFP team agree on it.

4. Once the outline is developed and reviewed by the "writers," have them revisit and confirm that they can complete their work within the scheduled time.

5. Once requirements have been written, write the evaluation criteria for each requirement. How will you measure a supplier's response to a requirement?

6. Compare the completed RFP and evaluation criteria to the budget. Have you underestimated the budget or overestimated the requirements?

7. Reestablish contact with suppliers prior to sending out the RFP. Ensure that your contact is still there and that the supplier is still interested—and still in business.

8. Publish the RFP. You may consider providing an electronic version of the RFP on a Web site for the suppliers to download. You may want to secure the site with passwords if there is sensitive information in the RFP.

9. Be prepared to hold the RFP conference if required. Ensure that you are prepared with a presentation, have the RFP team available, and can produce any other resources that are needed, as promised in the RFP.

10. Be prepared to receive and respond to suppliers' questions as they come in. In some cases suppliers may not be able to move forward until you respond to their questions.

11. Be as helpful to suppliers as possible during this period, but be careful of suppliers who try to work around the RFP team by going to senior management or who try to talk to the RFP team directly without the benefit of written communication.

It is the responsibility of the RFP team leader to ensure that these activities are handled quickly and that the schedule is kept.

Post-RFP Activities

✎ When proposals have been submitted, the next round of work begins.

Here are examples of activities to be performed once proposals are submitted. Each activity described below is discussed in more detail in Chapter 7, "Evaluation Guidelines" and Chapter 2, "RFP Planning and Preparation."

1. *Evaluate proposals.* The first activity is to evaluate proposals in an effort to separate potentially viable proposals from those that do not meet basic requirements. As little time as possible should be spent on proposals that *obviously* do not meet the RFP requirements. The initial evaluations should consider mechanical elements such as whether the proposal arrived on time, whether it followed the administrative instructions, and whether it took exceptions to major requirements.

2. *Eliminate the first round of suppliers.* The first proposals eliminated may be poorly written, priced significantly above or below other

suppliers by a factor of 50 percent, or on closer review lack the right product. Eliminated suppliers should be notified and should have the opportunity to understand why they were eliminated. Notification need not wait until the contract is awarded. It is important to document the rationale for eliminating a supplier, as this information may be used later when justifying the winning proposal.

3. *Establish a shortlist of suppliers.* The next step is to try to winnow the remaining number of suppliers down to two or three. This shortlist comprises suppliers with the potential to win the contract.

4. *Call references.* For suppliers on the shortlist, it is now time to call references. This call should be scheduled, and all of the RFP team members should participate in it. Only references for the shortlisted suppliers should be called.

5. *Host demonstrations.* The RFP may require that suppliers demonstrate their products, either at the supplier's factory or on site, so that the RFP team and other users in the community can get direct experience with the supplier and the products.

6. *Reference site visits.* If site visits were part of the RFP, these should take place prior to any final evaluation. The site visit is to a reference site designated by the supplier and is generally only for the final two suppliers in the competition. In a very close competition, site visits can make the final difference in the choice of supplier.

7. *Supplier site visit.* In some cases you may want to visit the supplier's factory or headquarters and meet the management team. This allows you to make certain that the supplier is financially sound and that all support groups proposed actually exist.

8. *Best and final offer (BAFO).* As part of the give and take during the evaluation period, there is a reasonable chance that the supplier overestimated a requirement's impact or overscheduled part of the implementation. The BAFO allows suppliers the opportunity to rethink and fine-tune their pricing by submitting their best and final offer.

9. *Supplier selection.* Consider this the last step in the RFP process and the first step of the project itself. You have done the homework, selected the best supplier possible, and are now ready to get started.

10. *Review the selection process with management.* It is possible that a formal internal document will need to be generated to explain why suppliers were eliminated and why the winning supplier won. Such a report will draw heavily from the evaluation forms and the notes taken during the meetings to compare evaluations. Remember to keep all of those notes taken during the meeting with suppliers, reference calls, site visits, and any other interaction with suppliers.

11. *Debrief suppliers who did not win.* Many suppliers are truly interested in why they did not win and how they could improve their proposal writing or products and services being proposed. Make room in your schedule to allow for supplier debriefings.

12. *Cleanup and storage of proposals.* It is advisable to keep at least one copy of all proposals in an accessible place for at least six months. While this is not a legal obligation (for commercial companies), it is possible that a losing supplier will question your decision three or four months after the award of the contract. Also, there may be good information in these losing proposals that you may want to review and profit from. Quite often, a supplier may raise a valid point about requirements, contingencies, or scheduling that you will want to incorporate into the final project.

As with any project, these activities must be coordinated and kept moving by the RFP team leader. Most of the RFP team will be off catching up on their "real" jobs, but the above tasks still need to be accomplished.

The Importance of the RFP from a Contract Perspective

The primary purpose of an RFP is to transmit your understanding of the requirements for a project to suppliers who you believe can provide solutions.

The RFP is a written document that both you and the supplier use to establish your joint understanding of the requirements, which become the project's baseline. This baseline, or the final proposal and RFP as written and agreed to, becomes the statement of work for the contract and is an important historical document if the project begins to experience problems.

Problems can begin at any point in the project and may include any aspect of the project from the schedule to the deliverables. If a problem becomes serious and begins to affect the project itself, the baseline documentation will most likely be used to determine where the problem originated. The origin of the problem must be established before a resolution can be determined.

If we agree that both the buyer and supplier in most cases operate in good faith, we can further agree that if the original cause of the problem can be pinpointed, the party responsible should accept responsibility for the cure. Having the RFP, proposal, and all associated documentation helps avoid the instinctive "finger pointing" when a problem is discovered and further puts the issue on the table in an objective fashion, allowing both buyer and supplier to determine jointly the cause, the potential effect on the project, and the possible resolution.

It is crucial to maintaining this "audit trail" to insist that every change, no matter how small, be put in writing and formally accepted by both parties. This change documentation should become part of the amended contract and should include any changes to the project schedule and other aspects of the original deliverables. For example, a "small" change or addition may affect the initial deliverable schedule, the internal and external testing schedule, the final documentation deliverable, and the final project deliverable itself. Even small additions must be accounted for in all of the areas that may be affected.

If the problem goes beyond the "good faith" mode of operation and the parties end up litigating the issue, the RFP and proposal will become the primary documents involved in the effort to establish the root cause of the issue. Maintaining current copies and insisting on documenting every change in writing will provide the detail necessary to determine who is at fault.

 One of the more common problems in projects is when two system engineers, one from the supplier and one from the buyer, decide to make an innocent change based on a conversation that goes something like, *Supplier:* "Can we move the text query box from the second page to the first so it can be accessed directly?" *Buyer:* "That's a good idea and I don't see why not. What's involved?" *Supplier:* "Not much. I'll handle it."

This change is then discovered during *final testing* by the marketing person, who says, "Who changed my design? The query box is not supposed to be on the first page because . . . so change it back."

Problems can range from schedule issues to feature issues and can be blamed on either party. While schedule issues may be the more common problem, "schedule creep" is typically the result of changing requirements or adding requirements to the project. Capers Jones, in his paper titled "Conflict and Litigation between Software Clients and Developers,"[2] states:

> Software development has been a difficult technology for many years. Compared to almost any other manufactured object, software development requires more manual labor by skilled craftsmen.
>
> Further, many software applications are designed to automate manual activities that were not often fully understood by clients in sufficient detail. Therefore as software development proceeds, new requirements and new features tend to occur in a continuous stream.

---

2. Capers Jones. *Conflict and Litigation between Software Clients and Developers.* Copyright © 1996–2001 by Capers Jones.

> Software contracting practices have often been highly ambiguous in determining the sizes of various deliverables, development schedules, and other quantitative matters. More often than not, the contract would deal only in generalities or discuss only part of the situation such as the number of staff to be applied. Unfortunately, most software development contracts contain insufficient language and clauses for dealing with changes in the requirements during development.
>
> The most common root cause of contract litigation where we have been expert witnesses are [sic] new or changed requirements added by clients after the basic contract has been signed and agreed to. The clients think these new requirements should be included in the original agreement while the contractor thinks they should be funded separately. Unfortunately, the contract itself is usually ambiguous as to how new requirements should be handled, and hence the contract itself adds to the probability of conflict and litigation.

By maintaining good documentation for the project, you will be able to minimize the "fix the blame, not the problem" mode of operation and be able to assess objectively how to handle project changes. Mutual assessment and agreement are preferable to allowing a problem to become an issue that may impact the schedule or the contract itself.

Jones' statement, "Unfortunately, the contract itself is usually ambiguous as to how new requirements should be handled. . . . " draws our attention to a potential area of concern over how changes will be handled and how suppliers accept (or reject) changes, track them, and report on the overall project status. Ensure that this topic is covered in your project management requirements section.

Conclusion

Writing an RFP and reviewing proposals are resource- and time-intensive activities. The costs for writing and publishing an RFP may be significant and may span six months (or more). Given the significant investment involved, the RFP process must be thorough and must be allotted sufficient resources and time.

Sending out an RFP is only the first step in the project: reading proposals, establishing evaluation criteria, visiting reference sites, performing a live test demonstration, and negotiating a contract will all be steps toward a final selection.

Remember that while your project may be significant to you, it may not be to a supplier. Suppliers are under no obligation to respond to your RFP if they feel it is poorly written, a technical "fishing expedition," not properly funded, irrelevant because they have evidence that you have already "selected" a supplier (". . . the RFP is *wired* for such and such" as they say), or if they believe that other opportunities appear to be better than yours. When they have multiple RFPs, suppliers will be selective and will work only on the ones that appear to be winnable.

Finally, the selected supplier becomes another member of your team and part of your company. Build a supplier relationship based on your mutual understanding of, and agreement with, the requirements and the work to be performed.

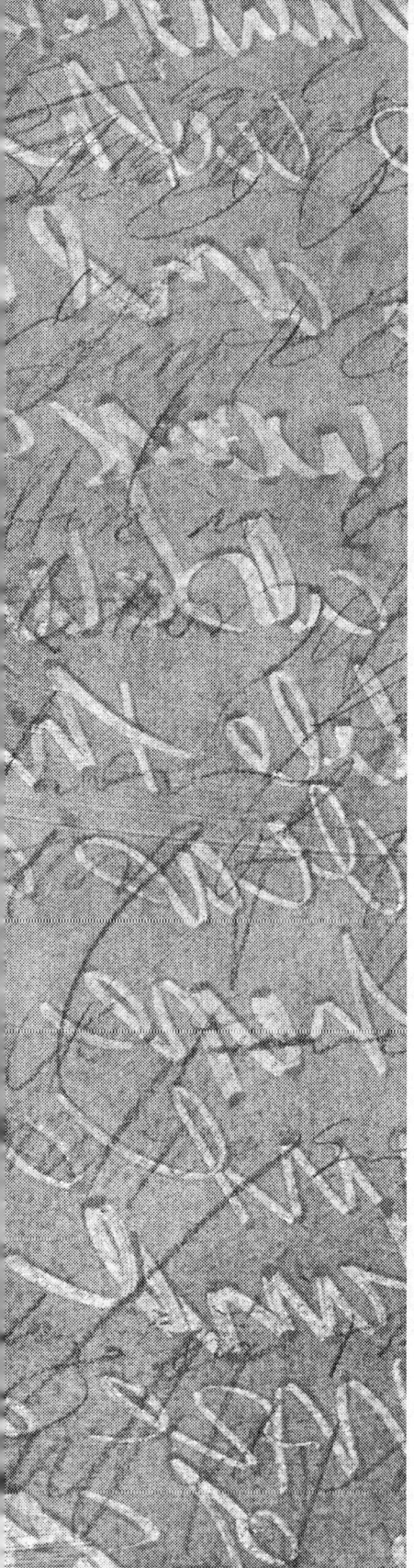

2

RFP Planning and Preparation

Introduction

Whether large or small, an RFP project should be properly organized and planned, just like any other project. An RFP is actually a segment of a larger project, in that some project work takes place before the RFP effort gets under way and the "real" project starts only when the supplier has been chosen. The RFP stage of the project takes the preliminary work and formalizes it into requirements and specifications. These requirements and specifications are then interpreted by suppliers and turned into proposals that are credible enough to allow you to move to the final project stage, which is to buy the products and implement them.

This chapter focuses on planning activities and preparing to move the RFP from the initial statement of need to implementation of the project. While the focus of the book is the RFP document itself, the "overall process" must of necessity include activities that happen before the RFP is written, such as a needs assessment, as well as activities that happen after the RFP is released, such as proposal evaluation, contract negotiation, and the overall project plan.

For example, prior to writing an RFP, someone on a committee said something like, "We need a new parking lot because we have run out of parking spaces in the staff parking lot and teachers and staff are parking in the student lot and sometimes off campus." In this scenario, before a team even began to write an RFP, a study group may have been formed to study the problem, arrive at possible solutions, and—most important for this project—determine how much it would cost to expand the staff parking lot. If the project then moves forward, the results of this work would become the basis for the RFP and provide the RFP team with some of the requirements and perhaps some ballpark pricing. To avoid duplication down the road, it makes sense for this valuable work to be undertaken in a manner consistent with the components of an RFP.

On the other hand, the initial study may have shown that eliminating the students from the staff lot would result in adequate spaces being available for teachers, so that no further work was needed. Or the project team may have found that adding space to the staff lot would involve significant work, that ballpark estimates were much higher than the school district could afford, and that no RFP was needed because the project was too expensive to pursue.

The following are the most typical tasks associated with developing and writing an RFP.

1. *RFP project organization.* Who is on the RFP team, and what are team members responsible for?
2. *Project schedule.* This includes the RFP but must also include all activities following the RFP, as well as supplier selection.
3. *Technology and supplier education.* How do you begin to understand what technologies and suppliers are available for your project?
4. *RFP budget development.* This includes the budget for the RFP phase but may also include one for the complete project.
5. *Project development and implementation.* Once a supplier has been selected, what tasks need to be performed to start the project?
6. *Post-RFP activities.* What tasks need to be done after a supplier is selected and before the project is started?

The project schedule shown in Table 2.1 is only an example of the type of schedule and planning that needs to take place once a project starts. The actual schedule should be in the form of a Gantt chart and should include assigned tasks, start and stop dates, constraints, and other details as needed and requested by your company.

Table 2.1   Sample Project Schedule

Item	Activity
1	**Pre-RFP Activities**
2	Identify need.
3	Perform initial study.
4	Write project justification.
5	Estimate budget for project.
6	Approve RFP project.
7	**RFP Activities**
8	Identify RFP team.
9	Identify project schedule and key dates.
10	Identify high-level requirements.
11	Start vendor and/or technology education.
12	Identify and interview users.
13	Develop technical requirements.
14	Review requirements with users.
15	Review requirements against corporate standards and constraints.
16	Finalize technical requirements.
17	Develop management requirements.
18	Review requirements with users.
19	Review against corporate standards.
20	Finalize management requirements.

continued

Table 2.1   Sample Project Schedule

21	Write RFP.
22	Develop evaluation criteria.
23	Develop RFP schedule.
24	Review finished RFP.
25	Send RFP to suppliers.
26	**Post-RFP Activities**
27	Allow question-and-answer period.
28	Receive proposals.
29	Evaluate proposals.
30	Ask suppliers' questions if needed.
31	Select shortlist.
32	Hold supplier presentations, site visits, demonstrations, and reference checks.
33	Select winning supplier.
34	Negotiate contract.
35	Provide supplier debriefings for losing proposals.
36	Review, clean up, and store losing proposals.
37	Start project implementation.

Pre-RFP Planning Considerations

Project Organization

The RFP project team should balance equally the skills required by three business departments: (1) business operations (the user group), (2) information technology (IT) and systems, and (3) purchasing.

Figure 2.1 depicts a typical functional organization chart for an RFP project. Bill S. from the IT group will be the RFP project manager and will

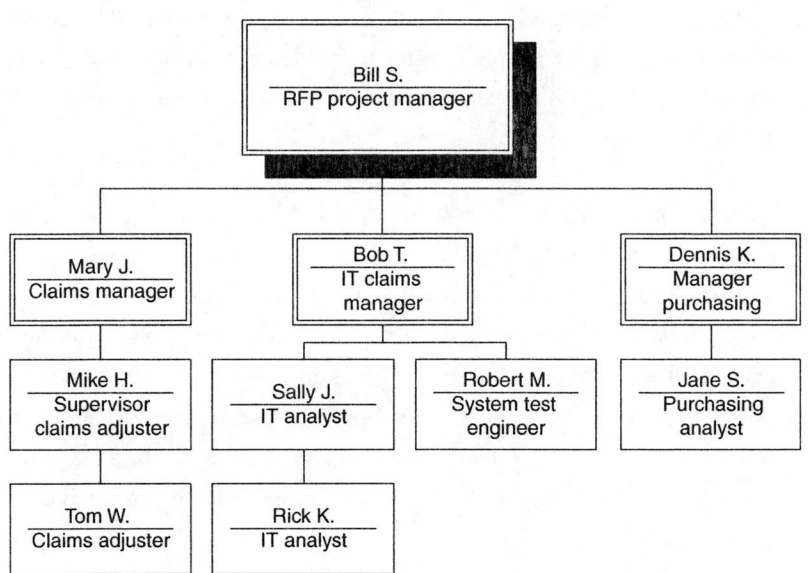

Figure 2.1   Typical RFP Team
Organization Chart

provide the overall project plan and direction. Mary J., the claims manager, represents the user community. Mike H. and Tom W. have the day-to-day working knowledge of how a claim is processed through the claims group and will support Mary in this effort.

The IT group position is staffed by the IT manager for the claims group and supported by two system analysts. The two system analysts may, for example, interview users in the claims group to establish the workflow and step-by-step tasks that are involved in the processing of claims that are entered. The system test engineer may be brought into the project early so that he or she begins to understand the technology and can start developing the testing requirements.

The purchasing department also has a role, and staff members will participate in the initial meetings so that they know what the project is about and what type of technology is being considered. Since a cost justification has been requested, purchasing has assigned a purchasing analyst to help the users and the IT staff develop the cost justification.

The organization chart in Figure 2.1 shows a group for a small RFP effort. For larger efforts, more people may be drafted from the user and technical communities, along with outside personnel such as consulting companies or industry experts.

Business Operations

✎ RFPs are sponsored by a department.

Business operations (which could be human resources, accounting, customer service, and so on) is usually the department that conducts the business for which this technology will apply and may be the sponsoring department for the RFP. Business operations staff understand the basic day-to-day work of their department, know how they use information, and are familiar with the current problems in a business process. When a new technology or system is being planned, operations should be the group that determines what work steps the new system should provide, how the information should be presented, and how a new system would improve upon the old work methods.

As part of the project team, operations is responsible for making the suppliers understand how the organization's employees do business in their current environment.

These same people should also be responsible for understanding how technology will resolve current issues or problems. The operations group needs to become familiar enough with the technology to assess its impact on their current processes and what benefit it would provide.

Operations staff typically provide the following types of information:

1. Definition of the current work process.
2. Development of the product's functional requirements.
3. Breakdown of workflow or business processes within the organization.
4. Definition of operational problems that limit the amount of work processed.

5. Description of operational processes that may not be changed.

6. Description of operational processes that can be changed or eliminated.

7. Analysis of work volume and throughput requirements.

8. Description of internal resources required (mainframe access).

9. Description of external resources required (regular outsourcing of work to a specialized company).

The job of operations personnel is to explain to suppliers what it is that the organization's employees do, why they do it, and what is limiting that work in the current environment. Operations must also be familiar with the technologies that can resolve these work limitations in order to describe to suppliers what they hope new systems and technologies will provide for them.

Information Technology (or Systems)

An information technology or systems (IT or IS) department is generally responsible for supporting corporate hardware and software needs, including the network and other communications. Technologies that might be needed to accomplish the organization's business objectives include the following:

- ❑ communication networks
- ❑ central computer systems and facilities
- ❑ personal computer systems
- ❑ business application software
- ❑ corporate standards

IT is charged with understanding how the new system will fit into the current computer environment, what changes might be required to support the new hardware and software, and what will be needed to support the image system. IT may also be responsible for local support operations once the system is installed. During the supplier identification period before the RFP is written, IT might be responsible for reviewing potential suppliers' technologies to determine whether they are appropriate for the project's application.

✐ IT typically handles legacy applications within a company.

As operations views the company from the perspective of how to get the work done, IT views the company from the perspective of what tools are needed to support that work. If either group dominates the planning process, the requirements that *both* groups would normally contribute might be lacking, and the resulting system might not meet either group's expectations.

In terms of contributing to the RFP, IT would be responsible for areas such as the following:

1. Development of RFP technical requirements (based on the functional work description supplied by the operations staff).
2. A complete description of the current equipment environment.
3. Description of any unique technologies with which the new system must coexist or communicate.
4. The setting of standards in the RFP regarding, for example, the communication's network, the GUI/workstation interface, or programming and development standards.
5. Identification of basic technologies.
6. Technical qualification of potential suppliers.
7. Development of RFP project requirements.

✎ IT reviews the potential technology that is correct for the application.

During their technology discovery process, IT might determine that certain technologies fit better than others, and this information becomes part of the planning process. For example, IT might find that certain internal paper forms (expense reports, vacation requests) can be stored more effectively as electronic Intranet-based forms, with users filling in the information online instead of submitting a paper copy. Following a review with the project team and an analysis of electronic forms technology, electronic forms would become a requirement in the RFP.

Purchasing (or Procurement)

The third group in the planning process is the purchasing department. Purchasing staff are normally associated with post-RFP work such as negotiating contracts and developing payment schedules. However, purchasing can and should provide a valuable service during the planning of the system.

Of course, the way in which purchasing helps you will depend on that department's traditional role within your company; some of the suggested tasks discussed below may not be appropriate in your case. It is advisable, however, to offer purchasing the opportunity to participate in the earlier stages of the project and not suddenly to "appear" when it is time to sign the contract.

In addition to the contract negotiation normally performed, purchasing could also be charged with helping to identify and validate suppliers, developing industry standard prices for equipment, and ensuring that potential suppliers are economically stable (reviewing D&B reports, 10K reports, annual reports, etc.).

A purchasing staff member should become a regular member of the team and participate in meetings. During the RFP period itself, purchasing can become the channel through which suppliers communicate with the technical team and, in turn, the channel for communications back to the suppliers. While this process might add a layer to the communications cycle, it insulates the technical team from the suppliers. It also allows the assigned purchasing person to keep up-to-date with the project and better understand the technology and the suppliers who are bidding.

This is not to say that suppliers and the technical team may not communicate directly (via a formal question-and-answer format). However, when that communication precipitates a change to requirements, that change should be formally documented and acknowledged by all suppliers. Purchasing, then, is responsible for maintaining the overall integrity of the proposal process. Purchasing should be responsible for the following tasks:

1. Developing and maintaining a list of potential suppliers and component suppliers.

> ✎ Purchasing can monitor the suppliers as well as review their business documents.

2. Developing and maintaining an estimated pricing list for budget development and providing a financial analysis of suppliers and suppliers' pricing.

3. Participating with IT and operations in the project cost justification by providing financial data and support.

4. Developing basic contracts and additional amendments for the project.

5. Formalizing the RFP for suppliers (the requirements and responsibilities) with IT and operations.

6. Participating in contract negotiations with selected suppliers.

Each of the three groups can play an important role in developing the RFP. In one sense, the RFP will become a better document because of the diversity of opinion and expertise represented by each group. Also, having each of the three separate business areas represented will foster team building within the company in general and for the project in particular.

Project Schedule

Developing a project schedule requires a basic understanding of the project's size, the technology involved and its unique application to the project's requirements, and the estimated amount of development and testing. The project schedule will most likely be a "best estimate" of the work that is needed; only after a supplier has been chosen will the actual schedule be confirmed.

The overall schedule can be broken down into the following three stages: (1) initial project planning, (2) procurement, and (3) supplier selection to project implementation and start.

Initial Project Planning

This period lasts from the time the project is approved until the time the RFP or procurement cycle begins. It includes such tasks as familiarizing the team with the technology, going to conferences and trade shows, having suppliers make presentations, and visiting operational sites where the technologies or products are in use.

This phase must also allow time for writing and presenting a project justification to senior management (if needed), making mid-course corrections to the project direction, establishing a budget, and getting management approvals. If a cost justification is required, this phase must be extended.

This stage is separate from the RFP because the project might be canceled due to lack of funding, scheduling problems, a poor cost justification, or other reasons; in that case an RFP is not written. The following are some typical reasons why a project may not move forward:

1. It offers a poor ROI compared to other projects.
2. The estimated budget is too high.
3. The project risk is too great.
4. Business operations change during the initial study, negating the need.
5. From a management perspective, the timing is poor.

Procurement

Once the project and budget have been approved, the procurement cycle begins. This phase must allow time for writing the RFP, having suppliers write and submit proposals, evaluating proposals, carrying out site visits and reference checking, and negotiating contracts.

A complete RFP schedule may include the following:

1. Initial project phase.
2. Preparation and distribution of RFP to suppliers.
3. Time for the suppliers to ask and respond to questions.
4. Evaluation of proposals.
5. Shortlist activities:
   a. presentations

b. demonstrations

c. site visits

d. reference checks

6. Negotiations.

7. Contract award.

✎ Use a reverse calendar for the project schedule.

Appendix K contains what is called a reverse calendar. A reverse calendar starts from the date you need the project to be in production and works backward to establish the various tasks needed to get to that point, setting the dates for each task to be completed. It is important to establish the date when the project should "go live" for this type of calendar. If the project doesn't have a firm completion date, estimate one and use that to establish the rest of the calendar.

The calendar in Appendix K contains steps that you may not think are appropriate for your project, but take care not to underestimate the many tasks that are needed. Once you have made a first attempt at the calendar, pass it on to other team members for their comments and additions. When this draft is complete, use it as the basis for the many planning activities that will be part of your project.

Supplier Selection to Project Implementation and Start

This phase begins when the contract is signed. Time must be allowed for suppliers and the RFP team to build the business applications, install equipment and communications links, train IT and operations personnel, and initiate project cutover. For some projects, the new system might be brought online in increments instead of an all-at-once switchover. There might also be a period of testing in which only parts of the system are operational, while final checkout is performed prior to final supplier sign-off.

Pay special attention to the tasks required for the project cutover. If you have an existing system that is being replaced, you may need to plan these activities very carefully; and you may also need to involve the supplier in the planning. In some cases, you can turn one system off on Friday and turn the new system on over the weekend. Many projects are more complex, however, and require user training in addition to changes that may affect your customers.

Since the amount of time needed for your project depends totally on your individual situation, rules of thumb are not applicable. However, it could take more than twelve months to move large systems from initial project planning to the installation of equipment to full operations. Given this amount of time, contingencies such as budget reversals, personnel changes, and supplier (technology) changes must be anticipated.

If the project is going to involve extensive business process reengineering, for example, the schedule will be affected in two ways. First, the reengineering analysis must have been carried out before the RFP goes out, so that the suppliers have all the pertinent new information. Since the goal of reengineering is to make work processes more efficient, applying the concept will substantially change the current work environment as part of this project. These changes need to be documented in the RFP. Second, more extensive training of personnel will be required after the system is procured, because the old processes and methods will have been replaced by completely new ones. In addition, the transition period might extend for some time as personnel adapt to their new environment. For projects in which the reengineering process is less extreme, training and transition times might be less dramatic.

Estimating the overall project time can be very difficult. The natural tendency is to be overoptimistic, causing the project to run over the scheduled time. It is best instead to approach the calendar with conservative estimates and to bring the project in ahead of schedule if possible.

A poorly planned RFP will cause confusion for both the supplier and the RFP team. The result of a poor RFP effort can seriously undermine a company's market position and strength if the issues driving the RFP directly affect the business operations of the company. The purchasing process and installation of equipment will take longer, cost more than anticipated, and may not provide a satisfactory long-term solution. Here is a typical chain of events resulting from inadequate planning.

1. The RFP team does not release the RFP on time because of an incomplete understanding of the problem and the technology needed to resolve it. Insufficient staff are assigned to the effort and they are given inadequate product training.

2. More supplier and product evaluation time is required, which necessitates keeping staff together longer, adds more travel, and perhaps causes you to revisit the RFP project budget.

3. Pre-RFP cost overruns quickly develop, and additional money is required to complete writing the RFP.

4. Technical risk mounts because additional funds are not approved. (All possible solutions are not explored due to the lack of funds and personnel resources.)

5. Once the RFP is released, the RFP team is quickly overloaded with questions and requests due to poorly developed and documented RFP requirements.

6. At least one question leads to the reevaluation of a principal requirement, thus resulting in a change in scope due to a restatement of the RFP requirement.

7. A change in scope requires a delay in the proposal due date, which delays all subsequent dates for the project.

8. When finally submitted, most proposals have not followed the requirements section contained in the RFP due to the changes caused by questions and general confusion on the part of suppliers.

9. The evaluation of proposals is delayed because of the team's inability to develop an equal baseline from which to compare the various proposals' features, benefits, and costs.

10. The suppliers now have to ask extensive questions in order to clarify proposals, further delaying the contract award.

11. RFP budget money is now in the red. The budget will have to be increased again to complete the evaluation.

12. If approved, additional budget money is taken from the project budget, which means that the project plan must be scaled down.

Technology and Supplier Education

The key to an RFP effort is understanding what you are buying from a technology point of view. It is absolutely essential that the people responsible for the RFP and writing the requirements are familiar with the technology and the differences between various suppliers' products. One of the most common pitfalls is to write a requirement that combines several needs; no single supplier can respond to or write requirements for products or product features that do not exist.

Therefore, technology and supplier education is an essential step in the RFP process. It is entirely possible, and reasonable, to invite a number of suppliers to give demonstrations and presentations about their products and companies. While each one may give a one-sided view, if you invite three or four suppliers, you will begin to see the differences in their products while learning more about the basic technology itself. As you interview suppliers, ask them for a reference so that you can learn more about how another company installed the product and whether the project was successful. (Suppliers may resist giving you a reference this early in the game.) If you are able to speak to some referees, they will often offer you tips about things they learned as part of their project.

Ask if the supplier has a user group in your local area, find out more about it, and attend a meeting. At the meeting you will find companies that have installed the product and use it, and you may be able to visit sites where the suppliers have installed their equipment. User groups are dedicated to helping other users (of a supplier's products), and they often publish a newsletter and hold an annual conference. This type of setting may be invaluable for learning about a product and finding out how other users view the supplier.

To help you establish a budget, you may also ask the supplier to provide you with sample product pricing. At the same time do not forget to ask suppliers for a thumbnail of how much a typical implementation costs. Budget development is discussed in more detail later in this chapter.

Attend conventions and conferences to see the products being demonstrated and hear speakers talk about the technology and the suppliers. You may be able to find other people with similar interests to yours or find speakers who are giving presentations about their implementation experience. At large conferences, there is typically an area in which suppliers can demonstrate their products and services. Contact the suppliers you want to see before the conference to ask if they offer private demonstrations; if so, request an appointment. Anybody who has gone to a large conference knows how difficult it is to get a good understanding of a product with 30 other people looking on and asking questions.

Consider hiring a consultant who specializes in that particular technology and can either become part of the RFP team or provide an appropriate training session on the technology and the differences among the most popular suppliers. Often, a consultant can save you time because of his or her experience and knowledge of the supplier community.

Once you have become familiar with the technology and the suppliers, make a list of the suppliers. If the list is large, you may want to do some pruning to limit the number of contenders. It is, of course, easy to send an RFP to any qualified supplier, but this approach is not the best. Limit the RFP distribution to those suppliers in whom you are interested, so that you can concentrate more on qualified proposals and not waste time on unqualified suppliers.

Budget Development

As an integral part of the RFP planning process, you must develop a project budget in order to establish funding for the project. The project budget can be broken down into three distinct areas:

1. RFP project budget.
2. Project acquisition budget.
3. Ongoing yearly costs (based on three or five years).

RFP Project Budget

The first budget item is to establish a budget for the project team and outside resources. The job of the project leader is to develop a project budget that may include items such as the following:

- ❑ number of personnel assigned to the project
- ❑ time commitments for the project team
- ❑ facilities and computer resources
- ❑ outside resources such as conferences, trade shows, and supplier visits
- ❑ outside support such as consultants or purchasing industry reports
- ❑ travel reference sites
- ❑ additional equipment for testing or demonstrations

It would be reasonable for the project team to expect to travel to trade shows and conventions, suppliers' headquarters, and several sites where similar technology has been installed. The project team might also elect to install (whether by purchasing the product or obtaining an evaluation copy) a small stand-alone system in order to become familiar with the technology, principles of operation, and proper methods of testing. This system would also allow operations personnel to "test drive" a prototype of the application and other uses for a test system.

This part of the budget, which may or may not be rolled into the larger project, is necessary to establish the overall budget for the project based on the number of people involved, potential purchases, and travel. The budget should encompass the project from the beginning until the signing of the final contract.

The Project Acquisition Budget

The project team is charged with developing a budget for how much the project and/or equipment will cost. The estimate can be based on the previous work accomplished while the team learns about suppliers and finds out their basic pricing. However, as already noted, large projects consist of more than just the physical equipment; installation charges, training, development charges, and possibly additional personnel also need to be accounted for. Appendix D, "Budget Planning and Investment Analysis," provides a general overview of how to establish the budget while also gathering information for the investment analysis.

One of the primary goals of the project team, therefore, is to establish the overall system costs, which would include at least the following components for a hardware and software computer system:

1. System hardware.
2. System software.
3. Application software (application development).
4. Communications hardware and software.
5. System maintenance.
6. Training.
7. Project management.
8. Facilities upgrades/site preparation.
9. Ongoing or recurring costs such as magnetic tapes, optical disks, or even printer paper and toner.
10. Miscellaneous costs.

Developing system costs can be accomplished through a number of methods. The first method is to work with several suppliers to establish basic equipment and software pricing. Suppliers will usually provide a "one-only list price," the suggested list price offered by the supplier for each piece of equipment and software. Getting these prices means that your budget will be conservative because final pricing may be lower but would not be higher.

The second method is for the project team to develop the equipment list and use an information service or a consultant to develop the pricing. But these prices might not be as accurate or up-to-date as those obtained directly from suppliers. Prices received by this method are generally as current as the last time the supplier's database was updated by the consultant or information service company.

The larger information technology services, such as Gartner Group or Giga Information, will also have current product pricing and may be able to put together a preliminary budget for your system and equipment. However, if you are not already a member, the costs can be substantial.

Another component to establishing budgetary pricing is determining the software development and project management costs if your RFP is for a computer application. Software development might in some cases equal or exceed the price of the hardware and application software. If this factor is not taken into account or is given only marginal attention, the final budget may fall significantly short of the actual costs.

The same is true for project management. For a long-term project in which the supplier is expected to provide assistance and coordination during the development cycle, there might be significant costs associated with the supplier keeping a team of people together for development, travel, and preparation of project summary reports.

Ongoing Yearly Costs
The third component of the budget is the ongoing support and recurring costs associated with both the project itself and the equipment being

installed. For example, additional power and air conditioning, extra insurance, recurrent training, and consumable supplies such as paper and toner for printers would all add to the total costs.

If the project is for a computer system, the yearly license fees, maintenance, and any other annual fees should be added to the costs. As reviewed in the pricing section, support costs can be significant and could make the difference between a winning and losing proposal. But even more important, these costs must be estimated and included in the budget.

These costs are reviewed in more detail in the pricing section, but they must be estimated at an early stage to establish a valid project budget. In some cases, this estimate may dictate alternatives and help you to decide whether, for instance, to purchase equipment or outsource the project. If the estimated project budget is higher than the "real" budget, you will either need to rethink the project goals or obtain approval to increase the real budget.

Post-RFP Planning Considerations

Project Development and Implementation

Depending on the type of project, a significant amount of work may need to be accomplished after the contract has been signed. This work may range from completing facilities improvements to developing the business application.

These activities will begin once the project has a final contract and the supplier is able to sit down with you to establish the schedule and the project start date.

It should be understood that the project plan required in the RFP was a supplier's best estimate given the facts in the RFP, and that after you and the supplier are able to have your first meetings, the project plan may change, and most likely will. This does not mean that the supplier will have the freedom to redevelop the plan, but there is a reasonable chance that a change will occur. If it does, it could affect the final project timeline and completion date. Such a change may also cause you to alter your final estimates of what resources are needed and for what length of time.

In addition to the project plan, it is also possible that changes will be made to the equipment, hardware, systems software, or final design of the project or application. These changes may or may not be absorbed by the supplier, as it depends, for example, on who was responsible for either missing a requirement or finding a "new" requirement during the initial project meeting. Change is inevitable, especially in a large project.

Additional Post-RFP Activities

When the supplier has been selected and you are ready to negotiate a contract, there are several important steps you may want to consider.

1. Make sure that the contracts person has all of the information that he or she needs to negotiate the contract effectively: copies of the winning proposal, copies of the contracts from the supplier, and any documentation that fell outside the original proposal such as amendments to the RFP or amendments to the proposal. If you supplied a contract with the RFP and suppliers commented on the contract, make sure these comments are read before negotiation starts. Ensure that the contracts person fully understands the pricing proposed and is aware of any "verbal" agreements between you and the supplier's sales representative. For example, the sales representative may have "thrown in" a development license for your development machine, but if the contracts person is not aware of this, it will not appear in the contract.

2. Do not just throw away the proposals that did not win. Keep at least one copy of all proposals and associated documentation. These proposals may become your "audit" trail for why you selected the winning supplier in case there is ever any question by other suppliers or

your management. Also, what if the contract negotiations with the winning supplier fail, or the winning supplier is disqualified for any reason after the project starts? It would be difficult to ask the second-place supplier to send you another copy of his or her proposal.

3. As with item 2 above, try to keep all of the evaluation forms for all the suppliers as part of their proposal file. Evaluation forms are not always returned to the RFP manager and can easily be discarded as soon as the evaluation period is over.

4. Make sure that all the notes taken during the supplier reference calls, supplier site visits, and supplier reference visits have been collected, consolidated, and retained. It is alarmingly easy for this information to slip between the cracks and be lost, and it is extremely awkward to call a referee back for the same information the person already gave you—along with precious time and goodwill.

5. Losing proposals often contain good information that is either not acted upon or is lost in the heat of selecting the winning supplier. Often, proposals will point out holes in your RFP or missing information that could be important. Make sure these comments and supplier insights are not forgotten when you start the project with the winning supplier.

6. If other departments within your company have been part of the project, ensure that they receive a copy of the RFP and the winning proposal. For example, you may have a department or group that specializes in testing new products or equipment, which is brought into the project only after the contract is signed. This puts the testing group at a disadvantage and may put you at the bottom of their testing schedule. It is possible that such a delay in final testing will set back the project completion date and that the original go-live date will be missed. (Testing should have been part of the original RFP if your company has mandated testing requirements.)

Another example may be the facilities department. What if the supplier's proposal requires additional air conditioning or other physical changes to the existing facilities? Be prepared not only to provide them with a copy of the proposal but also to review both their action items and the project plan. As with testing, if a project is going to involve change to a facility, the appropriate facilities people should be involved from the beginning.

7. During the period that contracts are being negotiated, take time to revisit the project plan. If you have made a plan, ensure that you fold the supplier's additions into your plan. If you have accepted the supplier's plan, ensure that you or the supplier fold your additions into the plan. Use this time to review the losing proposals and search their project plans for any potential ideas or tasks that you would consider including in your own plan. Try to have a good solid overview plan ready when you have the first meeting with the supplier. Remember that the project plan is a joint venture between you and the supplier. The supplier must be able to participate in the plan and schedule.

Conclusion

The RFP is an intermediate step in a project. It facilitates someone's desire to buy new technology or replace old technology, but it is only a means to an end. On the other hand, the RFP builds the foundation for the project implementation but is not the project itself. As with any undertaking, if the foundation is not solid, the project will be on shaky ground. An effective RFP is the key to a successful ongoing project.

Given that it is the intermediate step between two projects, it is essential that an RFP not only be properly planned but also be allocated the resources needed to make it successful. This means having the right people at hand; getting their undivided attention when needed; allotting enough time and not rushing the RFP; and having the budget for demonstrations, travel, and other essentials.

A second important aspect of planning is to include the supplier's input when the contract has been awarded. Quite often the proposed project plan and schedule will change depending on the availability of people and other resources. For large contracts with many people involved on both sides, it may take several days of meetings before a final schedule can be hammered out. Ensure, however, that if there is a firm date by which the project has to be completed, the supplier is aware of it.

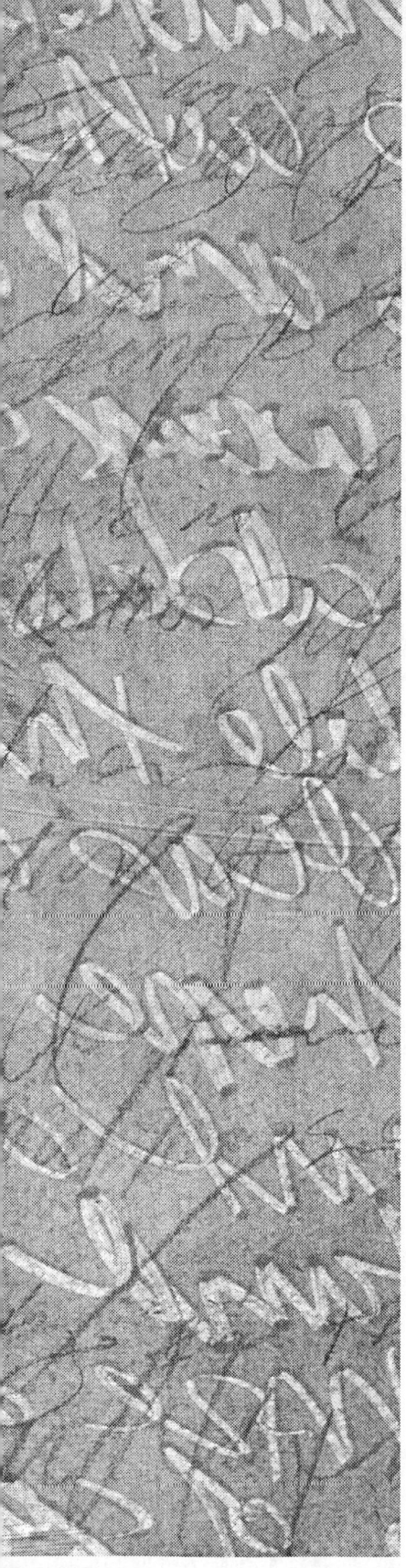

3

RFP Administrative Requirements Section

Introduction

The first section of the RFP is the administrative section. The purpose of this section is to provide suppliers with a framework for their responses so that all proposals received present the same information and follow the same structure. This "sameness" facilitates the proposal evaluation process.

The administrative section contains the following information:

- ❏ Introduction and statement of the problem.
- ❏ RFP roadmap.
- ❏ Time and place to submit the proposal.
- ❏ Date of a bidders' conference, if one is being held.
- ❏ Relevant dates for the procurement process.
- ❏ Requirements for preparing proposals.
- ❏ Description of how proposals will be evaluated.
- ❏ RFP contact names and addresses.
- ❏ Any other information suppliers may need in order to respond adequately.

Failure to comply with the administrative requirements might be grounds for disqualifying a supplier's proposal or lowering the supplier's overall score during evaluations. Instructions are mandatory requirements and should be treated as such by suppliers. Also keep in mind that the instructions should not make excessive demands and that suppliers should not be required to shoulder unnecessary expenses as part of their proposal efforts.

✎ RFP adminis-
trative requirements
are mandatory.

How to Use This Chapter

This chapter reviews and discusses, when appropriate, what goes into the administrative section. This section provides examples of RFP instructions and discusses why you may want to include a particular instruction in your RFP. *Note that not all of the ideas and examples presented below will apply to your RFP.* You may consider either adding additional instructions and requirements for your RFP when needed, or simplifying the list to suit your particular situation. A more complete example can be found in Appendix A, "Administrative Information."

Anatomy of an Administrative Section

Whether it is the first or last section suppliers read, the administrative section is their roadmap to responding correctly. If they do not have such a roadmap, the proposals you receive will be different in structure, content, and pricing. Evaluating five to ten proposals that have no relationship to each other or to the requirements is a difficult task. However, even though you lay down mandatory requirements, many suppliers will choose to ignore them, thus disqualifying their companies and products.

Most of the content of the administrative section is straightforward. Below is a list of those areas that warrant discussion and comment.

RFP Overview

✎ Administrative
requirements are
the ground rules
for proposals.

The RFP overview introduces your company and briefly states the reason for the RFP. Supplement information about your company with annual reports, appropriate marketing material, and the location of your Internet address in an RFP appendix. Suppliers will require background material on your company so that they can better understand why the RFP was written and how their products will fit into and help your company.

A sample company introduction may look like this:

ACME Bank is a federally chartered, publicly traded bank that ranks among the nation's top five banks and internationally among the top ten banks. Our main financial products range from private and personal banking to multinational loans for large construction projects.

ACME leads the field in large construction loans in North America and is among the top banks in Europe, Asia Pacific, and Latin America participating in multinational and multibank loans. ACME has one of the largest and most secure bank balance sheets in the world.

A world leader in multinational construction loans, ACME also dominates the market in risk management, financial structuring, fixed-interest issuance and trading, and foreign exchange dealing and derivatives. It maintains leading positions in corporate finance and equities throughout the world.

Additional information on ACME can be found in the appendices to this RFP; readers may also visit *http://www.acmebank.com/history* to find out more about ACME Bank.

This introduction by ACME Bank gives suppliers a rough picture of who the buyer is, what types of products and services they provide, and where they operate. A supplier can use the introduction as part of a summary to management when qualifying ACME as a bona fide sales opportunity.

The second part of the overview tells suppliers the reason for the RFP. Written at a high level, it introduces the basic problem that is being dealt with in the RFP. The problem statement may look like this:

ACME is releasing this request for proposal (RFP) for the implementation of an electronic document management system for loan servicing and processing. ACME is seeking to implement a global solution with a potential user base of approximately 20,000 users worldwide and would expect a solution of an appropriate scale. Currently, loan documents and portfolios are managed in their paper document form and kept in secure vaults, with copies being faxed or couriered nationally and internationally when needed for review or signature. Electronic document management technologies will eliminate the need for faxing and courier services while providing secure storage, faster access to documents, and disaster recovery capabilities.

✎ The RFP problem statement should be in the first section.

This RFP focuses primarily on the following areas:

- electronic document management
- digital imaging (scanning) of documents
- local and remote document retrieval (worldwide retrievals)
- workflow to facilitate the management and approval process (worldwide workflow)
- common international interface to facilitate user access for international users

ACME fully expects suppliers to provide a comprehensive solution on an international level that meets or exceeds all requirements as stated in this RFP. ACME expects suppliers to demonstrate their international management capabilities and to assume responsibility for all requirements in this RFP. ACME expects a single supplier to assume full "primary supplier" responsibility for the design, installation, and maintenance of the proposed system. While teaming and subcontracting are permissible, one firm shall be the prime supplier on the contract.

✎ Review with suppliers the business reasons that are driving this RFP.

There are several important messages in the above statements. First, we know right away that (1) the RFP is for electronic document management technology and (2) the application involves loan servicing and processing. Second, ACME states that the system will be international in scope. This point is important because some potential suppliers may not have international experience or capabilities and will either have to refrain from bidding or team with another supplier who can provide an international presence. Third, ACME is providing the first indication of its "hot buttons," such as, "eliminate the need for faxing and courier services while providing secure storage and disaster recovery capabilities." By telling suppliers *why* they need this technology, ACME is telling the suppliers to concentrate on the electronic transmission aspects and on "secure storage and disaster recovery capabilities."

A key element of the RFP introduction, and of the RFP as a whole, is to show suppliers how technology relates to a business problem. Technology is not normally bought for its own sake, but rather to solve a business issue or problem. By identifying the business issues (cost of faxing and courier services, delays inherent in courier services, weak disaster recovery capabilities) instead of making the supplier guess, ACME is allowing suppliers to focus on the business problems, not just on the technology.

Repeat your business needs and technology responses in all sections of the RFP to ensure that the supplier recognizes them and responds appropriately.

Supplier and Supplier Reference Information

While you may have done your homework in order to create the list of suppliers, you may still want to have the suppliers formally introduce themselves in their proposals. As shown in Appendix B, "Sample Supplier Information," this list of questions allows you to ask for and receive information about suppliers that you may feel is important to your project and the overall effort. Consolidating this information into one section or area of the supplier proposals provides you with a quick and easy glance at a supplier's business. If you do not request this information in a centralized place, chances are that you will be digging for the details in the supplier's proposal and annual reports, or even doing research to get some of the information. One of the primary purposes of requesting this information is to allow you to assess the supplier's financial strength and stability.

The same is true for the references that a supplier is asked to submit for your project. Prior to calling a reference account, you may want to have information about that company's business and the products that have been installed. Having this information included with the proposal allows you to determine early on if the supplier has large or small accounts (you may be a "large" account and want references of a similar size), how long the products have been installed, and what type of work the reference is using the products for; for example, if you are an insurance company, you may want to see references from similar companies doing similar types of work. You may also be able to require the supplier to provide other references if you find that the ones listed are not suitable.

The request for supplier information can be made either in the administrative requirements section, the management section, or the pricing section (pricing because contracts and licensing are often part of contracts, and supplier information is often considered the same type of information).

It is also possible to create a separate section in the RFP in which suppliers are asked to provide information about themselves.

Company Confidential Information

Your RFP may contain information about your company that is confidential or proprietary. For example, you may have to supply factory production numbers, accounting information, or information about your customers or your customer base. Protect this information by stating clearly in the administrative section that this information is confidential and by having suppliers sign and return a nondisclosure agreement (NDA). A sample NDA is provided in Appendix E.

If the information is highly confidential, you may consider requiring prospective suppliers to sign and return the NDA in order to receive the RFP. You may also choose to warn suppliers not to share the RFP with other suppliers or subcontractors unless they have been approved by your company and have also signed an NDA.

It is reasonable, in the case of confidential information, to ask suppliers to sign and return a notice of "intent to bid" (see below) and to include an NDA with this form. In this situation, a supplier may have to sign and return the form before receiving the RFP.

Intent to Bid

In order to understand and prepare for the proposals, it is often a good idea to require potential bidders to tell you whether they intend to bid on your RFP. Some companies require suppliers simply to write back by a certain date declaring their intent to bid or not; other companies send a form that must be filled out and returned.

The letter or form also requires the supplier to submit the name and contact information of the person responsible for the proposal effort. In many companies, the person who responds to an RFP is not the person to whom it was sent. In some cases, if you call and ask suppliers if they are planning to bid, they may not know which person in their company now has your RFP. By signing and returning the letter, suppliers are also indicating their acceptance of the terms and conditions as stated in the RFP.

> Suppliers shall complete and return this form within the time specified in the RFP schedule in the administrative section. Suppliers who do not return this form will be disqualified from further participation. The undersigned authorized person has read all RFP instructions and requirements and will submit a proposal in compliance with those instructions. Return this Intent to Bid form to the name and address listed in the administrative section.

The form may also ask why a supplier is choosing *not* to bid on the RFP, if that is the case. Quite often suppliers do not bid on RFPs but no effort is made to ascertain why. Appendix G contains a sample notice of intent to bid.

Proprietary Information Notice

Along with the NDA, you may also need to add a proprietary notice of confidential information to the front of your RFP, as in the following example:

> This RFP contains proprietary and confidential information of (YOUR NAME), which is provided for the sole purpose of permitting the recipient to respond to the RFP submitted herewith. In consideration of receipt of this RFP, the recipient agrees to maintain such information in confidence and not to reproduce or otherwise disclose this information to any person outside the group directly responsible for responding to its contents. There is no obligation to maintain the confidentiality of any information that was known to the recipient prior to receipt of such information from (YOUR NAME), or becomes publicly known through no fault of the recipient, or is received without obligation of confidentiality from a third party owing no obligation of confidentiality to (YOUR NAME).

Basically, this notice protects you against the supplier allowing confidential information from your RFP to be released or viewed by people not covered in the statement. This sample "Proprietary Notice Statement" is also available in Appendix F.

For those who are not familiar with this type of notice, it simply states that the supplier cannot share your information. However, if a supplier has already received confidential information from another source, such as a public site, the supplier is under no obligation to maintain the confidentiality of that information.

This is the same notice that a supplier may place in his or her proposal to protect company information, as described in the next section.

Supplier Confidential Information

Suppliers may provide confidential information in their proposals including information about how a product works, marketing strategies, financial details not publicly available, or future product offerings not yet released to the public. Suppliers may require you to sign an NDA, hold their proposal in confidence, or restrict the readership of their proposal to those personnel on the RFP team.

Typically, a whole proposal cannot be considered confidential because it contains some information that is publicly available. Therefore, in the administrative section, you should request that suppliers mark *only* the pages that contain confidential information.

Subcontracting

A supplier may need to subcontract with other suppliers in order to meet the requirements of your RFP. Most RFPs allow subcontracting but require that only one supplier (the prime supplier) submit a proposal; that company is considered solely responsible for agreeing to contract terms and for contract performance.

> The supplier selected shall be solely responsible for contractual perfor-
> mance and management of all subcontract relationships. This contract
> allows subcontracting assignments; however, suppliers assume all
> responsibility for work quality, delivery, installation, maintenance, and any
> supporting services required by a subcontractor.

The RFP may require any subcontracting relationships to be listed in the supplier's proposal. If a single subcontracting relationship exceeds 25 percent of the contract value, for example, the RFP may require that subcontractor also to submit financial and company information.

Even though a prime supplier has signed a contract accepting sole responsibility for subcontractors, a subcontractor with over 25 percent of the contract could substantially damage the overall effort if that company were to experience problems or not be able to complete the work. Thus, it is in your best interests to understand fully, and approve, major subcontracting relationships.

Interestingly, it has happened in the past and will no doubt happen in the future that a prime contractor and a subcontractor do not always see eye to eye, resulting in trouble for your project. While you may have an ironclad contract that binds the prime contractor to performance, if the subcontractor is experiencing trouble, is not being paid, or is on the brink of bankruptcy, your project will suffer.

In many cases the trouble revolves around money; for example, if the prime contractor, for any number of reasons, does not pay the subcontractor, the subcontractor may withhold all further work. Remember that while the two sides argue, your project may suffer, so be prepared to step in and mediate the problem, or in the worst case, agree to pay the subcontractor directly to keep the project moving.

RFP Contacts

The next piece of information that appears in the administrative section is whom to contact when there are questions about the RFP. It is wise to limit a supplier's contacts and not allow the supplier to speak directly to members

✎ Keep the number of contacts to a minimum.

of the RFP team. Such informal discussions of the RFP can be damaging to the overall effort, because one supplier may be given information that provides an unfair advantage. Alternatively, if incorrect information is given that causes the supplier to be eliminated, that decision may then be protested, causing extra time and money to be spent.

Advise suppliers to submit all communications in writing and specify that oral communications will not be allowed. It is usual to give suppliers only one name from the RFP team as a contact, thus ensuring that all communications are funneled through one person. Note: this person has to be present and available during regular business hours and throughout the life of the RFP. If suppliers' questions go unanswered or unacknowledged, they may justifiably ask for an extension to the due date or protest a final decision.

Below is a typical format for the contact:

1.1 RFP Coordinator

All requests, questions, or other communications about this RFP shall be made in writing to ACME Bank. Address all communications to the person listed below: communications made to other ACME personnel or attempts to ask questions by phone or in person will not be allowed or recognized as valid and may disqualify the supplier. Suppliers should rely only on written statements issued by the RFP coordinator.

> Ms. Jane Doe
> Director, Information Technology Services (ITS)
> 123 State Street, Building 4
> San Francisco, CA 94888
> (415) 555-1212 voice
> (415) 555-1313 fax
> janedoe@acmebank.com e-mail

To ensure that written requests are received and answered in a timely manner, e-mail correspondence is acceptable, but other forms of delivery, such as postal and courier services can also be used.

It is important for suppliers to recognize that a single contact will be maintained throughout the RFP process. Indeed, many sales representatives often cultivate friendships and business relationships with corporate managers, vice presidents, presidents, and board members. For a particularly lucrative contract, it is very possible that an "account manager" for the supplier will try to initiate contact with senior management in an effort to gain unfair competitive insight into the RFP. Ensure that your management is aware that a major RFP is "on the street" and that communication with suppliers is restricted.

RFP Questions and Answers

Suppliers will often have a variety of questions about all facets of the RFP, ranging from procedures to requirements. In some cases a supplier may not be able to complete a proposal until the question has been answered. Therefore, it is important to receive, distribute, and respond to questions as quickly as possible.

Distribute questions to RFP team members based on the type of question. A question concerning project management and implementation would go to the person responsible for writing those requirements. Questions about administrative requirements would be answered by the contracts team member. A typical question would be, "Can proposals be accepted if postmarked on the due date and received the next day?" (Answer: no.)

Questions mean that the RFP is being read and analyzed.

Responses to questions are held and periodically released to all suppliers at a set time, such as every Friday. In the released set of questions, the supplier's name and identification are removed so that other suppliers cannot determine who wrote them.

This procedure occurs for several reasons.

1. It is more efficient to gather responses as a group, and it saves time for the RFP team and question coordinator.
2. Allowing suppliers to see other questions and their responses should free your team from the need to answer the same questions repeatedly.
3. Suppliers can be directed to past questions for an answer.

Specify the format for submitting questions. Questions will be easier to read and understand if they are all presented in the same format. A typical format requires suppliers to specify the RFP section number, paragraph number, and page number and to quote the passage that prompted the question. This ensures that the question can be quickly found in the RFP.

Questions should be sent only to the specified RFP coordinator. Attempts by suppliers to ask questions of the RFP team directly should not be acknowledged. The paragraph with instructions regarding questions and answers should be placed directly after the paragraph containing the name of the RFP coordinator.

Below is an example of such instructions:

1.2 RFP Question and Answer Process

ACME will allow written requests for clarification of the RFP. All questions will be consolidated into a single set of responses and e-mailed by 12:00 PM each Friday. Suppliers' names will be removed from questions in the responses released. Questions should be submitted in the following format. Deviations from this format will not be accepted.

Section number

Paragraph number

Page number

Text of passage being questioned

Question

Questions not submitted electronically shall be accompanied by a diskette and questions shall be formatted in Microsoft Word (ver. xx).

Handling the questions electronically will save the RFP team many hours. Otherwise, each question will need to be retyped when the responses are prepared for posting.

Questions and responses are one of the most important parts of an RFP process. Questions demonstrate that suppliers are reading the RFP closely and that they are seriously committed to understanding your requirements and to writing a good proposal. If you have a complex RFP and receive no questions or only a few questions, you may consider calling several of the suppliers to ensure that they are responding to the RFP and to let them know that they are encouraged to ask questions.

You should set a deadline for final submission of questions. The final date forces suppliers to ensure that they have fully read all sections of the RFP in a timely manner. It also provides the RFP team with enough time to receive, analyze, and respond to questions prior to the proposal submission deadline.

It is important that the final date for questions be earlier than the proposal due date. A question such as a request for an extension, or one that results in a change in the requirements, could require that the proposal due date itself be extended. A good rule of thumb is to allow questions to be submitted up to two calendar weeks before the due date for proposals.

Responding to Supplier Questions

Suppliers may ask questions on topics ranging from the RFP requirements to the budget. It is the responsibility of the RFP team to determine how they will respond to a question. For example, many suppliers will ask if the project has approved funding and the amount. This question would be answered as follows: "The project has an approved budget, and that budget will not be disclosed to suppliers."

In publishing responses to suppliers' questions, the following format is commonly used:

1. Question
How many documents listed have printing on both sides?
Response
Approximately 25 per cent of all documents are two-sided.

2. Question

[Supplier name] requests an extension of five working days because staff are unable to complete a response on the date required.

Response

The request for an extension is denied, as there have been no changes to requirements and no other suppliers have requested an extension.

3. Question

Are alternative technologies that still meet the technical requirements permitted?

Response

Supplier is directed to review the proposal instruction paragraph 1.9, Submission of Alternative Proposals.

Responses to questions should be brief and, when possible, direct the supplier back to the applicable RFP section for further review. Responses should neither anticipate future questions nor provide information that has not been requested.

It is entirely possible that a question will cause you to rethink a critical portion of your RFP and to add or modify a requirement. While this may generate some concern on your part, consider it in a positive light; we all know that it costs much more to alter a requirement after the product has been built than to change the initial design.

If a change is mandated, consider the impact to the suppliers and to their proposal-writing schedule. A significant change may necessitate an extension to the proposal due date so that suppliers can rethink and perhaps reengineer their solution to accommodate the new or changed requirement. An example of the question-and-answer format is provided in Appendix H.

RFP Reference Library

An RFP Web site can be a valuable resource for suppliers.

Consider establishing a Web site for the RFP to publicize such things as the questions and answers, standards to which your company subscribes, and more detailed information about the project and the RFP. This "RFP reference library" makes it easy, for example, to post the questions and answers on the date and time you said they would be posted, and it becomes the supplier's responsibility to log on to the site and retrieve the information.

You may also be able to provide more detailed information that may have been too bulky to send to suppliers and is referred to in your RFP appendices. The reference library may not only be more convenient for the suppliers but also provides you with the opportunity to distribute more information in an electronic format.

The RFP library may also be used to maintain and update the RFP schedule and activities. By posting changes to the site, you are no longer responsible for sending large numbers of updates by letter or overnight courier.

RFP Schedule

The RFP schedule provides suppliers with one consolidated listing of the key RFP events and their respective dates. The following events should always appear in the schedule:

1. Pre-proposal conference.
2. Last day for questions to be submitted.
3. Posting of answers to last questions.
4. Proposal due date.

The schedule lists all events by name and date. If it is necessary to change the schedule during the RFP open period, send the page containing the new schedule to all suppliers either via courier service or e-mail. Request that suppliers acknowledge the new schedule so that no supplier can later claim not to have received it.

Pre-Proposal Conference

The pre-proposal conference allows both the RFP team and the suppliers to meet face to face. Each supplier who attends will see the competition, hear

   ✑ The pre-proposal conference is an important first step for understanding how suppliers will respond to your RFP.

their questions, perhaps gain insight into a competitor's strategy, and understand that more than one supplier is competing for this business, which is good for you and the RFP.

The agenda for the meeting can vary, but a typical meeting will cover the following areas:

1. Introduction of the RFP team and the suppliers.
2. Overview of the project's business needs and "hot buttons."
3. Review of the primary technical requirements.
4. Review of the current business process and application.
5. Responses to written questions submitted prior to the conference.
6. New questions and answers.

In the overview the presenter should reinforce the idea that the purpose of the RFP is to solve a business problem, not simply to acquire technology. This point is important, because you want suppliers to explain how their technology will not only solve your business problems but will potentially exceed your expectations. This in turn provides you with the ammunition needed when making a final supplier selection presentation to management. The following are examples of business-related goals and objectives:

❑ To enhance company growth, which is limited by outdated technologies.

❑ To improve customer service.

❑ To increase productivity (related to company growth or lack thereof . . .).

❑ To reduce the number of employees (related to productivity).

❑ To offer new products and services (related to company growth).

In the RFP paragraph about the pre-proposal conference, suppliers should be advised that questions submitted prior to the conference will be answered during the conference, while questions asked during the conference will be answered if possible, but may also be written down and answered after the conference.

The pre-proposal conference can be either mandatory or optional. The decision may rest on the overall size of the procurement and on the importance of the information provided at the conference. It may be financially onerous for suppliers to send one or two representatives across the country for a minimal opportunity.

 In one pre-proposal conference in which I participated, the incumbent supplier was very vocal about being the incumbent. This supplier was so persistent in reminding everyone that he "knew the account and had product installed" that I finally had to make a statement to the group that each supplier was going to be treated equally and that no supplier, including the incumbent, was positioned to win. Even so, several suppliers asked me after the conference for assurance that the RFP was "real" and not a ruse simply to show management that we had held a competitive RFP.

Proposal Format Requirements

One of the primary issues arising from RFPs is how to compare their requirements with the responses in suppliers' proposals. Suppliers, for the most part, are earnest in their proposal efforts *but would fall short if left on their own when organizing proposals.* Sales representatives and sales organizations are not typically organized around producing written documentation and proposals. Even though writing proposals is a necessity, many companies do not have a dedicated proposal support group. (Larger companies that frequently respond to federal and state RFPs usually do have a proposal support group.)

It is therefore in your best interests to provide suppliers with a roadmap for writing their proposals that forces all of them to respond in a consistent manner. The instructions provide an outline of the proposal and request suppliers to follow the outline when writing their proposals.

When outlining the proposal format, ensure that your instructions clearly follow your RFP structure and make it easy for suppliers to match requirements in the RFP to responses in their proposal. Also, emphasize in the instructions that suppliers must follow the prescribed format or risk disqualification.

Proposals may be divided into two volumes: (1) a technical and management volume and (2) a price volume. The reason for this division is that some companies try to evaluate the technical and management proposals prior to reviewing the prices, since they believe that pricing will unduly influence reviewers. You may also consider a third volume for all marketing material from suppliers.

Below is an example of the proposal response instructions:

All proposals submitted shall conform to the following format requirements. Deviation from these requirements may disqualify a supplier from the competition. A transmittal letter signed by a person authorized to engage your company in a contract shall accompany your proposal.

Volume 1: Technical Proposal

The proposal shall be divided into sections and tabbed as follows:

Section 1	Cover letter or letter of transmittal
Section 2	Proposal executive summary
Section 3	Response to administrative requirements
Section 4	Technical solution and description
Section 5	Project management description
Section 6	Response to demonstration requirements
Section 7	Supplier section for additional information
Section 8	Pricing section
Appendix A	Supplier references and qualifications

Appendix B	Supplier financial qualifications and annual reports
Appendix C	Supplier purchase contract
Appendix D	Supplier software license agreements

Suppliers are cautioned not to refer to a brochure as a response to a requirement. Suppliers are expected to write full answers for each requirement and not refer to previous responses using "See above" or "See the technical whitepaper, page 4."

If you choose to have a separate price volume, it would be laid out as shown below instead of being included in the main proposal as Section 8.

Volume 2: Price Proposal

| **Section 1** | Pricing response |
| **Section 2** | Contracts |

 Having spent many years both as a supplier and as an RFP writer, I can assure you that suppliers do not handle RFP scenarios very well. Even given precise instructions to follow, many suppliers simply do what they want and respond in a manner that is inconsistent with the RFP instructions. While it is easy to throw out the proposals that do not respond to requirements, you still want to have as many competitive proposals as possible to ensure that you have a "choice" among solutions. The worst case is when a supplier's solution is technically correct, with good pricing, but the salesperson has made a mess of the proposal. Are you confusing the salesperson with the product? Should you ignore the messy proposal? These are challenging questions for which there are no easy answers.

In addition to providing formatting instructions, you should also provide the supplier with information about how many copies of the proposal to send, whether an electronic copy should be included, and what type of binding is expected, such as a three-ring binder or a plastic comb binding.

The Cover Letter or Transmittal Letter

The cover letter shall serve as a letter of transmittal formally accepting the requirements of this RFP and shall be signed by a representative of your company who is authorized to commit your company to a contract.

The cover letter is an important document in the supplier's proposal: it is the company's commitment to stand behind the proposal. This means that only someone authorized to commit the company can sign the proposal and thus demonstrate that the supplier (1) has read and understood the requirements, (2) has accepted the conditions as stated in the RFP, and (3) is committing the company to the products and prices included in the proposal.

While it is unlikely that you would ever need to take issue with a supplier about this commitment, it is possible that whoever was primarily responsible for the proposal may have left the company and may have underpriced products and services.

The Executive Summary Required in Proposals

As part of your evaluation and decision-making process, you may be required to provide your management with a summary of the two or three leading candidates. Often, senior management will ask for the leading candidates' executive summaries.

To ensure that suppliers provide you with an executive summary, make it a clear requirement. The executive summary should be a summary of the project written at management level, which means that it should address the business problem, the technical and management solution, and summarize the pricing in nontechnical language understandable by someone (an executive) who is more concerned with the business than the technical issues.

The following paragraphs from a book on writing sales proposals state the purpose of an executive summary from a supplier's point of view.

The Executive Summary is an abstract of your proposal. It presents a summarized view of each major section, reviews any unusual features and benefits contained in your proposal, delivers the major selling points, and provides any pertinent information not requested in the RFP.

The Executive Summary is a real workhorse for your proposal. It not only summarizes the proposal, but it educates people not familiar with your products and company; it produces the first impression of your company; it translates complex technical concepts into understandable benefits; and it sells those benefits to the reader. To be effective, the Executive Summary shall do the following:

1. Tell the reader what he/she is buying in simple understandable terminology.
2. Explain complex technical concepts in terms that will be grasped by non-technical readers.
3. Convert complex technical concepts and features into understandable benefits.
4. Sell the reader on the benefits of the proposed solution.
5. Sell your solution over the competition's solution, features, and (perceived) benefits.[1]

If you think suppliers may not understand what is being asked for in an executive summary, be as explicit as possible. You can even outline the executive summary for suppliers, as shown if you think it necessary:

Suppliers shall provide an executive summary to familiarize ACME executives and evaluators with the key elements and unique features of their proposal and by briefly describing how they will implement this project. It should at a minimum do the following:

- Summarize your overall approach.
- Describe the business features and benefits for your solution.
- Discuss the risks and concerns arising from our RFP.
- Explain what is needed on our side to begin the project.
- Provide a summarized budget to include
  –pricing summary
  –how pricing was computed

1. Bud Porter-Roth. *Proposal Development: How to Respond and Win the Bid.* Central Point, OR: Oasis Press, 1998, p. 3-3.

–any pricing constraints on your part

–hidden or related costs that ACME may not have anticipated

Remember that this is your chance to have the suppliers do some work for you and for the suppliers to help you sell their solution to your management. It becomes very difficult to ask for this information after proposals have been submitted.

Pricing Section

The pricing section instructions review with suppliers how they must submit their pricing. As with the other sections, it is important that a supplier's pricing section relates to the technical and management requirements.

The pricing section may contain a variety of items, depending on what is being purchased. The key to a pricing instruction, however, is to require that suppliers break up their pricing into different products and services. Suppliers prefer to list one total price in order to prevent comparisons of specific product pricing among many different suppliers. If you received five proposals that ranged from $100,000 to $1,000,000 and the products were not broken into their component parts, it would be impossible to determine why one supplier's prices were ten times higher than another's. Generally speaking, prices from suppliers on the shortlist should be within a 25 percent range.

The following example, for a computer hardware and software system, not only breaks the major pricing areas into components but also breaks large components into subcomponents. Requiring each product to be listed allows the RFP team to determine whether one supplier is over- or under-pricing certain components. It also allows the team to determine where suppliers differ in their estimates and to form the team's baseline estimate, which helps to establish the budget.

Suppliers shall provide ACME with a firm, fixed price. Suppliers shall submit pricing both in writing and electronically in Microsoft Excel format.

Suppliers shall break prices down by their component parts as follows:

Hardware

    Data servers

    Communications servers

    User workstations with monitors

Software

    Application software

    Communications software

    Server operating system

    Workstation operating system

Implementation and Development

Suppliers shall price the implementation and development effort in accordance with the number of project personnel and their time. Pricing shall include all projected travel expenses.

Maintenance Costs

    Hardware

    Software

Training

Suppliers shall show the cost for each class that is required for initial start-up. Suppliers shall also show the cost of each class required over a five-year period.

Documentation

Suppliers shall show the cost of all documentation required.

Other Costs

Bidders are to specify any other costs that have not been specifically requested. Any cost listed should be tied to a specific task or product in the proposal.

Expendable Materials for a Three-Year Period

Taxes

One area that needs to be clearly defined and discussed is whether a product being proposed requires another product to be present for operation.

For example, a customer relationship management (CRM) system may require a full operating version of a major database product. If you do not have this type of database product installed, you would have to purchase it in addition to the CRM system. Suppliers may incorrectly assume that you know this already or have a suitable database product installed.

The above is only one example of a large system installation. One of the key elements to be reviewed will be the implementation and development costs. If, for example, one supplier prices this at $450,000 and eight months, while another supplier estimates $100,000 and three months, the discrepancy is too large. However, without the price breakdown, both companies might be within 25 percent of each other in total pricing.

Appendix C provides another example of proposal preparation instructions.

Best and Final Offers

✎ The BAFO is optional but can be useful when prices need to be revisited.

After proposals have been reviewed and a definite winner or two potential winners have been selected, you may request a best and final offer (BAFO). Having a BAFO is an option used most often by government agencies. However, the idea is generally sound, because after proposals are reviewed and suppliers have answered questions, suppliers may realize that they have overestimated some requirements. The BAFO offers them a mechanism for formally changing their pricing where they feel it is needed.

A note of caution: A BAFO is not the place to change requirements and have a supplier respond to new or lessened requirements. A BAFO is based on the original requirements of the RFP but allows the winning supplier to reinterpret areas in which he or she has gained a new understanding.

If you were to change the requirements in the RFP and request new pricing, suppliers who did not make it to the final stages of the competition might protest, in effect claiming that the rules were changed after they were eliminated and demanding the opportunity to consider the new requirements.

Alternative Proposals

An alternative proposal is one that offers you a product that may be different from what has been requested in the RFP. The alternative proposal may be so different that the proposed product may not "meet" the requirements as specified in the RFP. The challenge for the RFP team is to decide whether to accept such a proposal or to disqualify it immediately without further consideration.

Some RFP instructions state that alternative proposals will be considered, but only if the supplier also submits a proposal that does meet all of the requirements in addition to the alternative product being offered.

This restriction, of course, forces the supplier to write two proposals (which is a terrible burden on both you and the supplier) and assumes that the supplier can satisfy the original requirements, which is generally not the case.

An alternative proposal can either be a radically new product or approach to your RFP problem or a new way of approaching several of the requirements in the RFP while responding to the majority of the requirements within the letter of the RFP.

In submitting alternative proposals, suppliers must clearly note that they are taking exceptions to a requirement as stated but are in fact satisfying that requirement in an alternative manner.

For example, suppose you may have specified a live standup lecture presentation for the training requirement but a supplier has shown that an Internet classroom is just as effective as a live presentation, with the added benefit of being 50 percent cheaper. In evaluating this alternative, you may find that you agree with the supplier and accept their modification.

Compliance Matrix

A compliance matrix is a table that lists your requirements in one column and whether the supplier has complied with them in another. Requiring suppliers to provide you with a compliance matrix allows them in effect to summarize their proposal in one easy table. An example of a compliance matrix is shown in Appendix I, "Compliance Matrix."

This type of matrix allows you to skim the supplier's effort and determine immediately whether they have taken exception to your requirements or can only partially meet them. If too many exceptions are taken, you may decide to disqualify that supplier at this stage and not spend more time on a proposal that is noncompliant.

A compliance matrix also allows suppliers to *track their proposals* to ensure that they have responded to each requirement in the RFP. However, to complete a compliance matrix, suppliers must be clearly aware of and easily able to find all of the requirements. If you have tracked and developed a list of requirements, this information can be the starting point for a compliance matrix. Some RFPs supply the matrix and the requirements, while other RFPs require the supplier to create the matrix from scratch.

Including a compliance matrix is optional on your part and depends on how well you have defined your requirements and what type of RFP you are writing. In some cases, a compliance matrix may not be applicable.

Informational Paragraphs in the Administrative Section

✍ Additional information can be added whenever it is needed to help suppliers understand your RFP.

The administrative section may also contain informational paragraphs to help suppliers write better proposals. These items are informational and are not "requirements" that a supplier must follow in order to remain competitive.

For example, the RFP overview discussed in the first part of this section is informational and is provided to help suppliers better understand why an RFP is being written.

Definition of Requirements

Suppliers may not always understand what is a requirement and what is information but not a requirement. In government RFPs, the word *shall* always denotes a mandatory requirement, as shown in the following examples:

> Suppliers shall provide Annual Reports for the past three years.
>
> The noise level of any hardware component provided shall not exceed 70 dB.
>
> Suppliers' products shall meet the XML XX.XX standards.

Even if you do not use the word *shall* in your corporate culture, you should choose consistent wording to designate a requirement. Therefore, if you use the word *must*, suppliers should understand that whenever they see the word *must*, it is part of a mandatory requirement and they "must" respond to that requirement in their proposal.

Present this information in your administrative section in this way:

> 1.8 Definition of Requirements in this RFP
>
> To prevent any confusion about identifying requirements in this RFP, the following definition is offered: The word *must* is used to designate a mandatory requirement. Suppliers must respond to all mandatory requirements presented in this RFP. Failure to respond to a mandatory requirement may be cause to disqualify your proposal. Following are examples of requirement statements [provide several examples]:

As this definition of a requirement is crucial for suppliers, ensure that your RFP team uses language consistently. Many suppliers, if provided with an electronic copy of the RFP, will search for the word that denotes a requirement and pull those sentences and paragraphs out of the RFP and into a "requirements list" that they will use to guide them when writing their proposal.

Consider choosing among the following words to designate requirements: shall, must, will, or should.

Once you have selected a word, you may wish to develop a style guide for your RFP and provide examples of usage. When the RFP is completed, you may also consider performing a search for the chosen word to ensure that nonrequirements have not been inadvertently written into your RFP as requirements.

Additional discussion and information on this topic can be found in Chapter 4, "RPF Technical Requirements Section," in the section How Do Suppliers Recognize Requirements in Your RFP.

Production Environment Requirement for Products

Many companies writing RFPs do not want to become a test site for new equipment, services, hardware, and software products being developed. Furthermore, many companies do not want to be the first customer for a new product. Thus, many RFPs state that all proposed products must be in production and in use by at least three other customers in a production environment.

> ACME Insurance requires that all hardware, system software products, and application software products included in proposals be currently in use in a production environment by at least three other customers, have been in use for at least six months, and have been generally available from the manufacturers for a period of six months. Unreleased or beta test hardware, system software, or application software will not be accepted.

Interestingly, many suppliers have good products that will meet your requirements, except for their not being established and sold for years, or even months. New and unproven products should be considered, but the company itself, if also new, should be given a more thorough review to ensure that it is financially sound and will be able to service your account.

A company with a new product may also be more willing to negotiate the price or other contractual items, such as service charges, in order to sell you the product. The additional price concession may somewhat mitigate the risks involved in purchasing the product, as long as the company is stable.

Errors or Omissions in Proposals

As a means of protecting your interests, it is reasonable to tell suppliers that they are responsible for any errors or omissions in their proposals. In addition, state that you will not be liable if the winning supplier's proposal, which is incorporated into the contract, later proves to have math errors, for example, or if a product now required was not listed in the proposal.

> ACME will not be liable for any errors or omissions in supplier proposals. Suppliers will not be allowed to alter proposal documents after the proposal due date without permission from ACME. ACME may correct simple math errors and alert the supplier to the error, or if the error appears to be significant, ACME may either disqualify the supplier or require the supplier to make the recalculation and resubmit the data.

Proposal Evaluation Criteria

Suppliers should feel comfortable that their proposals will be given fair treatment and that no single supplier has "wired" the RFP. The evaluation instructions will help to confirm that all proposals will undergo an objective evaluation. A question that often arises is, "To what extent should evaluation criteria be provided in the RFP?"

There are two sides to the debate. The first side is generally against providing any evaluation criteria because suppliers will fine-tune (or heavily weight) their proposals to meet criteria provided and will pay less attention to those factors that are not being evaluated.

The second side argues that suppliers should know what the most important are and should be able to weight their proposals heavily toward those requirements.

Most RFPs will provide some level of evaluation criteria but will not go so far as to share the actual point values for each requirement. Below is an abbreviated example of an RFP's evaluation criteria. A more complete examination of evaluation criteria is provided in Chapter 7, "Evaluation Guidelines."

✍ Evaluation criteria tie RFP requirements to proposal responses.

Evaluation Criteria

ACME is interested in obtaining a complete solution to the stated requirements. Proposals that meet the proposal instructions and requirements will be given a thorough and objective review. Proposals that are late, do not comply with proposal instructions, or take exceptions to mandatory requirements will be eliminated without further consideration.

ACME will evaluate proposals using a number of factors, as described below.

Technical Solution

Primary consideration will be given to meeting the mandatory functional requirements as listed in this RFP.

The following are factors in the evaluation:

1. Fulfillment of the requirements as stated in this RFP.
2. Understanding of the work to be performed.
3. Technical approach and methodology to accomplish the work.
4. Completeness and competence in addressing the scope of work.
5. ACME will take a hands-on approach to building future applications and will favor solutions that allow ACME to develop applications internally using the provided toolset.
6. Discussion of the potential constraints of the proposed system that should be addressed and suggested approaches to resolving those issues.

Project Management

ACME believes that effective project management is essential for a successful implementation. Bidders will be evaluated on the completeness and responsiveness of their project management plans and the project team assigned.

As part of the project management plan, bidders must demonstrate adequate experience in developing and implementing similar corporate Intranet projects. ACME's confidence in the bidders' ability to meet deadlines and *successfully manage* similar projects will be a primary consideration.

Special consideration will be given to bidders who propose a detailed project plan with sufficient breakdown of tasks and steps to demonstrate a complete understanding of the project.

Cost

ACME will consider cost as part of the evaluation criteria. Low cost is not essential to win; however, large cost differentials between bidders will be carefully examined. Cost will be used as a final indicator for determining the finalists when all other criteria have been normalized.

Demonstrations

Bidders' site visits and the live test demonstration (LTD) will be evaluation factors. Bidders may not refuse to participate in either the site visits or the LTD.

References and Site Visits

ACME will contact bidders' referees. References will be questioned on the bidder's technical capabilities, project management skills, and ongoing support. If ACME requests a site visit, the visit will be a factor in the evaluation.

Proposal Costs and Expenses

Although the point is generally understood, it may be worth reinforcing that suppliers are responsible for all costs associated with preparing a proposal, participating in a demonstration, and traveling to reference sites.

ACME is not liable for any costs incurred by suppliers in the preparation and presentation of proposals, demonstrations, and site visits.

Product Demonstrations

As part of the evaluation process, a product demonstration may be called for in the proposal. Depending on the product, it is often beneficial to see and touch the actual product after the proposals have been read and a shortlist of suppliers has been selected. Generally, only suppliers on the shortlist are required to participate in demonstrations.

> ✍ Product demonstrations can cast aside any final doubts about the supplier.

There are several types of demonstrations:

1. *Supplier-provided "canned" presentation.* This type of presentation is typically provided by the supplier, who does a standup presentation using either presentation graphics or actually running the product. This is usually nothing more than a sales presentation.

   However, after reading and evaluating proposals, the RFP team can ask questions during the presentation about features and functions that were not well documented. Being able to see the product while asking questions is often worthwhile for many of the RFP team members. This also gives you one last chance to interact with the supplier's personnel, which can be meaningful.

2. *Demonstration of working software or product.* A second type of demonstration is to have the product installed and working, allowing the RFP team to work with it directly or under the supplier's supervision. Many suppliers have "canned" test applications that can show the functionality of the product so that all users can try different features and functions. This type of demonstration is better than a presentation, though not as good as seeing the product do the type of work that has been spelled out in an RFP. However, seeing and touching the product will give the RFP team a chance to verify requirements firsthand, which may lead to other insights that would not have been possible when just reading about a product.

3. *Live test demonstration (LTD).* A third type of demonstration requires the supplier to install the product at your site and to have the product perform a limited set of functions that are specified in the RFP. This means that the RFP team will see the product doing work that it will be doing if purchased and installed. It may also allow you to see how easy or difficult it is to set up the system and operate the system.

4. *Paid limited functionality demonstration.* In some cases it may be possible to pay a supplier or suppliers to install their products and to have them perform the tasks that were specified in the RFP. In this case, the supplier is paid for the time and resources involved in making the product perform the required functions. For a software program, for example, the supplier would customize or program the software to perform your application. Depending on the extent of the application, the program might generate a complete set of functions or a more limited set of functions. Once the product is operating, the supplier leaves it at your site for 60 to 90 days and allows you to operate the product on your own.

If you request a demonstration, it must be part of the RFP instructions and must be explained to suppliers. Suppliers must have time to prepare for the demonstration. In addition, the RFP team must prepare evaluation criteria and must be able to determine if the product performs as expected. The evaluation of the test becomes part of the final proposal evaluation.

One side benefit of such demonstrations is that the RFP team is actually able to work with the supplier for a short period. This interaction may indicate how well the supplier will work with the team after the contract is awarded.

Notifying Winning and Losing Suppliers

There are several chances to notify losing suppliers during the RFP period. The first opportunity comes when the RFP team decides on a shortlist of suppliers. This is typically the first cut and reduces the number of suppliers from ten (for example) to two or three. Some companies hesitate to notify suppliers early and prefer to wait until the final supplier has been selected.

If you are able to remove three suppliers from the competition immediately because of poor proposals, wrong products, and so on, there is no reason why these suppliers cannot be notified right away, since there is no longer a chance that they will be considered.

If suppliers who did not make the second cut or the shortlist are no longer going to be considered because they offered the wrong product, a terrible proposal, or astronomical pricing, they should be notified and removed from further consideration.

Proposal Debriefing

It is customary to offer to debrief suppliers who have lost. This courtesy is extended because (1) these suppliers may participate in other RFPs in the future and you should avoid alienating them and (2) many suppliers are seriously interested in learning why they were not chosen. It must be made clear, however, that this is not a chance for them to try to challenge or argue

✍ Suppliers who are disqualified or eliminated from further evaluation can be notified right away.

with the decision. It is also important not to provide competitive information, such as pricing, in these debriefing sessions. You may say that in addition to not having the "right" product, the supplier's pricing was very high, but do not disclose the actual winning price.

If a supplier seriously wants to dispute your decision after this session, this must be done in writing. However, you must have the ability to handle a dispute of this type, or else you must inform the supplier that the decision is final.

 I participated in a supplier debriefing in which the losing supplier wanted to know about the winning supplier's product features. The intent was to dispute that the winning supplier could actually perform as stated and to cast doubt in our minds. After the supplier tried several times to get these features identified, I finally said that I could not disclose proprietary information about the winning supplier, just as I would not disclose proprietary information about this supplier's product.

What Should Not Appear in the Administrative Section

The most common mistake people make when writing the administrative section is to confuse it with the contract, contract administrative information, and contract terms and conditions. If you include a sample of your purchase contract with your RFP (and you should), refer to it in the administrative section, and make it a requirement that "Suppliers shall review the attached contract and list in their proposal any potential issues."

Keep the contract language separate from the RFP and proposal instructions, because the RFP focuses on finding the right supplier first, then getting the contract signed second.

The reason for sharing the contract with suppliers is that there are items in the contract that they will budget for in their proposal. For example, in the second example that follows, the cost of parking in a city lot for several months can be expensive and should be considered a reasonable out-of-pocket expense. The supplier will either budget for it along with other items or ensure that you will pay for it as part of the out-of-pocket expenses projected for the project.

Here are some common examples of contract terms found mixed with basic RFP instructions:

1. ACME will not be responsible for the loss of equipment or materials left on ACME's premises or in ACME's departments by a Contractor during the performance of work covered by this purchase contract.

2. No free parking facilities are available or will be provided for the Contractor's employees during the course of this project.

3. Until the expiration of four (4) years after the furnishing of the services provided under this contract, Seller will make available to the Secretary, United States Department of Health and Human Services, the United States Controller General, and their representatives, this contract and all books, documents, and records necessary to certify the nature and extent of the cost of those services. (Note: This was a hospital RFP.)

4. Invoices must show purchase order number, plainly identify all applicable discounts, be itemized, and be submitted in duplicate.

5. Suppliers are required to supply ACME with proof of Workers' Compensation Insurance or Independent Contractor's Exemption covering the supplier while performing work for ACME.

6. The contract will be subject to termination by either party upon thirty (30) days' advance written notice of intention to terminate.

7. An MSDS for all hazardous substances must be included with each deliverable. (Note: This was for a software project—an MSDS is a Material Safety Data Sheet required to be supplied with chemicals.)

8. Code and software documentation for all customized workflow scripts, indexing and retrieval screens, and special functions, along with all associated intellectual property rights, shall become the

property of ACME. (Note: It is especially burdensome for the supplier to face a requirement like this placed in the middle of the administrative section between the "Acceptance Test" and the "Proposal Outline" paragraphs. Software contract items must be in the contract, not in the RFP.)

When writing the RFP, you are not negotiating the contract and therefore should not expect suppliers to agree to contract terms and conditions as part of their proposal. It is, of course, good to know that suppliers have read the contract and have noted their "issues," but the real contract negotiations can only start once a supplier knows he or she is the winning candidate for the project. Otherwise, most suppliers will feel it is a waste of their time to negotiate a contract that they may not win.

Conclusion

The administrative section of the RFP provides suppliers with instructions for responding to the RFP, items that are required in a proposal, and information about other areas, such as evaluations. The proposal format instructions are particularly important, because they require suppliers to conform to a specified format. The purpose of these instructions is to ensure that proposals can be (1) easily reviewed against the requirements in the RFP and (2) compared equally and fairly. The reason for comparing proposals is to ensure that there is a degree of consistency across all proposals and that suppliers are not creating radically different solutions. If that is the case, the RFP team may not have done its homework, and it may be difficult to select the correct technology.

It is also important to understand that the instructions contained in the administrative section are not cast in stone. Obviously, more or fewer instructions can be written than are contained in this section and in the examples at the end of this book. Also, the administrative section may be a supplier's first "test" in the evaluators' eyes: if suppliers cannot follow instructions on how to submit a proposal, will they follow other, more important instructions relating to a contract and the actual work involved?

Finally, be creative in this section if you need to, but be fair in your demands. The rules presented in your RFP are also the supplier's first impression of you as a potential customer.

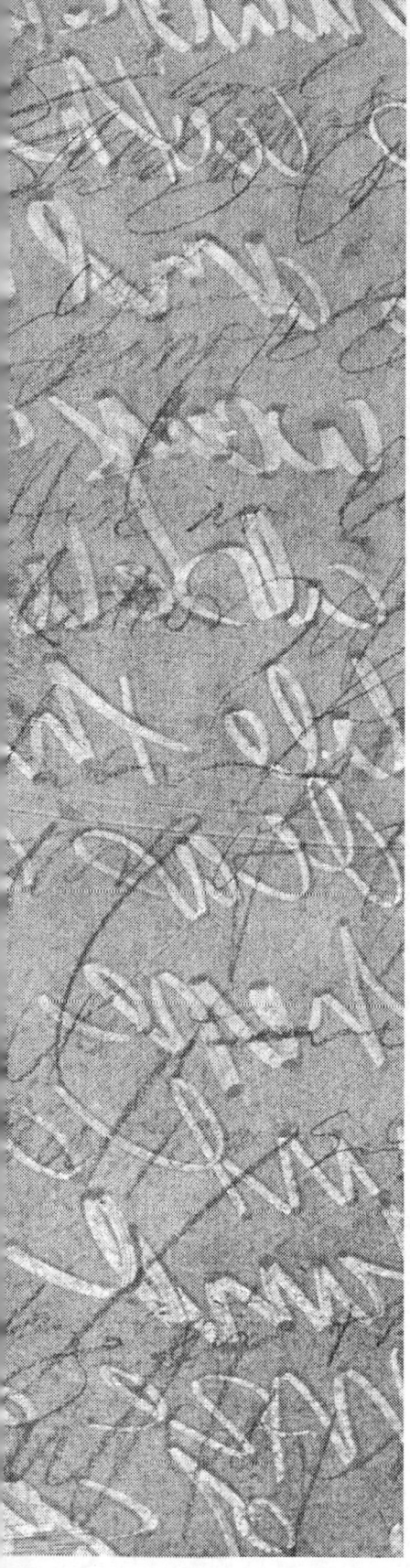

4

RFP Technical Requirements Section

Introduction

The objective of this procurement is to implement a corporate Intranet system that best meets the functional requirements as identified in this RFP. The successful supplier will be responsible for the design, development, purchase, and implementation of all hardware and software for the Intranet, purchase and development of a content management system (CMS), and purchase and development of a search engine for the content on our Intranet site.

The technical requirements section contains the requirements for what you are buying, whether it is consulting services, training, outsourcing, computer systems, accounting systems, or a corporate Intranet. The technical requirements are the foundation for a supplier's technical solution, but they also drive other sections such as project management and pricing.

The technical section is the heart of the RFP and is where suppliers should spend the most time initially. It provides details of the amount and type of work that a product, service, or person has to accomplish. If suppliers cannot provide the "product," it doesn't matter whether they have superior project management or low pricing or a great story to tell about their company.

Nevertheless, many suppliers will try to "sell" you their solution, which may not exactly meet your requirements (remember that proposals are selling documents). The degree to which this will happen depends on how tightly focused your requirements are and to what extent you allow the suppliers to interpret

> 🖎 Vendors will "interpret" requirements if they are not clear.

them. There is a huge difference between saying, "I require a car that can hold six people" and saying, "I require a blue car with four doors that can travel at 70 miles per hour, average 35 miles per gallon, and hold six people."

In some cases it is entirely right to provide minimal requirements in an RFP in order to receive the most innovative proposals. The downside to casting such a wide net is that you may receive a bewildering number of proposals with potentially acceptable solutions that differ greatly in price and functionality, making it almost to impossible to evaluate them.

On the other hand, providing requirements so tightly focused that only one or two suppliers can meet them means that you have severely limited your choices in terms of products and prices. If you know the industry and have thoroughly researched the products, it can be good to limit the participation in an RFP because it allows you to spend more time reviewing and evaluating every proposal.

> 🖎 Use an RFI if you cannot determine whether products or services exist for your project.

If possible, the requirements should reflect a reasonable understanding of the products and services being requested in the RFP. If this is not possible, it may be better to lead with an RFI first. The proposals received in response to an RFI should help you to focus on (1) the correct technology and (2) the appropriate set of suppliers.

The answer, as usual, lies somewhere in the middle, but it also means that the RFP team has to agree on how open or narrow the RFP will be; to do this, the team must have a good understanding of the project and the technology.

The first part of this section will review what constitutes a requirement and how to document requirements. The second half will review what constitutes a typical technical section.

Writing Requirements for the Technical Section

Definition of a Requirement

Since an RFP is a collection of requirements that specify a product or service, perhaps the first question to ask when developing an RFP is, "What is a requirement?"

A requirement is a statement of need: "Vendors shall provide an electronic document management program." It may start out as a larger generalized statement of need as above, but be broken down further into subrequirements until all aspects of the intended product (or project) have been defined. Furthermore, a requirement must be measurable in some manner that allows you to determine whether a supplier has fully met, marginally met, or not met the requirement. Ralph Young, in his book *Effective Requirements Practices*, defines a requirement as, " . . . a necessary attribute in a system. It may also be defined as a statement that identifies a capability, characteristic, or quality factor of a system in order for it to have value and utility to a user."[1]

> A requirement states a need and is measurable.

A requirement, then, is a definition of a need, and the supplier's solution to that need must be able to be verified and measured against some defined criteria. Thus there are always two parts to every requirement: (1) the requirement itself and (2) the evaluation or measurement criteria.

We may also argue for a third criterion, which may seem obvious but is commonly overlooked: A product or service must exist in order to satisfy the requirement. If we write a requirement for which there is no existing product or service, that requirement is considered not feasible. Requirements and their attributes are discussed further in the following paragraphs.

---

1. Ralph R. Young. *Effective Requirements Practices*. Boston, MA: Addison-Wesley Information Technology Series, 2001.

For example, if our RFP involves printing within the office environment, we may interview users, that is, the people who need to print documents, to understand what they need (or require) in a printer. The following requirements were identified by users:

1. Printer shall be able to print in color.
2. Printer shall not be noisy if situated locally.
3. Printer shall print envelopes.
4. Printer shall have four trays so that letterhead, memo stock, envelopes, and plain paper can be printed without reloading different types of paper.
5. Printer trays shall hold at least one ream of paper.
6. Printer shall be jam-resistant.
7. Each member of staff shall have his or her own printer.
8. Printer shall be efficient in its power usage, reverting to a standby mode when not in use.
9. Printer shall be fast and adequately handle the group's needs.

Representing what the average user thinks is needed in a typical office printer, these items become the basis for the printer requirements section in an RFP. The nine requirements listed represent the "statement of need" for a printer. There may also be a list of technical requirements that satisfy the information technology (IT) department's needs, such as network accessibility, error notification, and so on.

After the initial user requirements have been established, they must be validated to ensure that (1) they are real requirements and (2) they are feasible, that is, there is a product that exists to meet the requirement.

In the previous example, we may question requirements 1, 4, 7, and 9 to determine if the need really exists and if the requirement is feasible. During this review of the first requirement, we may find that 99 percent of all printing jobs are memos, reports, and so on, with only 1 percent representing a real need for color. Therefore, we may choose to eliminate this requirement as not cost-effective.

As requirement 4 is reviewed, we find that no standard office printer has four trays allowing four individual types of paper to be selected. The requirement is thus eliminated because no product can meet it, that is, the requirement is not feasible. Another approach to this requirement may be that printers with this capability exist, but are not considered general-purpose office printers and are typically found only in large printing centers, in addition to costing several times what the budget allows.

When requirement 7 is reviewed, we find that the volume of individual printing does not warrant purchasing individual printers for each staff member. This requirement is eliminated because it is not cost-effective.

Requirement 9 represents the users' view of the requirement or need, but it is not a valid requirement because, as currently written, it cannot be measured—what do "fast" and "adequately handle our group's needs" mean to a supplier? Since such subjective language is not meaningful to a supplier, this requirement has to be reexamined and quantified in order to represent something that a supplier can measure and respond to. After the math is done, it may be determined that a group of 15 people needs a printer that can print at 40 pages per minute (ppm). It should then be rewritten to say, for example, "The printer shall print at 40 ppm."

For the remaining requirements, we try to determine how they can be measured to ensure that the requirement has been met. For example, for requirement 2, we have found that our corporate standard is that office machinery should operate at 70 decibels or less and have therefore added this requirement to the list. When evaluating proposals, we would look for suppliers to state the decibel level of their printer when it is operating. If we wanted to test this measurement, we would also state in the RFP that during the demonstrations, the decibel level would be tested using a decibel meter.

Who Writes Requirements?

The second question to ask when writing an RFP is who will document, verify, and write the requirements in your RFP? If we assume that the RFP team includes both users (people responsible for a business process) and IT or engineering personnel (people responsible for managing the equipment required for that process), who should be responsible for writing each type of requirement? We may also throw into this mix a hired consulting company, which may be responsible for writing some requirements and sections of an RFP.

✎ Who writes requirements?

If the team were composed of users and IT staff, the users would write the requirements based on the business application or problem being addressed in the RFP. For example, in the case of an accounts payable application, the users would develop the accounting-related requirements for a new system, based on the way the business currently operates and what they expect of the new system.

IT personnel would help define the current technical environment (servers, PCs, network) and what suppliers would require to work within this environment. IT would also define new technical requirements, a software development environment, and system administrative and support functions, if applicable.

Companies have, over time, developed their own working cultures that dictate how RFPs are developed and written and who is responsible for them. It may be that in your company, the IT department is responsible for RFPs and serves as an in-house consulting group, interviewing users and developing user functional requirements.

In their book *Customer-Centered Products* Ivy Hooks and Kristin Farry develop what they call "operational concepts," which are, ". . . scripts describing how a product will be used, manufactured, tested, installed, stored, and decommissioned. . . . Operational concepts are a simple, cost-effective way to build a consensus among all stakeholders and to discover missing requirements."[2]

Developing an operational concept for each requirement in your project allows you to build a working outline for that requirement in which you trace how that particular feature will be implemented by the typical user. In other words, you may "role-play" what happens when a requirement is actually put into practice, and by sharing this information within your group, you may uncover other hidden requirements or find that a requirement is actually not that important.

For example, many writing and drawing programs include a feature that allows you to add annotations to files as you read them by, for example, inserting boxed comments, highlighting a sentence with a color electronic highlighter, or electronically circling a word in question. A basic requirement for such a feature would read, "Word-processing program shall have the ability to add annotations to the file." If we were to develop an operational concept for this requirement it might look like the following:

1. User opens the file and begins to read it.
2. User highlights a phrase and adds a comment that requests the author to clarify the highlighted phrase.
3. User closes the comment field.
4. User wants to secure that comment so only the author can review the comment and other reviewers may not open it; however, this security feature is not part of the original requirement.
5. User wants to color-code comments to distinguish them from other comments. Color-coding is not part of the original requirement.

Based on the comment in number 4, the requirements team decides that it is important to be able to secure comments by user ID so that a comment can

---

2. Ivy F. Hooks and Kristin A. Farry. *Customer-Centered Products.* New York: AMACOM, 2001.

either remain open for all to read or be secured so that only the author of the document can see it. The team disagrees with the proposal for color-coding the comments, and this idea is dropped from the operational concept. The original requirement, "Word-processing program shall have the ability to add annotations to the file" is therefore amended as follows; "Word-processing program shall have the ability to add annotations to the file. Users shall have the ability to secure annotations by their user ID so that only the author of the annotation and the original author of the document can view the annotation. If no security is invoked, the annotation shall be viewable by any person who opens the file."

By developing an operational concept and working through how the required feature may be used in a real scenario, we have "tested" the stated requirement in a simulated scenario and found that a potentially important subrequirement was missing.

Operational concepts can be developed for almost all types of requirements and may be especially effective for "user-driven" requirements in which typical users are asked to walk through how they currently perform a task, demonstrating what tools are needed to perform the task and how they would perform the same task with the new technology or system.

Operational concepts are generated by having the team create the RFP requirements; they should be developed in a standardized format to ensure completeness and consistency throughout the project. As Suzanne Robertson and James Robertson note in their book *Mastering the Requirements Process*, " . . . requirements . . . will not always be fully formed. They are ideas or intentions for requirements. On the other hand, the requirements specification that you produce is the basis for the contract to build a product, and so it shall contain clear, complete and testable instructions as to what has to be built."[3]

---

3. Suzanne Robertson and James Robertson. *Mastering the Requirements Process.* Harlow, UK: Addison-Wesley, 1999.

By performing operational concepts, you will perhaps try and discard several "trial requirements," and it is through this process that the "real" requirements emerge. Numerous studies have shown that it is much more expensive to fix flawed requirements once programming has begun or when other materials needed to implement a requirement have already been purchased. Using operational concepts enables the team to "measure twice, cut once" during the initial stages of a project.

 In my experience it has always been necessary to involve the user community when developing requirements for systems that will affect how a user works. Only the user, who faces the day-to-day challenges in his or her work, truly understands what is wrong, what is right, and what can be improved. Too often I see RFPs in which the user was not adequately interviewed and the requirements were at too high a level to be properly addressed.

When developing requirements for a system, ensure that the people who will use the system daily are involved. For example, after involving users in a study and then completing a feasibility document for a business process reengineering study, we brought in several suppliers to give demonstrations of the technology. We did this because the recurring theme among the users was, "I won't use it because it will slow down my work." And in a conspiratorial voice they added, "but don't put that in your report . . . ."

After the technology demonstrations, the users were even more resolute in their opinion that the technology proposed would hinder rather than help them in their work. The project was ultimately cut back and included only functions that did not affect the users' work processes. Again, when designing a system, pay attention to the people who will use it.

However your company approaches writing RFPs, two basic types of technical requirements have to be written: (1) The business application requirements, that is, what the product being purchased is required to do and how it is required to perform; and (2) the technical environment in which the product has to function.

How Do Suppliers Recognize Requirements in Your RFP?

✍ How do you define a requirement?

The third question to consider when writing requirements is how will a supplier recognize a requirement versus a statement of fact or a narrative description of a process? Historically, most federal and state governments have solved this problem with the use of three words:

1. *Shall.* The word *shall* indicates a requirement. Whenever it is used anywhere in an RFP, what follows is a requirement. There are no exceptions, and this rule is so rigid in government RFPs that suppliers will immediately search for and pull out all sentences containing the word *shall.* These become their checklists to ensure that they have identified and responded to all requirements.

2. *Should.* The word *should* is used to describe project goals. For example, "With the implementation of the XYZ system, ACME Insurance should realize an ROI within two years." In this context, *should* does not indicate a requirement but rather an informational statement about something that is expected to occur as a result of the project.

3. *Will.* The word *will* is used to denote statements of intent. For example, "ACME will, at its discretion, conduct Oral Presentations. Or "Specifications for Oral Presentations will be published in the RFP."

Just as government departments invariably use these words in a specific way, you too can establish your own vocabulary, as long as you use it consistently throughout the RFP and make it absolutely clear to the supplier when you are stating a requirement. Many RFPs from the commercial business sector also use the words *shall* or *will* to denote requirements, as in the statements, "Vendors shall provide annual reports for three years" or "Vendors will provide annual reports for three years."

If you are using the word *shall* to denote a requirement, ensure that team members do not lapse into other methods of denoting a requirement, such as (most common), "Vendors are required to provide annual reports for three years," or, "Vendors should provide annual reports . . . ."

It is advisable to use the administrative section to review with suppliers how you have written your RFP and exactly what terms you have used to denote a requirement. Note that not being able to determine what is a requirement is one of the biggest problems suppliers encounter when responding to RFPs.

What Is the Difference between Specifications and Requirements?

Specifications and requirements are sometimes used interchangeably, but they are not the same. A specification is the sum of a group of requirements. For example, a laser printer is specified in an RFP, but the specification for the printer includes the following requirements:

> What is a specification?

1. Printer shall print in either black and white or color.
2. Print speed for black and white shall be 20 pages per minute.
3. Print speed for color shall be 7 pages per minute.
4. Printer shall have two feed trays, for letterhead and plain paper respectively.

> ☑ A supplier I know of has a policy of not questioning poorly written or confusing requirements because it allows him to respond with minimal capabilities and a low price—knowing that the RFP writer will not detect the lack of or completeness of a response. Once the contract is won, the supplier will bring these inconsistencies to light and thus be able to negotiate a new higher price based on the "additional features" and work that was "not" called out (at least not *clearly* !) in the RFP.

This printer, however, may be a requirement in a larger overall specification for an accounting system that includes workstations, scanners, printers, a

RAID storage system, system software, and application software. The sum total of the specified components may in turn be called a system. The members of your RFP team should fully understand the distinctions between requirements, specifications, and systems and should be careful to use the terms consistently throughout the RFP.

Written Formats for Requirements: Questions, Statements, or Narrative Description

Requirements should be straightforward, easily identified by suppliers, and unambiguous. Requirements can be presented to suppliers in several ways, but the most important point to keep in mind is that the language should ensure that a supplier will not confuse narrative description with a requirement. While there may not be a "best" way to present a requirement, let us review the most common options.

Presenting Requirements as Questions

✎ How will you state your requirements?

Many RFPs provide suppliers with a description of the current business and technical environment and describe the business application for which the RFP was written. Once the supplier is given that essential information, the RFP concludes with a set of questions, for example:

1. What workflow capabilities exist within your product?
2. Does your system integrate with the Internet?
3. Can users fax information from their desktop workstations?
4. How many users can log on to the system simultaneously?

Questions, as in the above examples, are a joy to the supplier but pose a hidden problem to proposal evaluators. The first question is so broadly stated that suppliers would not know how to respond or what type of information is being requested. They could either write pages and pages, hoping that some of the material would provide the correct information, or they could ask you to clarify what specific capabilities you are asking about. In fact, this question is analogous to asking Microsoft what capabilities the

Windows® operating system has—and the response would most likely be nothing more than a repeat of a datasheet, a technical brochure, parts of a manual, and perhaps a technical white paper. (As a proposal writer, I have been in this situation and have literally thrown such books into the answer, hoping that something would click.)

Requirements that are too broadly stated, such as "The AP software package shall include workflow capabilities…" should be reexamined and broken down into measurable requirements to which a supplier can respond.

The problem with questions 2 and 3 is that they could be answered with a simple yes or no, but would that provide the information requested? For this type of question, suppliers are likely to take the easy path and either answer yes or no or provide the least amount of information possible. For example, a supplier may answer yes to question 3 but not mention that user workstations must first be linked to a fax server. (Remember the supplier who does not question poorly written requirements?)

Question 4 could be answered simply with the statement, "All 10,000 users at ACME Insurance can log on simultaneously." But, this response fails to mention that four servers are needed to handle that amount of traffic, or that the software can only "see" 1,000 user requests at a time, rendering the capability to have 10,000 users logged on meaningless.

The danger with questions, therefore, is that they may either be so broad as to be meaningless or so narrow as to provoke a single-word response. To be effective, questions must be used carefully and only when a very limited response will provide a meaningful answer. For example, you might ask, "Does your software incorporate the XML standard XX.XX?"

Simply asking a question does not necessarily convey that the issue is a mandatory requirement. Should suppliers assume that any question represents a mandatory requirement? The question about XML could be a

✍ A question may not indicate that it is a requirement.

simple request for information rather than a requirement that the supplier "shall" meet that standard. It might be acceptable for the supplier to be one or two versions behind or not at all. It is thus much clearer to state the issue as a definite requirement, for example: "Vendors' products shall meet the XML XX.XX standards." This leaves no doubt as to what is being requested.

From the suppliers' point of view, questions do not generally allow them to "explain" their products or to "propose" solutions. They feel relegated, or compelled, to provide simple answers without having the chance to explain why their product is a giant technology breakthrough or why their product solution has advantages over other product solutions.

Since the ability of suppliers to "sell" their solution is impaired when an RFP is nothing more than a list of questions, you may end up making a decision based on incomplete answers because you didn't present your needs in the right way.

Questions that are not requirements may also invite suppliers to provide you with half-truths about their products. Since the question does not define a requirement, suppliers may feel freer to describe vapor-ware, refer to future products as released products, and spin positive answers that really do not say anything.

Below is a question from an RFP and the supplier's response. Note that the supplier provides a positive response but does not answer the question.

Training

Question: Can you provide training internationally? If so, please provide details.

Response: Yes, we provide training internationally. We have consultants trained who reside in Europe. We also have significant recent experience of providing consulting support worldwide to support the deployment of a worldwide system solution.

Let's look at this more closely. The question asked for training "internationally," which generally means training has to occur worldwide, but the response said merely that the company has "consultants trained . . . in Europe." First, Europe is generally not considered to be worldwide and second, "consultants trained" does not generally refer to professional trainers with actual classroom experience. The supplier, after asserting for you that "Europe" means "international" and that consultants equal trainers, goes on to claim worldwide "experience" and "consulting support," which supposedly adds up to international training.

Another supplier's response to the same question was, "Yes, we can provide international training when requested." This is a positive response and therefore gives that supplier an evaluation point, but it provides absolutely no details. This type of answer generally indicates that a supplier is willing to commit to something in a proposal and will worry about it later—when and if asked.

However, because the preceding question seemed to be just a question about capabilities and did not indicate that it was a requirement, in both cases suppliers felt safe in fudging the answers. The question was therefore not only ineffective but would make additional work for the RFP team if more substantial answers were needed.

A supplier will try to determine whether an item being requested is actually needed or was just thrown in and will never be implemented. If suppliers sense that a requirement is not real, they have little to lose and much to gain by answering positively. Once a contract is won, it can be manipulated to a supplier's advantage.

Presenting Requirements as Statements

Many RFPs provide all the essential background information but present all the requirements as statements, for example:

> Vendors' products shall meet the XML XX.XX standards.
> Vendors shall provide 24/7 support.
> Vendors shall provide 19-inch desktop monitors.

Although this approach is very similar to asking questions, it forces the supplier to provide a potentially incomplete answer or one that is pages long, with the information you really want buried somewhere in the middle.

As with questions, you may not get the type of information that will help you to decide which supplier has a better product; all the suppliers may say that they can provide "24/7 support or 19-inch desktop monitors." Like questions, statements are more effective if they are narrowly focused so that the answer provides the basic information requested.

However, be careful not to state a requirement as a request to describe a product feature. The statement "Describe how you meet XML standard XX.XX" does not make clear to a supplier whether it is a requirement or a simple request for information. You may just want to know how the company integrates a standard into its product line. It may, however, also be written as a requirement:

> Vendors shall meet the XML XX.XX standard and shall describe how the standard is incorporated into their product.

Presenting Requirements as a Narrative Description

Presenting requirements as a narrative description allows you to write them in such a way that they are clear to the supplier, but also tell a story in a natural way of writing. Narrative description does not preclude the use of questions or statements, and in many cases facilitates the use of those writing devices.

> The noise level of any hardware component provided shall not exceed 70 dB. Tests will be performed on equipment operating within listed normal range, and measurements will be obtained during all normal modes of

operation. Measurements will be taken using a general-purpose sound-level meter, at a distance of no less than 3 feet and no greater than 4 feet, from any part of the equipment. ACME shall perform these tests with the equipment on site.

This narrative paragraph incorporates the requirements into each sentence. While the primary requirement is that the noise level not exceed 70 dB, there is clearly also a requirement that tests be conducted to ensure compliance.

In the following example, the RFP writer has combined the requirements with a good narrative description. The narrative in the first paragraph contributes to the supplier's understanding of why the requirement is being requested and why it is important to the overall effort. After the narrative, four requirements are stated that support the need for reporting. Notice that in the second paragraph the requirements are statements, the last one being a list. This example is from an Intranet search engine RFP.

Reporting capabilities will play an important role in the ongoing improvements and fine tuning of the new system. Currently, we do not have adequate reporting capabilities and therefore cannot fine-tune the system based on usage. We believe that with good reporting capabilities, we will be able to continuously monitor system usage and be able to improve the system based on the terms or phrases being searched for.

Vendors shall describe the reporting capabilities that are available as part of the standard product offering. Vendors shall provide sample standard reports as part of an appendix to this proposal. Reporting shall include the following:

1. Number of searches performed.
2. Number of positive search hits.
3. Number of negative search hits.
4. Number of searches per hour/day/week.
5. Average length of time spent using the search function.
6. Most popular search terms.
7. Search terms not found.

Vendors shall describe how custom reports can be generated.

The potential problem with narrative requirements is that it must nevertheless be clear to the supplier what is a statement of fact, what is narrative description of a process, and what is the actual requirement.

Qualities of Well-Written Requirements

Because the success of your RFP depends entirely on the ability of suppliers to understand what you are asking for and describing, the requirements that are provided in the RFP must have the following qualities: They must reflect real products or solutions, be unambiguous, not use subjective terms, be measurable, be meaningful, and be complete. They must not include the solution or unnecessary characteristics.

Requirements Must Reflect Real Products or Solutions

Requirements must be achievable. That is, whether based on a ready-made product or something that is to be custom-built, the supplier must be able to buy, integrate, or build what is in the requirement. If we revisit our search engine project, perhaps users have confused the search engine itself with supporting technologies such as content management systems and have stated that they need a search engine that can automatically metatag the content of their Intranet. This then becomes a requirement that is put forth by the people who manage the corporate Intranet and the content managers who supply the content for the Intranet.

While this may sound like a good requirement and actually have a good justification because it reduces the work for the content managers, there is no search engine technology available that automatically metatags content prior to searching the content. Therefore, this requirement, if released in the RFP, would cause the suppliers some amount of confusion. One supplier may think another has "leapfrogged" them in technology and begin to beat on the product developers to include metatagging technology in the next release. Meanwhile, another supplier decides to integrate the search engine product with another supplier's content management software in order to respond to the requirement. A third supplier may decide not to bid on the project because this requirement cannot be met.

It is possible to see a requirement like this because of what may be called the "shopping cart approach" to writing requirements. That is, one or several persons may contribute requirements based on their project research, user interviews, and supplier interviews; these requirements, taken from different sources, are then melded together to specify a single product that is not verified against supplier products or current technology. The result is that no supplier will be able to satisfy the requirement.

The lesson to be learned is that the RFP team must be knowledgeable about the existing products or services in order to write requirements that are feasible. If you feel that the requirements in your RFP are questionable, or that you don't have internal resources that can determine whether requirements are feasible, you may consider several options.

First, send the RFP team back for additional research for those requirements that seem to be questionable. Second, contact several suppliers and ask them if their products can do what is stated in the requirement. If you are still unsure, consider releasing your RFP as an RFI. Vendor responses from an RFI should provide answers to questions you have about product capabilities and indicate whether the questionable requirements are feasible.

> Review questionable requirements with suppliers before the RFP.

Requirements Must Be Unambiguous

Consider the following requirement;

> The noise level of any hardware component provided shall not exceed 70 dB.

This statement appears to be clear and unambiguous, since it provides a specific measurement (70 dB); but it does not state how that measurement is to be taken. If measured from a distance of 2 feet, the decibel level may be 85, whereas from 4 feet, the decibel reading may fall to 70. In fact the point where the measurement should be taken depends on how and where the machine is used. If users are active within 2 feet of the machine, it should be taken at that distance. If users are always at least 5 feet from the machine and no significant work is ever undertaken closer than 5 feet, the measurement should be taken at 5 feet.

Here is how this requirement should be rewritten to make it unambiguous:

> The noise level of any hardware component provided shall not exceed 70 dB as measured with a standard decibel meter from a distance of 5 feet, with the meter held at desktop (30 inches) height.

Requirements Must Not Use Subjective Terms

✎ Subjective requirements are hard to measure.

When writing requirements, continually ask yourself if what you have written can be measured. If not, the requirement may be too broadly stated, or it may use subjective wording. Subjective wording sounds good in a casual reading but does not hold up under scrutiny. Consider, for example, the following two requirements:

> Vendor shall provide *adequate* user training.
>
> *Application level software functions* shall be *intuitively obvious* and not require training by users.

In the first example, how would a supplier define "adequate," and how would you measure it? Without a good measurable requirement, suppliers will tend to exaggerate their response in an effort to cover all the bases. This approach leads to long, overwritten proposals that may have the correct answer buried somewhere among five to ten pages of boilerplate text. And if you find what you think is a good response, what is your personal interpretation of "adequate" versus that of the other five or six reviewers?

The second example poses the same problems and also invites several additional quibbles. First, in the RFP from which this was taken, the term "application level software functions" was not defined and therefore suppliers were left to form their own interpretations. The second problem is that the phrase "intuitively obvious" is totally meaningless by any objective standard.

Here's one last example of a subjective requirement:

> Vendor shall have *adequate resources* and the *financial stability* to provide the *funding necessary* to start up and follow through on this project to completion.

In addition to its use of subjective terms, this requirement is so poorly written that it doesn't make much sense. (This requirement was also placed in the technical section of the RFP as an afterthought, when it clearly should have been part of the vendor financial section.) We understand the intent: The writer wants to ensure that the supplier will not go into bankruptcy as a result of this project. Nevertheless, how do you measure "adequate resources," "financial stability," and "funding necessary" with regard to what is being asked for? Should the supplier list all the people who will play any part in this project and explain their function? If a supplier provides three years of annual reports, does that mean the company is financially stable? More to the point, would you know how much financial stability a supplier needs to work on your project successfully? And last, depending on the project, many suppliers are not going to let you audit their company and books for your project, so the responses to the foregoing requirement will not be measurable.

✒ Poorly written requirements will cause confusion.

Requirements Must Be Measurable

The key to well-written requirements is being able to look at the requirement and immediately know whether you can measure compliance with it. If the measurement aspects are not clear, try to understand whether the requirement is poorly written, perhaps due to subjective terms, or simply not feasible, and therefore not measurable.

> Response time will be measured as follows: With 1,000 users logged on and actively using the system, the delay between requesting and receiving a

file from the server will be no longer than 1 second as measured from the moment the "Enter" key is depressed until the file is displayed on the monitor.

Even this requirement poses some problems and a supplier may request clarification. First, what does "actively using the system" mean? Will all 1,000 users request a file simultaneously (i.e., press the "Enter" key within 1 second of one another)? When the file is received by the user, is it considered received when the first page arrives, or only when the whole file has appeared on the screen?

If suppliers are sharp, they will continue to press you for details like this, and you will have to continue to "write and modify the RFP," which will take up your time and resources. Such questions about a requirement will force you to rethink and rewrite it, which means that you will then have to send out a change addendum to the RFP. If the change is significant enough, you may also have to extend the due date for proposals in order to provide suppliers with enough time to consider the modified requirement and change their proposals accordingly.

Requirements Must Be Meaningful

Often, we write requirements that demand information from suppliers that is rarely used or even reviewed by the evaluation team. For example, requesting a list of "associated standards" used in the development of a product, or asking theoretical questions such as "How would you handle the following situation . . ." causes the supplier to spend additional time and resources that may be better spent on the primary requirements. Ensure that if you request something from a supplier, the information has value and will be used as part of the evaluation.

Sometimes a requirement is "thrown in" inadvertently because it is copied from a product datasheet or some other product description source. Let's go back to our previous example:

The noise level of any hardware component provided shall not exceed 70 dB.

It is possible that this noise level requirement was in fact copied from a datasheet, that no one on the RFP team requested it, and that the equipment would actually not be measured. In effect, the requirement may be moot because the equipment is going into a closed room where there are no people. However, it may cause the supplier to "tack on" some additional cost for testing and shielding.

 Many companies that I work with call for three years of annual reports or audited financial statements as a requirement in their RFPs. However, the RFP team rarely reads these reports, and upon questioning, many do not know how to determine whether a company is financially stable or not. If you request financial information but are not sure how to read and understand the report data, ask some people in the purchasing group or your CFO to review the report and give you their opinion. If there are still questions, you may decide that further financial analysis is warranted. In this case you may ask the CFO to solicit a Dun & Bradstreet report or other means to determine financial stability.

Requirements Must Be Complete

Another problematic situation arises when a requirement does not provide all of the data needed to respond to it. The following requirement was taken from an RFP in which the requirements were all presented as statements with minimal narrative information. The writers assumed that suppliers would understand what they were being asked for from the context of the statement and its place in the RFP.

Vendors shall state their approach to importing large volumes of data for initial implementations.

What is meant by "large volumes of data?" It could be electronic data, it could be paper documents, it could be documents already scanned but being converted to another format, it could be several other data types mentioned in this particular RFP. In this case, the fact that the RFP was not clear meant that suppliers had a very difficult time responding to this requirement. Also, the words "approach" and "large volumes" are subjective in nature and render this requirement meaningless.

To respond to this requirement, a supplier would have to ask the RFP coordinator a question and try to obtain more specific information. Also, as a supplier reading this requirement—and there were others like it in this RFP—I would become somewhat suspicious of whether adequate research and validation had been performed on the requirements of the RFP generally. Indeed, I would consider not bidding on this RFP because it appears to be poorly researched. Poorly researched RFPs go one of two ways:

1. No contract is awarded because the proposal prices are higher and perhaps more complex than expected.
2. A contract is awarded, but because the requirements were not clearly stated, the project never makes it past the roll-out phase due to project cost and time overruns.

If you have released an RFP and are receiving what you think are persnickety or nitpicking questions about your requirements, maybe the suppliers are trying to tell you something. In this case, it may be a good time to reassess the requirements and determine whether to proceed.

Requirements Must Not Include the Solution

> Requirements should not predefine the solution.

One of the dangers in researching different supplier products is that it is hard not to include a hint of the solution you are seeking when creating the requirement. For example, when writing the requirements for a data storage system, you might actually specify the type of storage media instead of functionally stating that suppliers need to store 100 terabytes of data. The requirement might read, "Each optical disk shall store at least 20 gigabytes and the total storage requirement is 100 terabytes." This requirement has mandated suppliers to use "optical disk" instead of magnetic disks, magnetic tape, or perhaps an even newer technology. In wording the requirement as being able to store 100 terabytes on optical disk, you have provided the solution, and you may thus actually limit not only the suppliers' proposals but also the number of suppliers. If there is a technical or legal reason for specifying a product or type of product, you should also explain why that type of product is being specified. Otherwise, you will receive many questions from suppliers asking why they cannot use some other type of product that they sell.

Requirements should be functional in nature whenever possible. State what is needed but don't presuppose a product or technology. Remember that RFPs are supposed to make suppliers think and propose what they believe to be the best solution for your problem. If you do their thinking for them, you should save the time and expense of writing an RFP and just buy the product you think is the best fit.

Requirements Must Not Include Unnecessary Characteristics

Just as you may inadvertently write the solution into your requirements, you are also almost certain to write a requirement for something that is not needed, or could be provided optionally if the budget allows. This is sometimes called "gold plating" the requirements. For example, you may require color printers for all print applications instead of regular black and white printers. This requirement may have come from a single user (office worker) who firmly believes that color documents are easier to read and provide more contrast on the page.

Is color necessary to print normal office documents such as e-mails and memos? Could one color printer suffice for a group while all other printers are black and white?

Poorly written requirements will jeopardize the RFP effort.

Prior to accepting the user's requirement for color printers, the team should validate the requirement itself. The validation process should determine whether there is a compromise solution that allows everyone to win but does not increase the budget too much. To support the validation process, you may have to go back to the person who originally wrote that requirement to understand how it was developed. The additional information gained during a discussion with that person may help validate the requirement.

One result of poorly written requirements is that suppliers spend additional time reading the RFP, as they don't want to look foolish for not understanding a requirement, and when they decide they cannot understand a requirement, they will have to write asking for clarification, and you will have to take the time to respond. This process can be a serious drain on the resources, both time and energy, of the supplier and your RFP team.

Poorly written requirements may also jeopardize further interaction with the suppliers. Vendors have been known not to bid on RFPs because it appeared to them that the requirements were not well researched, the RFP team was not well educated, the proposal would be a heavy drain on their resources, and there was a good chance that the RFP would not go to contract.

The results of poorly written requirements will inevitably show in suppliers' proposals. The most obvious sign may be that proposal prices are inflated and higher than expected as suppliers add an extra percentage to their prices to cover contingencies. The negative effects of poorly written requirements cannot be overemphasized.

Developing Technical Requirements

The technical section comprises a descriptive narrative that helps suppliers understand what you are doing and why, and lays down the technical requirements for what you are purchasing. In order to develop the narrative description and technical requirements, the RFP team will have to document both the existing environment, if there is one, and what the new product or system is going to provide.

Projects typically get started when someone expresses a need to do something or have something to improve a business unit's work process, or the overall business itself. The expression of this need is either approved for more formal review or rejected, in which case the potential RFP is dropped.

Here are several examples of a "need" statement:

- ❏ We need a better search engine for our Intranet because we cannot find anything using the current engine. Our users have frequently complained that the search engine does not find documents that they know are present, and they are forced to "hunt and peck" through the Intranet site to find material.
- ❏ Our accounts payable system cannot keep up with the current and expected future volume of work. Therefore, it is inadequate and needs to be replaced.
- ❏ We are running out of physical storage space for our paper files and need to either increase the space or find a different way to store and access documents. Since increasing the space is not an option, we must therefore find other means of storing the documents.
- ❏ If we had a corporate Intranet, we could distribute information more efficiently. We currently distribute company announcements via e-mail, which is inefficient, and then follow-up the e-mail with a printed memo, which is also inefficient and a waste of both computer time and paper.
- ❏ We need to write an RFP but do not have the in-house knowledge. We have been charged with writing the RFP for the Intranet search engine, but our group has never written an RFP. We are therefore seeking outside consulting assistance to help us write and manage the RFP process.

The relevant "need" can be expressed by anyone in the company, and when it is put into the "potential project queue," it will take more work to explain why the need exists and what benefits the company will receive if the project is implemented. Thus, someone begins researching the project, the result of which a preliminary set of project requirements and project benefits or business justifications is produced.

 I was engaged to perform a business process reengineering study for a company that had eight different business units that did similar work though each had different operating procedures. I was expected to map each unit's processes, determine where procedures could be standardized, and then recommend how the company could streamline operations for each unit. This information would then become the requirements for an RFP.

As it turned out, and to the chagrin of my project sponsor, I was not allowed to interview the people in the business units because they were too busy; the managers of all the units requested that I review their operating procedure books, which by their own admission were out of date.

The project was dropped because real user requirements could not be documented and verified.

If we take the first example of a corporate Intranet search tool, it appears that there is already a search tool available but that it is not effective, perhaps returning too many search hits or incorrect hits. So while the *need* is to replace the current search engine, the *objective* of the project (or one of many objectives) is to provide the user with more relevant search results. We need to do this because (1) we are paying for a tool that is ineffective, (2) users are spending too much time skimming through hundreds of responses, only to find that the correct result was not listed, and (3) the company information available on the Intranet is not being effectively located, distributed, and used. We now have good business reasons for buying a new search engine.

We now have the following:

1. Need—to have a better search engine.
2. Objective—to improve user searches.
3. Business reason—possibly save the company money.

If a project is given the approval to move forward and it is determined that an RFP should be written, the technical requirements must now be researched and written.

At this point the project team may be formed, and documenting the project then becomes a more formal process. For our corporate Intranet search engine, the team may first document why the current search engine is not effective and then, with that knowledge, begin researching new technologies and documenting the requirements for the new engine.

Following is an abbreviated view of the start of a project. Figure 4.1 provides a typical requirements development process.

1. A need is expressed, perhaps for a new product or system or to replace an existing product or system that is outdated.
2. The need is researched and verified before the project moves forward. It is possible that the research will show that the current product or system is being used incorrectly or is not working properly.
3. Once verified, the basic project is outlined and research begins. The assigned project manager will need to begin developing a project plan and assembling the project team.
4. Users are interviewed to gather information about requirements and to substantiate those requirements. This step and the next can be an iterative process. Users can help you outline and diagram what they

currently do on a task-by-task basis, but they may have trouble "conceptualizing" what a new product can do to help them if they have no knowledge or explanation of the new technology.

**Figure 4.1   Requirements
Development Process**

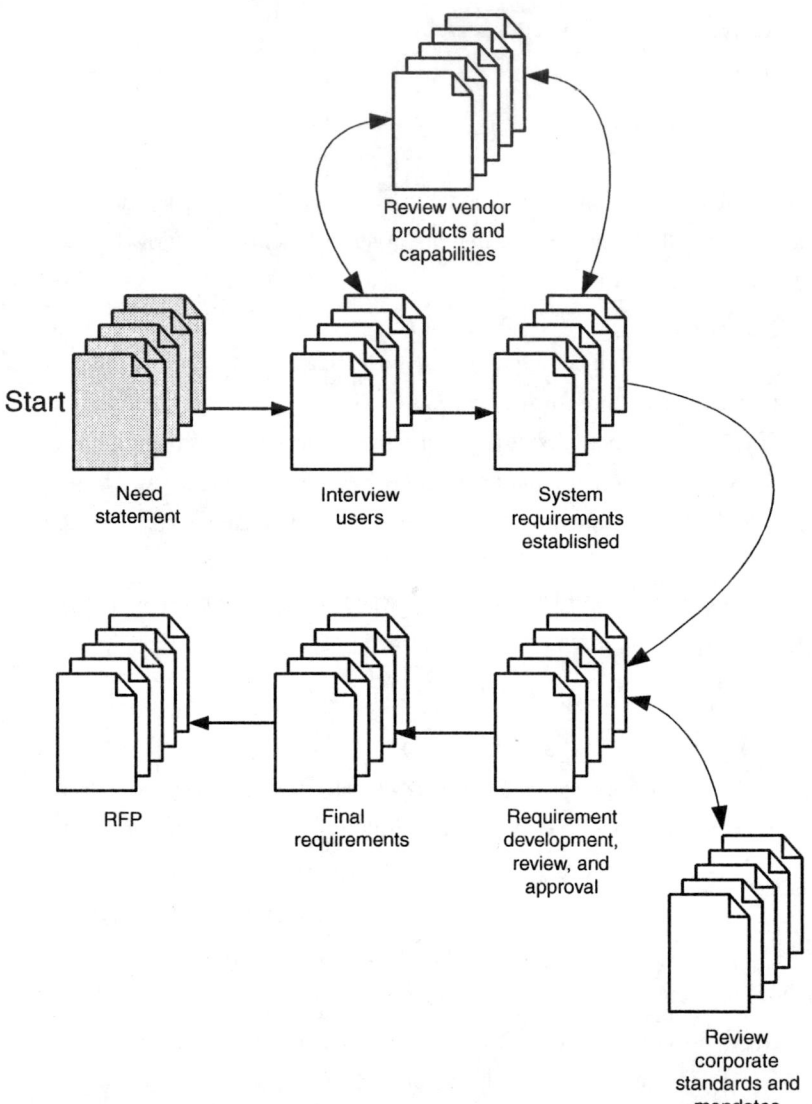

5. "Defined" requirements are tested against suppliers' products and capabilities to determine if they are available. Users and the technical team should educate themselves about potential vendors' products by attending conferences, demonstrations, and presentations, and by reviewing vendor literature.

6. These requirements are also reviewed against existing corporate standards and mandates to ensure that there are no conflicts. Vendor products will have to adhere to these standards and mandates in order to be considered.

7. The requirements are then confirmed, reviewed, and approved. This is a good time in the process to step back and conduct an internal review of the completed requirements before they are completely finalized.

8. The requirements become the basis for the RFP.

9. The RFP is written incorporating the requirements.

Perhaps the most time-consuming part is ensuring that users are interviewed, that the business process is thoroughly documented, that the requirements for the new system have been validated, and that the requirements can be satisfied with a product.

For example, in our search engine project we may find that content managers do not and will not include metatags with the content, because (1) the company never developed a standard list of metatags and (2) using metatags is too time-consuming given the amount of content published each day. As a result the search engine has to be effective without using metatags.

When the no-metatag requirement is accepted, two aspects need to be checked:

1. The requirement represents a real need and is neither overstated nor considered gold plating. In the above example, management may want to review whether the company should adopt a metatag standard and

whether there are more efficient ways of coding the files than having the content manager code them manually.

2. The requirement needs to be tested against the potential search engines identified as candidates. If all search engines require the use of metatags, the requirement is invalid, since no product can satisfy the requirement. If only one out of six search engines can satisfy the requirement, the requirement should be reconsidered, since one supplier cannot create a competitive environment.

Each requirement that is written must be reviewed and validated not only by the users but also against corporate standards and project standards. Project standards will help you to decide whether a requirement is actually needed or if it is overstated and can be eliminated or reduced to the essential needs of the project.

It is suggested that the RFP team use some type of consistent documentation process and that all the requirements be listed in a table in order to ensure that they are all considered for the RFP. Table 4.1 below is an example of this type of table. The table can be as simple or complex as needed to meet the project needs.

Once the requirements are written, validated against technology, and approved, the RFP is ready to be assembled.

Table 4.1 Sample Requirements List

Requirement	Objective	Measurement	Approved	Author
Search engine does not use metatags	Eliminate need to metatag documents	Search for content without using metatags	Yes	Bill Author
Search engine uses Boolean terminology	Help user to focus search more closely	Search for content using Boolean terms	No	Mary Smith

Prior to getting started on writing requirements, you should address one other point: try to graphically illustrate your requirements whenever possible. It is no secret that RFPs are pretty dry, technical documents; an illustration or two can really liven them up.

Illustrating Requirements

The value of incorporating illustrations into an RFP cannot be overemphasized. Through graphic representation, requirements take on a tangible quality, and complex concepts become easier to grasp. RFPs that are devoid of illustrations, especially in highly technical documents like an RFP, are more difficult to understand without the benefit of visual assistance.

Line drawings, workflow diagrams, photographs, tables, charts, or graphs can all act as powerful tools for conveying information that could not be communicated adequately in any other way. Illustrations effectively support the text and may well convey more data to a reader than pages of text. Illustrations also provide visual relief for the eye, especially when the reader is faced with many pages of complex technical descriptions and jargon.

Given the illustration tools that are currently available, including ready-made illustrations of computers, networks, and other sources of drawings, there is no reason why your RFP should not contain as many illustrations as needed to support the text. In addition, it is fairly easy to import "objects" such as a chart, for example, directly into your text to support a point being made.

Illustrations like those in Figure 4.2 may show your current document management system and may be embedded in the narrative description of the system itself.

Figure 4.2 Sample Technical
Illustration

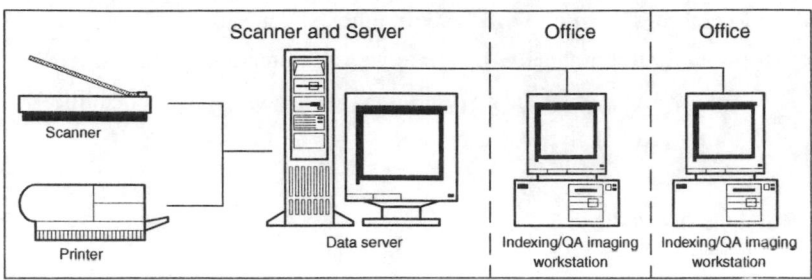

Figure 4.2 Sample Technical Illustration

Figure 4.3 offers a wealth of information about the content of a file folder and provides a visual map of the organization of the folder that is generally easier to comprehend than a plain text description of the contents. This illustration may also serve as the basis of a diagram for suppliers writing their proposals.

In the past, it was difficult for smaller companies without a graphics department or ready access to the tools needed to do the paste-up work to include photographs in an RFP. Today, with the advent of digital photography, anyone can incorporate a photograph into an RFP if it is appropriate and will help explain the material. For example, your RFP may be for changing or

Figure 4.3 Sample File Folder Illustration

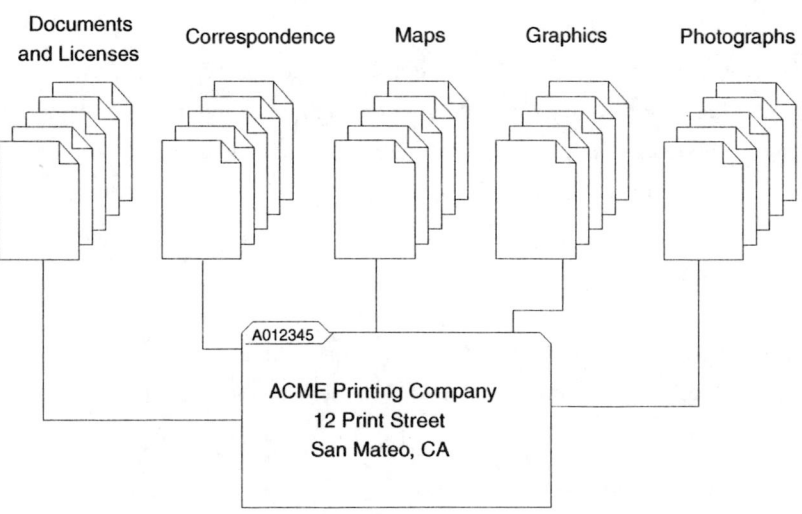

adding to existing facilities and equipment. The RFP should contain a dimensional drawing of the facility room in addition to including several photographs of the same room taken from different angles.

A series of photographs can also be placed in the RFP Web site library if it would be inconvenient to include them all in the RFP itself. In such cases it should be noted in the RFP that additional photographs and/or drawings can be found in the RFP library. A note of caution: ensure that your photographs do not include people or areas that should not be seen by suppliers.

Take care to ensure that all materials offered are in a common format for viewing. Many programs allow you to convert drawings, spreadsheets, project plans, and so on to html format for downloading and browsing with common Internet browsers.

Anatomy of a Technical Section

Now let's discuss the most common elements in a technical section. When writing your RFP, don't get locked into this sample format or any other—it is only a suggested format and a "typical" way of writing RFPs. Add more sections to clarify your RFP if they are needed, or develop a simpler approach if your RFP is smaller. However, don't sacrifice clarity for brevity; if you do, you will most likely incur additional work in the long run.

Current Business Environment

For almost any project involving a change in the current business environment, the existing environment must be documented. Only when suppliers understand how this part of your business currently operates can they determine how their products will fit into that environment and whether their solution will be successful.

For example, suppose ACME Insurance wants to set up a corporate Intranet to share corporate information within the company. Currently, their only methods for disseminating corporate information are a paper and electronic newsletter distributed on Mondays. But if you wanted to know about the vacation policy, you would either have to go to Human Resources and ask someone or look it up in a human resources policy book.

In this example, the description of the current environment would explain how people currently receive their corporate information and describe what types of corporate information would become part of the Intranet. ACME Insurance wants all of the business units to have a listing on the Intranet home page, allowing each unit to publish its information to a designated space on the Intranet. Human Resources may want to publish a policy handbook, a list of people to contact by phone or e-mail with questions, a frequently asked questions (FAQ) list, corporate training schedules, and other useful information.

The "current business environment" section states the business problem that the RFP is trying to solve. This statement should be followed by an explanation of how business is done in the current environment.

> ACME Insurance Company would like to develop and build a corporate Intranet that would allow each business unit, and departments within the business unit, to publish information directly to the corporate Intranet. Employees would access this information by logging on to the ACME home page.

> ACME currently distributes company information through a variety of manual methods, including e-mail, printed weekly newsletters, company policy bulletins that are printed and distributed, and policy manuals that are kept in Human Resources and in each business unit. We find that these methods are slow, inefficient, costly, and prevent the widespread dissemination of company information. They are also not suitable for distributing information quickly to all of our geographically dispersed business units.

In addition to a general description of the problem, you may also provide details on all aspects of how business is currently conducted. For the preceding example of a corporate Intranet publishing system, you might provide details on how each business presently publishes and distributes content.

This section offers suppliers a business perspective on the problem and suggests how you are justifying the expense of a new system. When writing their proposals, vendors should use this information to explain how their proposals will, for example, help to distribute information faster and less expensively.

This section may also outline the goals and objectives of the project in more detail. While these may have been covered briefly in the RFP introduction, it is often useful to expand on those themes. Common examples of business improvement goals include the following:

1. Increase productivity.
2. Reduce customer wait time.
3. Improve customer relations and customer service.
4. Build a more flexible business environment.
5. Reduce operating costs.
6. Provide for disaster recovery.

Here's an example of a project goal:

Reduce Customer Wait Time

Over the past several years, ACME Insurance has experienced tremendous business growth, which is expected to continue for the next several years. As a result of this rapid rate of growth, ACME has significantly increased staffing levels, but customers' telephone wait time has continued to increase—from an average of 3 seconds to 6 seconds. Our acceptable standard for customer wait time is 4 seconds. We believe that with the addition of this technology, ACME will be able to slow the hiring curve and decrease the wait time from 6 seconds to an average of 2 or 3 seconds.

Vendors should be able to conclude the following from the preceding statement:

1. ACME has strong growth and is therefore a very viable client.
2. Working with ACME offers long-term potential; in other words, this contract may not simply be a one-shot deal but may yield continuing opportunities.
3. ACME needs a technology-based solution to the customer wait time problem and recognizes this need.
4. Hiring additional personnel is not helping, and may be making matters worse, further justifying the need for technology-based solutions.
5. Reduced hiring provides part of the cost justification for technology.

The purpose of this section is to establish the need for this project and to interest suppliers in what you are doing. It should be comprehensive and informative, and any necessary additional information should go in an appendix. Additional information may be a study done by a consulting company, or a report documenting some aspect of the business. Do not skimp on the information if it is available; good suppliers will use it to their advantage to write a better proposal.

Current Technical Environment

While the following examples about the current technical environment relate to a computer system environment, they apply to any RFP in which equipment is being purchased, from a power generator, to new office facilities, to a mechanical system. If there is presently no equipment and the purpose of this RFP is to establish a new environment, the business reasons and environment may suffice.

The technical description may discuss your hardware, software, and communications environment. For example, you may use only UNIX machines and be unable to accept a solution based on Microsoft operating systems, or you may be open to any type of hardware and software operating system.

When needed, you may provide a catalog of equipment in an appendix listing such items as current server base, types of desktop PCs, printers (networked or personal, black and white or color), scanners (networked or personal), and so on. Also, if needed, provide a network diagram showing the type of internal network available within the building or campus and the external network available between business locations (such as a T-2 line) and, if needed, outside communications to the Internet.

An important aspect of the current environment to be defined is sometimes called the "speeds and feeds," that is, how much "work" is processed in an average day and a peak period or day. In addition, and this may be the reason a new system is being purchased, the expected growth in "work" should also be stated.

For example, suppose your current CRM system, purchased when the company was new and small ten years ago, has hit its limit for storage space and its ability to handle the daily transactions. Based on current projections, the system has experienced a steady 25 percent growth, and you expect a further increase based on projected company expansion. It is essential for you to give suppliers these data; otherwise, they will undersize your system from the beginning, and within a year or two you will have outgrown it again. The growth information, projections, and spreadsheets would be excellent candidates for an appendix or for the RFP's Web site.

In this section you may also list any technical constraints or limitations that are being imposed on suppliers. For example, software applications must be available on IBM's AIX platform; furthermore, they must be certified by the IBM porting center. Or perhaps your company uses IBM's Token Ring instead of Ethernet and applications must be compatible with this requirement.

✎ Constraints place limits on requirements.

When writing this section, be as complete as possible, especially with regard to any constraining requirements. Place any additional relevant information in an appendix. Remember that lack of information will most likely result in questions from suppliers, and you will end up having to provide the information anyway.

Be careful in writing the introduction, which should be narrative and informative but should not include requirements that need to be responded to as part of this section. Any such requirements, for example a constraining requirement, should be repeated in the next sections. If your current technical environment will change, the requirements for that change should be placed in the next section, "Proposed Technical Environment."

If the application or project that is the subject of this RFP is new, you may not have existing hardware and software. However, it is probable that you do already have a network, desktop PCs, and other equipment that allows employees to work. Provide technical details of the existing equipment so that suppliers can comment on this and your infrastructure in the technical section. In the technical requirements section, have suppliers review your existing equipment and verify whether it is sufficient or needs to be upgraded.

Proposed Technical Environment

The proposed technical environment section provides the supplier with information about the environment that will be in place when the project is started. For example, your RFP may be part of a larger project to update, modernize, or change from one technology to another. If there is going to be a change in the general technical infrastructure, this section will provide suppliers with that information. For example, if you now have some IBM OS2 workstations and some Apple-based workstations, you may be changing and consolidating to the latest version of Microsoft's operating system. Alternatively, if you are going to standardize on Ethernet instead of a variety of other communication protocols, Ethernet would become a requirement. Or perhaps you now store scanned images in a supplier's proprietary format and will have to convert them to the new standard, which will be ITU Group 4 with TIFF.

While this section provides suppliers with requirements for the technical environment and infrastructure, it does not necessarily provide requirements for the application or the work that is to be performed. Rather it tells suppliers that if the application needs a personal computer, that computer will be running the latest version of Microsoft operation system and a compatible CPU such as Intel.

If you have a document that describes the IT upgrade plan, and the plan does not include confidential or proprietary information, you may consider providing this plan in an appendix to allow suppliers to review it as part of their proposal effort. Once you have established these ground rules, it is time to describe the primary application that you are buying.

A Note on Hardware Requirements

For many companies, hardware is not typically part of a software application request, because it is assumed that users already have desktop PCs, that a communications infrastructure is in place, and that if hardware components are needed for the application, they will be purchased by the IT department based on hardware purchase agreements already in place. However, it is relevant for the supplier to provide hardware specifications so that the IT department can determine if current resources are adequate or if hardware needs to be upgraded and/or purchased.

✑ Software companies normally do not purchase and maintain hardware.

Furthermore, many software companies do not provide or supply the hardware components for their software. Most software companies have no need to provide hardware because their customers already have purchasing agreements with hardware suppliers. Most companies buy servers, workstations, printers, scanners, and communications gear and associated operating systems directly from their preferred suppliers.

If an application requires special hardware that is not currently part of a company's inventory, the company will use the specification contained in suppliers' proposals to purchase the needed equipment. Suppliers must therefore list the specifications for the required hardware so that the appropriately sized server, for example, can be ordered.

Hardware Specifications

ACME Insurance will be responsible for purchasing all required hardware for this project. Vendors shall provide ACME with the hardware specifications for all required hardware components. Vendors may propose components by brand name when the named product(s) have specific features or functionality that is integrated with the supplier's system. Vendors are responsible for providing a complete list of hardware and related purchasing specifications. The supplier is responsible for purchasing components that are not specified but are later determined to be required.

It is also possible that your company already has in place many hardware components that you would like to use. If this is the case, list each component and provide its specifications. The supplier is responsible for accepting the installed component, providing specifications for upgrading the component, or rejecting it as being insufficient for the application needs.

Current Hardware Component Configurations

ACME plans to use existing hardware components wherever possible. Below is a list of our installed equipment with their respective current configurations. Vendors shall determine whether each component is satisfactory for use with the supplier's software and state one of the following:

1. Component is satisfactory.
2. Component requires the following upgrades to meet requirements.
3. Component is not satisfactory.

If the component is a desktop computer, for example, you should also include the version of the operating system.

It may be that you have a unique application for which you would like the supplier to supply both software and hardware. If this is the case, that requirement should become part of the RFP itself. Some companies require suppliers to support both the hardware and software so that the company's internal Help Desk staff need only call one number when experiencing a problem. The supplier is then responsible for initiating the troubleshooting procedures, determining whether the problem is hardware, software, communications, and so on, and either providing the resolution or contracting with the hardware provider to shift the responsibility if the problem does not originate with the software supplier's program.

Single Source for All Components

Vendors may assume that ACME Insurance has no established hardware or software that can be used for this project. Vendors shall therefore purchase and support all components required as part of their overall solution. These shall include all hardware; system software; peripheral devices such as printers, scanners, communications and network hardware and software; and any other component needed to implement this project successfully. Vendors should refer to the paragraphs in this RFP on ACME equipment standards to ensure that the equipment proposed meets all ACME standards.

A Note on System Software Requirements

System software is typically referred to as the operating system software. A large, complex system may require system software for the servers, workstations, desktop computers, and network servers. If you have an established standard for system software, such as UNIX, LINUX, or the current version of Microsoft OS, you must present it as a requirement in the RFP.

✍ System software is not the application.

However, as with hardware, many suppliers do not provide the system software, because it typically comes with the hardware or is acquired separately through existing purchasing agreements. As above, if you have existing equipment that will be considered for reuse with this project, you should list the software operating system and current version in the RFP. This information allows suppliers to determine if their software is consistent with your system software environment.

System software may also include peripheral software that is installed and operating on workstations and servers. For example, if your project is for a corporate Intranet, you may already have a Web design software package, or several, and you may prefer to continue to use this instead of purchasing new software. More important, if your company has standardized on certain software applications, you should name these software products and require suppliers to integrate with these existing products. (Ensure that you do not include a requirement for something that is not possible. When requiring integration with existing software applications and company standards, they must be compatible with supplier products or no suppliers will submit proposals.)

Some types of system software may also require other software to be present. The supplier may assume that you already have this software or at least that you already understand that you need to purchase it along with the products being proposed. This point may not be clear to you or clear in the supplier's proposal.

Application Requirements

This section, also called the "Statement of Work," or "Scope of Work," contains the project requirements, whether for a computer system, a consulting engagement, a facility upgrade, or an outsourcing opportunity. These requirements mandate what a supplier must provide in order to be responsive to your RFP.

If the project is to hire a consultant, there may be no equipment requirements, nor any existing services such as are being requested, but it will be necessary to explain why you need to hire a consultant. You may also place "technology" constraints on the consulting company by stating that they must provide a project plan in a certain program or that they must be able to up- and download data from an FTP site.

If the project is to hire an outsourcing company to maintain existing computer facilities and software applications, you will need to describe the computing environment, outline what type of support is expected (since the outsourcing company will sit between you and the equipment manufacturer), and list a myriad of details.

A third type of project is one in which you are buying a product, such as hardware or software, either to replace an existing product or to install as a completely new product.

While it is not possible to document an entire technical requirements section, the two brief examples that follow show the types of requirements found in the statement of work section.

Request for Consulting Services

If your RFP is for consulting services, this section will provide the details of what is expected of the consulting company. The example given, for hiring a consulting company to study an accounts payable (AP) process, relates only to the actual statement of work requirements; it does not include the description of the problem and other introductory sections.

The following are the requirements for this consulting engagement:

1. Consultant shall interview all personnel associated with the AP process. The consultant shall follow the path of an invoice from the time it arrives in the mailroom until that invoice is paid and all work is completed. The following is a list of people who physically handle or work on an invoice: *[list not provided in this example]*

2. Based on the interviews and research, the consultant shall provide a workflow diagram of the AP process to include the following:

   a. Each process step and tasks, beginning when an invoice is received by that person.

   b. Functional name of person responsible for the task (mailroom clerk, junior payment clerk, payment clerk, and so on).

   c. Equipment used to complete a task including name of software program (ACME AP APP, Excel).

   d. Average time to complete each task in terms of a time value (seconds, minutes, hours, days).

3. Consultant shall review each step in the current AP process. For each step reviewed, the consultant shall suggest one of the following actions:

   a. Eliminate step.

   b. Implement a simple process improvement within the existing step.

   c. Implement a new process step incorporating new technology.

In this example, the consulting company is required to review all aspects of an AP system and assess whether that system is working efficiently or whether it can be improved with simple changes or a new technology solution.

In order to write this RFP technical section, your company must be able to lead suppliers through the work process itself and provide them with enough information to understand the extent of the consulting work; otherwise suppliers would have no basis for their proposals. From this RFP, suppliers must be able to estimate the number of people needed and the associated costs for people, travel, and so on.

Request for a Business System Application

This second application description is based on the Intranet search engine project example used previously in this section. Again, we have not included all of the preparatory material such as the description of the basic problems, current technical environment, and so on. The examples given show the types of requirements that would appear in this RFP.

Search Engine Functional Requirements

Below are the requirements for the search engine. Vendors shall respond to each requirement as listed below.

The following requirements are for the types of searches:

1. Standard key word search. Engine shall search for single words or multiple words such as "default insurance."

2. Advanced search using standard Boolean query terms. Engine shall be able to use standard Boolean query terms such as "default insurance AND risk mitigation."

3. Natural language search using phrases. Engine shall be able to parse multiple word phrases or complete sentences such as "I want to know about default insurance plans."

4. Proximity searching. Engine shall be able to search for terms that are near to each other as specified in the search parameters such as "default insurance NEAR risk mitigation."

Vendors shall explain and provide examples of how search results are returned for each of the types listed above.

The search engine shall be able to search the following types of documents:

1. All Microsoft Word and Excel files.
2. Adobe PDF-formatted documents.
3. Files saved in standard ASCII formats such as .txt files.
4. HTML documents.

In addition to the above requirements, the proposed search engine shall be capable of searching documents with attachments and shall be able to index the attachment along with the primary document.

Advanced search requirements. As shown in the example below, suppliers shall be able to provide users with an "Advanced Search" function that allows users to designate such parameters as "Language," track the number of search hits returned, construct a Boolean search, and other advanced search functions as shown in the example.

Users shall access this feature by selecting "Advanced Search," which shall be written next to the search terms input box.

The examples show that the RFP team understands basic search engine technology and terminology. However, what if the team does not want to limit the suppliers' responses to those items listed because there may be additional "unique" information that each supplier can provide?

In the example for searching types of documents such as HTML and PDF, for instance, perhaps other types of documents would be searched in the future, but they are not part of the immediate project. The requirement could be supplemented with the following sentence:

The search engine shall be able to search the following types of documents.

1. All Microsoft Word and Excel files.
2. Adobe PDF-formatted documents.
3. Files saved in standard ASCII formats such as .txt files.
4. HTML documents.

In addition to the document types listed above, suppliers shall also provide a complete list of all document types that can be searched. Vendors shall also state whether it is possible to customize the search engine for document types that are not listed.

In this example, the primary four document types are listed, but the requirement also covers those document types that may be searched in the future, such as graphic illustration files. The final sentence allows suppliers to explain whether they are able to identify document types that are not currently part of their engine and build a custom search routine for that document type. For example, perhaps the RFP team has long-range plans to search unstructured data within a database program, but that requirement, if needed, would be several years in the future. This additional requirement allows them to explore this possibility with each supplier.

The previous two examples of functional application requirements show that requirements must be directly stated, clear, and reduced to the lowest level possible. To write "good" requirements, the writer needs to provide enough information to get the meaning across, but not so much as to confuse the supplier.

Conclusion

The following conditions must apply in order for the RFP team to write an effective technical requirements section:

❑ The team must know in detail how the current system operates (if there is one) and must be able to communicate that knowledge to the suppliers.

❑ If there is no current system and this is a new application, the team must be able to design the system from scratch since there is no existing system to use as a basis for the new system. This means that the RFP team may have to do considerable requirements analysis with the users, in addition to researching and comparing requirements to potential supplier solutions.

❑ The team must know what is expected of the new system and must provide suppliers with direction.

❏ The team must know what are acceptable solutions, given that they have several valid solutions to choose from.

❏ The team must be able to evaluate intelligently the differences between the acceptable solutions.

Because technical requirements drive other sections of the RFP, such as management and pricing, the team must be able to ensure that a technical requirement neither conflicts with nor constrains requirements in other sections. For example, you may require a level of testing that drives the price beyond your budget, or you may require the software interface to be in English in the technical section but multilingual in the management section.

Ensure that technical requirements are correctly referenced, when needed, in the management section of the RFP and that the references are consistent. You cannot mandate "distributed personal printers" in the technical section and then require "centralization of printer facilities, services, and operations" in the management section.

Requirements have to reflect actual products and capabilities, not something that does not exist or cannot be built. Do not combine proprietary product features from several suppliers into one single requirement. This tactic results in a requirement that no supplier can respond to and may force suppliers to drive the price beyond the budget in order to be responsive. As requirements engineers and many others have said, "A camel is a horse designed by a committee."

Requirements must be measurable. If you call for a product to work "internationally" what does that mean, and how will you measure it? If the user interface "shall be intuitively obvious," how can you measure that quality?

Requirements should have a corresponding place in the evaluation criteria. If it is a requirement, it should be evaluated.

Requirements should be functionally stated whenever possible, allowing suppliers the latitude to propose differing solutions. Requirements that are too tight restrict the number of suppliers who can compete and therefore limit the number of possible solutions. Requirements that include a " pre-defined solution" further limit suppliers to your prescribed solution, not theirs.

Requirements should reflect the actual need; they should not be excessive or indulge in gold plating. Why request multilingual products when your company only operates within the United States? Why request that scanned documents be stored on local magnetic storage (expensive storage) when those documents are seldom, if ever, accessed?

Reviews of the RFP should include an effort to catch these common problems and to determine whether the requirement is valid or should be rewritten. If the author of the requirement cannot defend it, that requirement should be removed or rewritten.

In most cases, it is always possible to add something if it becomes apparent that it is needed, but almost impossible to return a product or service or unwrite program code once it has been implemented and discovered to be unnecessary.

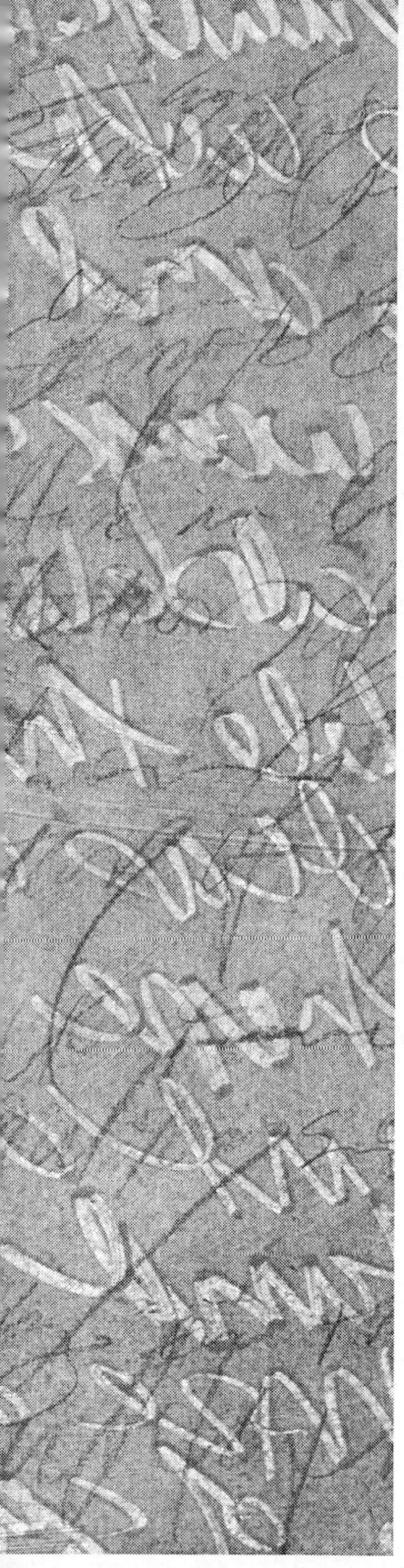

5

Management Requirements Section

Introduction

Suppliers shall include a project management plan for implementing the ACME project. The project management plan shall be detailed enough to assure ACME that the supplier can deliver the system on time, within budget, and meet all requirements as specified in this RFP. The project management plan should not be a tutorial on project planning and the benefits of a project plan. ACME is looking for preliminary plans that suggest step-by-step tasks, timetables, staffing numbers, personnel resumes, and responsibilities for both the supplier and ACME.

If the project under consideration requires the installation of equipment or installation and testing of new software programs, or if suppliers are required to be onsite at your facility, include a requirement for a project management plan in the RFP. The specifications in the management section require suppliers to demonstrate their approach to the design, development, installation, and maintenance phases of the contract, as well as to provide assurances that they have the necessary resources to complete these activities.

A supplier's response to the RFP's management section will clearly indicate whether the supplier's company has the requisite project management skills, resources, and experience to be considered for the project. A supplier may have developed the proposed technical product but lack the ability to develop and implement an effective management program. While it is possible to shore up a weak project plan with internal resources, such a plan may indicate that the supplier has more serious problems.

Research suppliers' project capabilities as well as their technical solutions.

Many companies spend resources on product development and product marketing but do not realize that post-sales activities are equally important. Many startup companies initially focus on product development and marketing and have little insight into the installation and maintenance issues involved when customers install their products. Many companies either neglect support issues or believe that third party system integrators or value added resellers (VARs) will handle the support and installation.

The RFP team should consider a supplier's project skills and capabilities as one of the qualifying factors for getting onto the preferred supplier list. If a supplier has poor installation capabilities, determine whether that supplier also provides the product through other channels such as system integrators, or whether the product may be bundled with other products by a supplier with additional capabilities. If there are other channels, consider sending the RFP to both the supplier and the other companies that carry the product. Otherwise, *caveat emptor.*

The project management section typically requires, but is not limited to, development of the following:

- ❑ project plan
- ❑ project schedule
- ❑ site preparation plan and responsibilities
- ❑ staffing requirements
- ❑ design, development, and implementation
- ❑ delivery and installation
- ❑ system acceptance test
- ❑ system maintenance
- ❑ training
- ❑ documentation

The requirements in the RFP, along with the supplier's response, will form the basis of a working relationship between you and the supplier. The completed management plan ensures that both you and the supplier have made your best attempt to describe what needs to be done, by whom, in what order, and at what time.

Requiring a well-documented project plan also provides a starting place for making changes in a contract. For example, after the contract is awarded, the winning supplier will develop a final requirements document in order to begin the design phase. It is not uncommon for both supplier and buyer to agree to a change based on information uncovered during the creation of this document. This modification could affect how work is processed, which could require additional work, such as software to be designed, or additional hardware to be added to the system. Without an overall plan that has been written and agreed to, it would be hard to assess the impact of modifications to the schedule, installation requirements, and price of the product.

The project plan is the foundation for the project.

Not all RFPs require the level of management planning presented below. However, the principles outlined here remain the same: if a supplier is required to install and maintain what is being purchased, a management plan should be required. In developing the management section, think through the project from the day the contract is signed to the day the system potentially becomes obsolete. The management section can be as broad or as narrow in focus as necessary, given the size and duration of the project being considered. You may for example, include a requirement for a disaster recovery plan, a technology obsolescence and replacement plan, or a production transition plan.

Writing Requirements for the Management Section

The management section is composed of information and requirements that provide suppliers with your vision for managing the project. In order to develop the management requirements, the RFP team has to be aware of the company standards and needs that are unique to the project being undertaken. New and unique requirements will have to be written for the

Be aware of company standards when writing requirements.

project that support its goals and objectives but are not in conflict with the supplier's product and capabilities.

 Readers may want to review "Writing Technical Requirements" in Chapter 4. The same principles apply to writing management requirements, especially with regard to defining requirements with subjective terms such as *adequate*, *sufficient*, *intuitively obvious*, or *flexible*. Requirements such as "User training shall be sufficient" are not valid because "sufficient" is not a measurable term.

For example, if the project is to purchase a new customer relationship management (CRM) software package, the RFP team will have to understand how the customer service representatives operate on a daily basis. The company may historically have operated Monday to Friday, 8:00 AM to 5:00 PM PST. However, a new service being offered means that the customer service group now has to have support coverage for the East Coast as well as Hawaii, which necessitates extending their business hours from 5:00 AM to 8:00 PM PST. The supplier will be required to have live support during that same period. Suppliers' support time, in which they are required to begin problem response and resolution, is called the "principal period of maintenance" or PPM. In this example, the PPM has to change from 8:00 AM to 5:00 PM PST to 5:00 AM to 8:00 PM PST.

The requirement may read:

Supplier shall maintain a principal period of maintenance (PPM) from 5:00 AM to 8:00 PM PST. The supplier shall offer a call-in help desk functioning as a single point of contact for servicing all ACME locations. This help desk shall be accessible via an "800" number. The supplier shall be able to provide on-site personnel to ACME locations within two hours of the initial report of a problem. Problem resolution shall be within four hours from the time the problem was identified. In addition, each supplier shall describe escalation procedures for addressing problems that remain unsolved after a four-hour period of time.

This example lists more than one requirement, and the supplier is responsible for dividing this paragraph into a list of all requirements that need to be addressed. The requirements in the above paragraph are the following:

1. PPM response time is from 5:00 AM to 8:00 PM PST.
2. Supplier shall staff a help desk during the PPM.
3. Supplier support shall be contacted through a toll-free number.
4. Supplier shall acknowledge the call and begin troubleshooting within two hours of the initial trouble call.
5. Supplier shall have a physical presence at an ACME location within two hours if necessary.
6. Suppliers shall fix all problems within four hours.
7. Supplier shall describe what happens after four hours if the problem has not been isolated and fixed.

In order to develop management requirements, the RFP team will have to analyze the project from an operations perspective. Figure 5.1 is a graphic representation of the process and is the same as Figure 4.1 from Chapter 4. The first step in requirement definition is to look at each management task as a discrete unit of work. In the PPM example above, the task is to provide system support during business hours. As a result of the analysis, other requirements associated with the support period include being onsite within two hours (corporate mandate and supplier capabilities review), providing a toll-free number (corporate standard), completing problem resolution within four hours (user requirement based on the service offered), and defining problem escalation procedures (corporate standard).

As when developing technical requirements, be careful not to specify requirements that suppliers cannot meet. For example, because this is a critical application in which customers are calling in to the customer service group to conduct business, the product marketing group determined

Requirements are dictated by how a business process works.

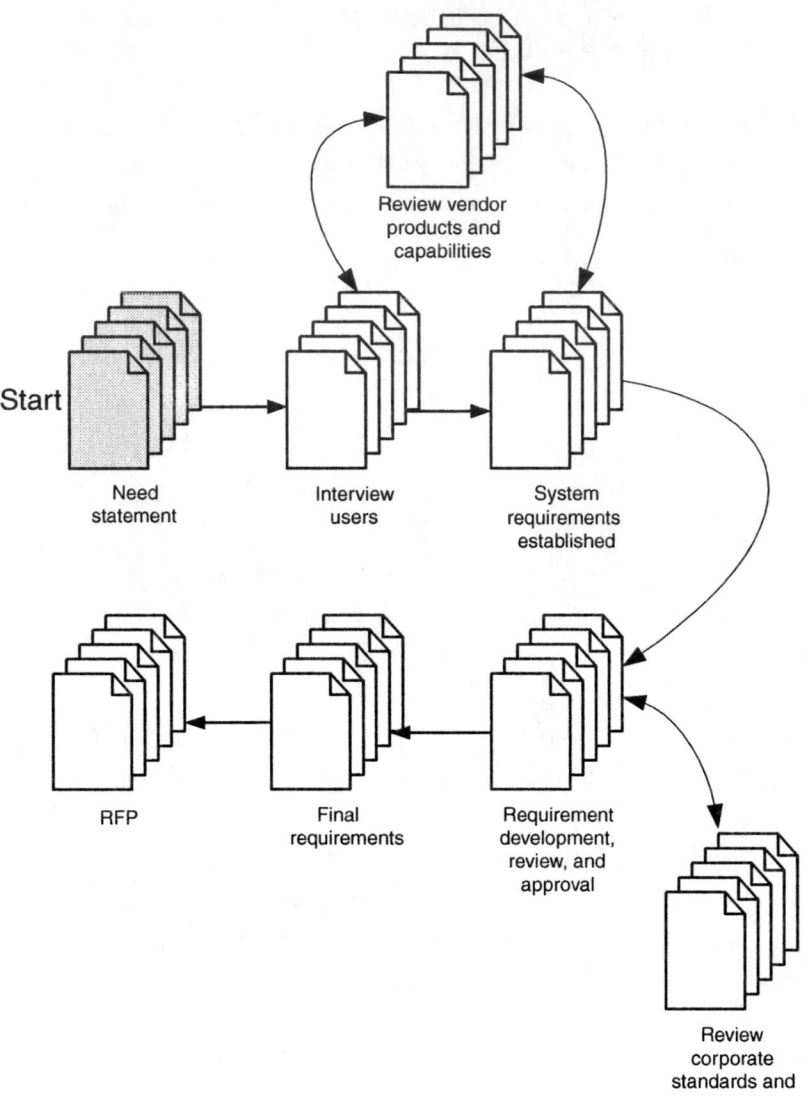

Figure 5.1
Requirements
Development Process

Review vendor
products and
capabilities

Start

Need
statement

Interview
users

System
requirements
established

RFP

Final
requirements

Requirement
development,
review, and
approval

Review
corporate
standards and
mandates

that all calls must be responded to and fixed within four hours. This marketing requirement drives the supplier response requirement to have support on site within two hours and to have the problem fixed within four hours.

By reviewing various vendor data sheets and support information, you may determine that no supplier in the competition could satisfy the physical on-site requirement. Suppliers would either have to fail to comply with this requirement or they would have to establish a support location within two hours of each ACME office, for which they would determine the cost and bill you. This option may be too expensive to consider.

Based on supplier capabilities research, the RFP team may have to rewrite the requirement to say:

> The supplier shall provide on-site personnel, *or remote diagnostic capability,* to ACME locations within two hours of the initial report of a problem.

This requirement allows suppliers to choose how to respond to this requirement. You would keep the requirement to have the problem fixed or escalated within four hours, because that is a promise you made to your customers.

Developing management requirements starts with knowing what the application needs to do operationally as well as technically. For example, in the above requirements for response and escalation, the RFP team may include a "fault tolerance" requirement in the technical section that complements the response-time requirement in the management section. The technical requirement may be written thus:

> All hardware, including servers, data storage, and communications network equipment shall have an uptime capability of 99.99 percent.

The technical and management requirements work together to satisfy the business application.

✎ Management and technical requirements must work together.

Examples of Poorly Written Requirements

Above all, requirements need to be unambiguous. As discussed in Chapter 4, suppliers should not have to determine whether a sentence is a requirement or just general information. The example from an RFP that follows is apparently about staffing requirements for the project, but there is no "requirement" for the supplier to propose staffing. The first two sentences are informational, acknowledging the need for staff and the fact that staffing will vary according to the supplier's proposed solution. The third sentence is the actual requirement, but it states only the need to have personnel who are capable of operating the system.

> Full-time, in-house staff will be needed to maintain the system. The staff required to maintain the proposed system will depend on the system and the installation complexity. Regardless of the suppliers or a particular implementation, ACME personnel who can operate and maintain the various components of the system will need to be available.

Written more specifically, the paragraph should require suppliers to propose staff for various types of work, the number of staff required, and their specific duties. For example:

> Full-time, in-house staff will be needed to maintain the system. Suppliers shall propose the type of staff required, technical or administrative, to support the system being proposed. ACME will be operating the system on a 24/7 basis in order to meet the national and international needs of our customers.
>
> For each type of support position proposed, suppliers shall propose the number of people required, the type of people required (including any prerequisites for the position), and the specific functions to be performed by each type of person.

The following paragraph is the documentation requirement from an RFP for an international system. It constitutes the entire requirement for documentation.

> Because of the international nature of this procurement, comprehensive, high-quality, and easy-to-read documentation is essential. Documentation shall provide a complete explanation of all hardware, system, application, and network software.

This requirement contains several subjective terms that will make it difficult for suppliers to respond: "comprehensive, high-quality and easy-to-read . . . ." How will these "requirements" be evaluated? Will the customers read the manuals and say whether they thought the documentation was easy to read? If a supplier's proposal is accepted and later the customer finds the documentation hard to read, will the supplier be responsible for rewriting it? Is there a grade-level reading standard against which the documentation is being prepared?

When writing your requirements, always be wary of the use of subjective terms such as "easy," "comprehensive," and "high quality." Also be aware of how a requirement can be evaluated. On the technical side, it is easy to require that communications be at T-1 speeds, or that a CPU perform at x.xx gigahertz, or that the system perform a particular accounting function. It is more difficult to be specific in the management section, for example, if you require a project plan. What is your idea of the project plan versus what a supplier may think? In order to be as precise as possible and avoid subjective interpretation by the supplier, provide examples of what you are asking for. For a project plan, you may include a complete plan as an example in an appendix. With an example to use as a reference, suppliers should be more exact in their response.

Anatomy of a Management Section

The management section provides a roadmap of how you expect to work with a supplier. Suppliers in turn respond to your requirements by providing you with a plan based on their experience. It should be noted that the plan requested in the RFP is typically a high-level one that calls out the

The project plan is the roadmap for the project.

major tasks and may provide detail on subtasks, but should not be considered the final plan. The final project plan is generally completed after the award of the contract, as a collaborative effort between you and the supplier. However, the supplier's management plan and schedule should be complete enough, with tentative times and dates, for you to evaluate against the RFP requirements and your needs.

The level of detail in a supplier's project plan is directly proportionate to the level of detail in the RFP. In most cases, the supplier will, after the contract is awarded, assess and validate the requirements as stated in the RFP as one of the first tasks in the project plan. This reevaluation may affect the final schedule and plan, but it should not lead to a major rewrite.

Project Plan

✎ If you don't know where you are going, any road will get you there.

The heart of a management section is the project plan requirement that itemizes major tasks, responsibilities, and schedules. The initial plan may be only a high-level plan in the proposal, but it becomes the basis for the full plan once the contract has been awarded.

> The supplier shall include a plan for implementing the project described in this RFP. The plan shall be comprehensive enough in scope and detail to convey the supplier's ability to manage this project. The plan shall include project tasks, dates, and staffing levels. The ability of the supplier to manage all aspects of this project is one of the critical success factors of the whole project. ACME uses Microsoft Project™ for project scheduling and requires that the supplier use the same program and version. The project schedule shall be submitted electronically as part of the electronic proposal.

The final approved project plan is a joint effort between you and the supplier. The initial plan submitted with the proposal should serve as an evaluation factor to judge whether the supplier knows how to develop a project plan. The plan submitted with the proposal should be reviewed for completeness and credibility.

A typical project schedule from a supplier should have a detailed list of project tasks and subtasks. Each task should list a start and stop date, along with the estimated number of hours required to complete the task. Each task should also have a person assigned, or several, and should include your personnel if required. Completion of major tasks should allow for some testing time to demonstrate completion or acceptance of the task to reflect your acceptance that the item was completed and approved.

Having the hours or "relative" time to complete a task is important. As stated before, the proposed schedule is an estimate based on information in the RFP, but the supplier's assessment of how long a task takes to complete should be fairly solid. This means that while the project may start four weeks later than anticipated and include several extra tasks, the basic time to complete the tasks listed should not have changed.

After the project is awarded, one of the first tasks for you and the supplier is to meet and begin developing the final project plan and schedule. This will be done in conjunction with reviewing the list of technical requirements.

Project Schedule

In order to provide a project schedule, the supplier will need to estimate both the start date and the completion date. A completion date may be required in order to meet management expectations for a product rollout, holiday schedule, or year-end schedule. That is, if the project is to be completed very quickly, the supplier may have to coopt extra staff to meet the deadline, thus adding to the overall cost.

If the project is more loosely structured, the RFP team may provide the supplier with an arbitrary start and finish date. The final schedule may depend on the supplier's assessment and validation of the RFP requirements. It will not be completed until after this first task is finished and both you and the supplier agree to the schedule.

More important than a start date is when the project needs to be up and running.

Site Preparation Plan and Personnel Responsibilities

Site preparation and installation involve the basic work needed to prepare a site for installation of equipment; checking power, communications, space, and ergonomics for users, and environmental conditions. Suppliers shall provide specifications and typical equipment layouts, including door swings, for the physical area where the server, communications server, and magnetic storage units will be installed. ACME's preference is to locate this equipment in Building 4 (see the attached building map in Appendix D). Suppliers shall also provide minimum desktop specifications for the user workstation monitors.

 Site preparation extends beyond the computer room.

When installing new hardware (computer or otherwise) or equipment, existing facilities may need to be modified, or new facilities built, to meet the requirements of the hardware. If these requirements are not requested in the RFP, the installation will invariably fall behind schedule while you wait for the facilities to be upgraded or built. Or even worse, equipment will be delivered to facilities that are not prepared or inadequately configured and will have to be either returned or stored.

> ☑ In one memorable instance of poor site planning, a piece of equipment that was purchased was so large that it would not fit through the doors to the computer room. The supplier had to dismantle the equipment, move each piece into the computer room, and then reassemble it. The equipment was complex and had to be exactly square and level, which necessitated calling in the manufacturer's technical specialist, who spent a day realigning the equipment. Three days were lost, and the company that purchased the equipment had to pay for the supplier's time as well as the technical specialist's travel expenses.

The term "facilities" covers a number of areas, for example:

1. *Equipment installation planning*. Some types of equipment require special installation procedures or may not physically fit through existing doorways, hallways, equipment elevators, or other physical

areas. Ensure that the supplier provides physical specifications and identifies equipment that is oversized.

2. *Computer room facilities.* This area may need supplementary electrical power, additional air conditioning, raised flooring, special cable runs, or other modifications as specified by the equipment manufacturer. Ensure that the supplier provides physical specifications for power, air conditioning, machine sizes and dimensions, and door swing layouts.

3. *Personnel work areas (cubicles, offices, work surfaces).* For example, if the project requires a 21-inch computer monitor, the existing cubicle desktop may be too small.

4. *Communications requirements.* The new project may require either new communications equipment and lines or upgrades to existing equipment and lines. These requirements could, for example, involve rewiring your building, which is a major undertaking.

In your RFP, ensure that suppliers are responsible for specifying equipment, hardware, and software requirements, and also make sure you specify who is responsible for installing upgrades or building new facilities. Roles and responsibilities should be part of the project plan.

> Who is responsible for making facility upgrades?

Project Staffing Requirements

Staffing is particularly important if either you or the supplier determines that the project requires additional staff. If that is the case, when are they needed? What qualifications must they have? Should they be trained before or after installation of the product?

Conversely, the new project may reduce current staffing and facilities needs. If that is the case, the supplier should propose the correct staffing numbers for the new system, allowing you either to reassign existing staff or release staff who are no longer needed.

✍ The supplier can help you determine what the project staffing needs will be.

Because the supplier is the technology expert, he or she should be able to determine what staff are necessary after reviewing who is available for the project. This means that the RFP team needs to provide current staffing information as part of the RFP. This information extends not only to personnel who work in the business applications area (claims adjusters, customer service representatives) but also to additional information technology (IT) staff (system administrators, system operations people).

Using the organizational diagram in Figure 5.2, you may add names or, as supplementary text, provide the names of your staff who will participate in the project. Also, if it is important, you may provide titles or skills as needed. For example, the list of your own staff who will work on the project might look like this:

> ACME project manager
>
> Mary Smith, manager of customer relations
>
> ACME systems manager
>
> Bob Jones, IT senior project manager
>
> ACME implementation manager
>
> Mike Henry, IT senior project leader

Figure 5.2   Sample Staffing Diagram in an RFP

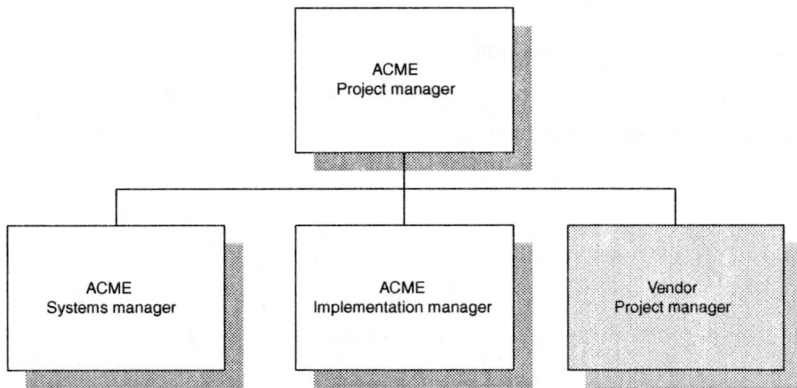

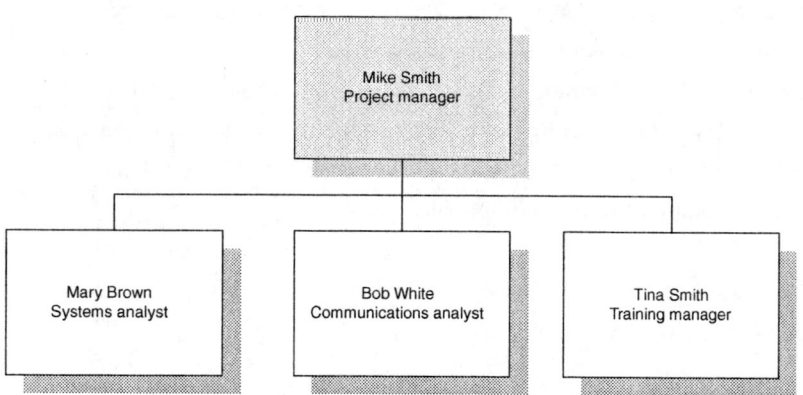

**Figure 5.3   Sample Supplier
Staffing Diagram**

The supplier also staffs the project team. For a large project, this team may include a project manager, various system-level people, and training personnel (see Figure 5.3). It is important for you to review and consider each person proposed, since the supplier may not have the right experience in your particular business application. Have the supplier provide names and resumes for all personnel.

It is also important to ensure that suppliers do not list their most qualified personnel in the proposal and then provide less qualified personnel when the project starts.

Project Staffing

Suppliers and their subcontractors shall describe the proposed management structure and identify key personnel who will be assigned to this project. Resumes for all key personnel shall also be included in this section. Suppliers shall designate key personnel deemed necessary to satisfy the requirements of this RFP. Once identified, suppliers may not change key personnel without prior notice and acceptance from ACME. ACME shall have 30 days' notice of any change in the project's key personnel.

Roles and Responsibilities

Whenever two project teams, such as yours and the supplier's, come together, it is important to understand each other's roles and responsibilities. Roles and responsibilities also apply to such areas as site preparation, in which it may not be clear who will make the facilities' physical changes that are required for new equipment.

Generally speaking, the lead project manager should be from your company. In the RFP, you may request:

> Suppliers shall define the roles and responsibilities of the ACME project team as well as those of the supplier's project team. ACME will appoint a project manager who will work closely with the supplier's project manager.

Design, Development, and Implementation

Design, development, and implementation are the core sections of the management plan. In this section, the supplier needs to explain how he or she will begin the design process, what is needed from your company, and what will be the basic steps and tasks. For example, one of the first tasks may be to validate the requirements in the RFP. This process may lead to a reexamination of some requirements, which may precipitate a change to the requirement itself.

This section of the RFP may be simple or robust, depending on your company's experience and the size of the project. Again, depending on the project, you may request a fairly detailed project description, reaching down to individual tasks. The following are typical major steps in a hardware/software project:

1. Validation of RFP requirements.
2. Final design and approval.
3. Development.
4. Prototype testing.
5. User testing.

6. Product installation.

7. Acceptance testing (30 days).

8. Production cutover.

9. Retirement of old system.

10. Production.

11. Training.

12. Support and maintenance.

Each of the above tasks may be broken down into subtasks in a project management program along with names of resources, dates, and contingencies.

In the preceding list, training begins after production, but this may not be true for your project. In some projects, training begins before production starts so that system users can begin to use the system immediately. However, many factors are involved in deciding when training actually begins.

Project Change Control

The project plan should show how changes to any part of the project will be recognized and formally agreed to by both the supplier and the buyer. Even for a smaller project, there should be some mechanism for capturing such items as bug identification and resolution, problem identification and reporting, engineering change requests, and product or application enhancements.

> Suppliers shall describe how they handle bug reporting, engineering change requests, and product enhancement requests during the implementation phases of the project. ACME prefers an Internet-based approach that allows us to enter the identified bug or enhancement and to view its status online. All open items will be discussed at the project review meeting. Supplier's program shall be able to provide reporting capabilities on the status of all open items.

This requirement allows you to list formally and track what you consider to be problems or issues during the installation process. You should also record when a requirement is changed or added as part of a project review meeting.

After the project is complete and in production, you will switch to the regular CRM program offered by the supplier.

A word of caution: While it is easier to make and request changes informally, it is always possible that two conflicting changes will be requested that may adversely impact the project, in addition to causing general confusion and delay while both are examined.

Delivery and Installation

Delivery and installation are two key elements in a project. Delivery should be within a week of installation time; otherwise, you will be forced to warehouse the equipment until installation begins. Also, under some contract terms, delivery may trigger a milestone payment, which should not be paid if the equipment will not be installed right away. Delivery should be carefully managed, because some suppliers may try to ship early in order to invoice, and therefore recognize revenue, within a certain financial quarter. It is never a good idea to warehouse expensive new equipment, whatever it may be, as the longer it is there, the more chance for damage or loss to occur.

 The supplier's first trip was a total disaster. We had requested a plan, a list of to-dos, and who was responsible for what, but the supplier was always too busy preparing for the trip, or was called to another site for an emergency. When the supplier's team arrived, people spent the first day doing what we could have done to prepare the equipment before their arrival. The second day was spent troubleshooting connections to the corporate network—something we could have done ourselves. The supplier had to make a second trip, at their expense, to complete the equipment acceptance test and debug several other problems. The consequence was that we were three weeks behind schedule after the first week of the project.

Installation should not proceed until all site work or upgrades have been accomplished.

Suppliers shall install all hardware and software components for the project. Suppliers shall anticipate lead times to ensure that all required hardware and software is received in sufficient time to meet the project schedule. The project schedule shall have specific dates for the installation of hardware and software, along with associated activities such as site preparation review and any facility upgrades that are needed prior to equipment installation.

Testing

As part of any implementation and installation effort, the supplier must perform a variety of testing. Typically, there should be a requirement in the RFP for the vendor to explain how the product will be tested, in addition to including product testing as part of the project plan and schedule.

Testing is your proof that the system or product operates as intended and meets the RFP requirements, as well as any subsequently developed requirements. For example, if you purchased an Intranet search engine along with the hardware, operating system software, and application, you might consider these basic types of tests:

1. *System level testing performed upon installation.* This test is to demonstrate that the hardware and software operate as warranted. It is performed as soon as the equipment is set up and operational but does not test the "application," since that has not been built yet.

2. *Application software testing.* This would be an acceptance test of the basic functionality and operation of the application. If you test the application at the same time as the system hardware and software, there might be a glitch or problem at the system level, which would complicate troubleshooting the application software.

3. *User testing.* This is the testing of the application itself after it has been developed. In our Intranet search engine example, this test would be performed when the initial screen designs have been accomplished so that users can verify that their "design requirements" were followed.

4. *Acceptance testing.* After you sign off on the user testing, the application is tested in production operations over a 30-day period. For the Intranet application, the search engine would have to search and index all intended databases within the company, display all of the search results properly, and provide the expected level of results or "hits" using a variety of search terms.

> Upon completion of acceptance testing, ACME will run the system and application software for 30 days to ensure that the system meets the functional and performance requirements stated in the RFP. After the 30-day test period, if the system conforms to the test requirements, the system will be deemed accepted.

Acceptance tests are generally run over a specified period of time to ensure that any potential bug has had a chance to show itself. The supplier will be responsible for troubleshooting and problem resolution.

5. *Acceptance testing reruns.* If the software or hardware application is performing in a critical line of business, the acceptance test is rerun when new versions of the hardware or software are installed or if the application software has been modified.

Testing can be a time-consuming and contentious activity. Contentious, because you and the supplier may have different ideas about what should be tested, how it should be tested, who should do the testing, and what the test criteria for passing or failing are. What happens if the product fails a test by a tiny margin, or partially fails a test? If the computer is to return a result within 3 seconds and the best the supplier can do is 3.2 seconds, has the product failed the test? Could there be degrees of acceptance? And finally, what is the end result of failing a test?

In a typical 30-day test, the supplier can fail initially, make modifications or fixes, and restart the test. The test criteria may allow the supplier to fail and restart twice in 30 days, but after that, the supplier has failed acceptance testing.

What happens at this point depends on the nature of the failure and on what is in the contract with regard to performance guarantees. If the failure is catastrophic, the supplier may be asked to remove all hardware, software, and other pieces installed and return any portion of any milestone payment made up to this point. This means that either the supplier in second place is asked to return and negotiate a contract or that the contract and project are reworked.

Testing provides both you and the supplier with a baseline in which both of you have agreed that the system performs as expected. This baseline serves as a starting place anytime there is a dispute about system performance or operational functions.

System Maintenance and Support

The system maintenance requirements must be consistent with the business application, as discussed earlier in the section on how to write a requirement. If the business application is a low-level, internal process and it is possible to operate that business unit for a while without running the application, then the maintenance requirement should reflect this type of operation. (24/7 with a 1-hour response time, 4-hour fix time.)

Maintenance is part of the return on investment (ROI) analysis. If business and income are lost because the system is down, then the maintenance requirements should be structured so that the system is repaired as quickly as possible. If the application is not a line-of-business application and business is not lost when it does not operate, there is no need to pay a higher maintenance rate for unnecessary service. You may be able to improve your ROI significantly by selecting the maintenance plan that most closely fits your needs. If you do not explain this point in the RFP, a supplier may assume that you want the highest-priced, most comprehensive maintenance, even though it is actually not needed.

Maintenance is that activity that is required both to prevent and to treat problems with your system. Maintenance includes troubleshooting the

Testing provides the baseline for all future measurements.

problem, sending out a maintenance team to repair the problem, and supplying whatever work and parts are involved in fixing the problem.

Support is the activity required to keep the system operational on a day-to-day basis: helping users log on to the system, adding new users, answering operational questions, or reviewing daily system reports. Support can come both from the supplier and from your internal staff.

From a supplier perspective, support is provided by the person staffing the supplier's help desk, who may answer a general question or look at a problem you are having via a remote dial-up line. If there is a problem, the support desk initiates a maintenance call and starts a maintenance log.

Support can also come from your company personnel, who must be able to staff a help desk and perform other administrative functions. If the project is large and a line-of-business application, then the requirements should request that the supplier outline the internal staffing needs.

If the product being purchased is used during business hours and you have people spread from New York to Hawaii, you may request that the supplier offer support coverage for different time zones. A supplier who provides support coverage only from 8:00 AM to 5:00 PM PST will have to add staff to cover your needs.

Training

If the product being purchased requires training, a training requirement must be written into the RFP. Training can be for a variety of personnel and a varying number of trainees. If you are purchasing a new customer service system, 100 customer service representatives (located across the United States) may have to be trained, as well as IT staff (located across the United States), including system administrators and system operations personnel.

> ACME requires that the supplier provide comprehensive training for all user, administrative, technical, and operational personnel. The supplier is

encouraged to propose innovative approaches to training such as programmed self-study guides, online tutorials, videotapes, CD-ROMs, and
computer-based training. All training shall include step-by-step detail that
will enable employees unfamiliar with the system to perform the described
activities.

You may require that the training be held on your premises, or you may
agree to send personnel to the supplier's training site. You may decide on a
combination of sending IT personnel to the supplier's site and training
users at home.

If you require training to take place at your site, several considerations
must be taken into account for a typical computer system application:

1. You must have the hardware present onsite.

2. You must have the software onsite.

3. You may need the "training database" that the supplier may require
   in order to train users.

4. Items 1–3 must be onsite and running before training can start. It is
   usually very difficult to use the same "production" system for training, since it is still being built, programmed, and developed.

5. If the training involves many people, you must have a suitable training
   facility within your company. If the training is for larger groups, you
   may want to ask the supplier how he or she has handled similar groups.

✒ Training
logistics may be
more complex than
you think.

You may also have a training standard stating that a regular training facility
will be used and that a lecturer will teach the class, as opposed to having
network-based training with personnel sitting at their desks.

Documentation

Documentation refers to the manuals that accompany the equipment, hardware, software, and other products that are in your RFP. More and more
suppliers seem to be providing CD-ROM versions of manuals instead of
hard copies.

Comprehensive, high-quality user documentation is essential for the success of this project. Documentation shall be provided that covers all system hardware, system software, and application software. All documentation provided *shall be in written form*. Documentation should also be provided in electronic form and shall be network-accessible. ACME requires at least two full sets of written documentation for all hardware and software components. One complete set of documentation will reside in the project's library and the other in the computer room. The project library set will be maintained as a "master" set. Changes to written documentation shall also be added to the electronic version.

If it is important that you receive physical copies of the documentation, you must specify that in the RFP. You may also request a copy in electronic form, if possible in a Web-enabled form such as HTML. If the documentation comes on a CD-ROM in Microsoft Word format, for example, you may have to convert it for Web usage; however, the conversion may have to be approved by the supplier because of copyrighted material. Web-enabled material may also have to be protected against being available outside your company Intranet or being used by personnel who are not working on the project.

 After we selected a supplier and received the software, we asked why the documentation had not been sent. The supplier stated that all documentation was on the CD-ROMs and that written documentation was no longer supplied. We reminded the supplier that there was a written documentation requirement in the RFP and that they did not take exception to it in their proposal.

We ended up printing our own copies, at our own expense.

Standards

If your company has developed a set of standards for your IT system and infrastructure that will apply to this procurement, you must list them in the RFP. A full set of extensive standards should be placed in an appendix.

There may be a wide variety of standards within a company. Standards can apply to hardware, software, networking, or data storage. Here is a list of communication and network standards from an RFP.

Suppliers shall comply with the following network standards:

- IEEE 802.3-I: Application of 10BaseT-T in Local Area Network (Ethernet)
- ANSI X3T9.5:FDDI
- EIA/TIA-568: Commercial Building Telecommunications Wiring Standards
- SNA 3770: native and emulation
- SNA LU 6.2
- SNA 3270 and emulation
- Netview management for SNA devices
- SNMP/Spectrum management for LAN and Bridges

There may also be a "standard software development methodology" that you may require a supplier to use.

The purpose of this section is to list all of the standards that your company uses for a project. Suppliers will compare this information to the standards their equipment meets. If a new standard needs to be implemented, suppliers will cost this into their proposal pricing.

Project Cutover

If your project is to replace an existing technology, system, or product, there should be a requirement for the supplier to help you with how and when to make the cutover from the old system to the new system. For some projects this may be of considerable concern, as the project may involve a key business application such as accounting, customer service, or product support.

Ask suppliers to provide you with examples of how they handled other, similar projects and options for handling the cutover. For some projects the

The cutover is a critical period in the implementation.

cutover can happen overnight or over a weekend, but for larger projects it may take a week or longer and involve phasing out the old system while simultaneously phasing in the new system.

Be especially concerned with not losing information—whether telephone calls, paper documents, or updated customer information in a database—during the transition period. Ensure that suppliers have included how to capture or recapture information lost during the cutover process as part of their plan.

Supplier Issues and Concerns

Inviting suppliers to question and/or comment on the RFP's management plan, schedule, and other requirements is always a good idea. These comments may include concerns about the project requirements, ideas for solving a requirement in a new way, or project requirements that were not made but should be considered.

✎ Suppliers should be encouraged to comment on potential issues within the RFP.

Comments from all suppliers' proposals may provide useful insights into the project—whether the particular supplier has won or lost. If the RFP team determines that a comment raises a valid issue, it should be reviewed and acted upon.

For example, suppose the application being purchased is a line-of-business application such as accounts payable and the RFP does not specify backup or disaster recovery procedures. A supplier may comment and then present a backup and disaster recovery plan in an appendix. This information gives you the option of exploring the disaster recovery plan further, though of course you are not required to adopt the plan.

This type of extra effort by suppliers demonstrates that they have compared your requirements against, perhaps, industry best practices. If you ask suppliers for a project plan using a project planning tool, such as Microsoft Project, you might consider comparing all of the plans, from both winners and losers, and adding or supplementing the winning plan with additional information gleaned from other suppliers' plans.

Conclusion

The management plan is a key factor in the evaluation of a supplier's implementation capabilities. Clearly stated management requirements are measurable, although some requirements may have a higher subjective factor than others. If you require suppliers to provide a "detailed project plan," how will you measure the "detailed" part of the requirement? If you state that suppliers "shall provide adequate user training" who will determine what is "adequate?" When you review the final RFP, ensure that subjective terms are clearly defined so that both you and the supplier know what *adequate* means.

Depending on the reason for the RFP, and the product being purchased, management requirements may carry as much or more weight as the technical and pricing section. Companies that discount the management section when writing their RFPs often get into trouble later when they discover that the supplier has no installation resources or skills. While the product may actually work well, the implementation costs may exceed the original budget.

When contacting potential vendors to put on the suppliers' list, include questions about their post-sales resources, such as installation support, training classes, project management personnel, ongoing support programs, and product documentation. If these areas appear to be weak, find out if they distribute the product through other channels.

If the product is technically strong but the post-sales support is weak, consider finding a system integrator who can work with you and the intended product, or add resources to your own internal team. However, if you are adding internal resources, ensure that you thoroughly understand the long-term costs associated with this. You may want to analyze these costs over five years or develop a life-cycle cost model for comparison.

Developing a management section may also be an indication of your company's strengths and weaknesses. If the project involves the development of a detailed project plan and your company has little or no experience in doing this, consider whether to move forward or drop the project. If you are determined to proceed with the project, think about adding project managers to your staff, or increase the budget to accommodate outsourcing project management to the chosen supplier or to a systems integrator who can manage the project.

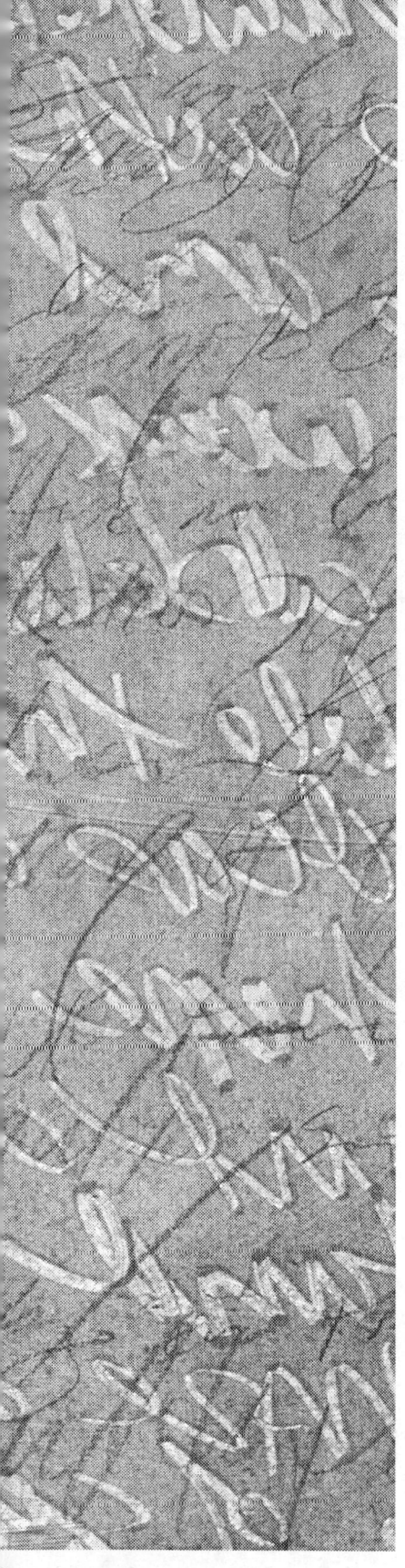

6

Pricing

Introduction

A successful RFP meets two basic requirements. The first is that suppliers and products meet the requirements; the second is that the products or services fall within the projected budget.

The pricing section brings together all of the previous work in the RFP and provides information for suppliers to follow in developing their price proposals. Depending on the type of project, the projected budget may influence how the technical and management section's requirements are developed and presented.

It is critical to the evaluation of proposals to have pricing presented in a consistent format and to give the products being priced a consistent nomenclature. It is also important for product categories to be broken into the same relative components so that a fair comparison can be made among suppliers.

Pricing will play an important role in the evaluation of proposals. Many companies do not award the contract to the lowest-priced supplier, but rather use the price to determine the overall value of the offers. If, for example, the supplier list is down to two suppliers and they appear to be technically equal, a comparison of their prices may decide the winner. (Many state and federal agencies evaluate on technical merit first and use price as a secondary award criterion.)

Anatomy of a Pricing Section

Introduction

Suppliers shall provide purchase prices and installation costs for each equipment item, software product, and service proposed. All elements of recurring and nonrecurring costs that must be borne by ACME Banking shall be identified. This includes, but is not limited to, hardware maintenance, system engineering, manuals and documentation, consultation, training, conversion services, shipping charges, installation costs, acceptance testing, and taxes.

The pricing section follows the structure and the requirements that are in the technical and management sections and any other section where requirements need to be priced or the supplier has been directed to provide a pricing response. The areas covered below are for a computer system RFP, but your RFP may be for services such as hiring a consulting or training company or buying equipment. The concepts contained in this section are applicable across RFPs for all types of equipment or services.

✍ Pricing should be broken down into individual components and tasks.

The pricing section generally contains instructions that direct the supplier to break the proposed system into individual components. These components represent the major pieces of equipment and services that the supplier is proposing. Each product, service, or task in the project management list should be in response to a requirement. For example, if the requirements were for a data server with 1 gigabyte of main memory and 120 gigabytes of hard disk space, the price would reflect the whole workstation and would not be broken down into the individual pieces that made up the workstation. However, the project management section may list installation and testing of the server as a separate task.

The following is an example of the breakdown of components for a typical computer system being installed.

Technical Section

1. Hardware

    a. Servers (by type: data, communications, and so on—don't forget to add in a development server and test server).

    b. Network storage devices or large magnetic drive repositories.

    c. PCs or workstations (may include hard drives or RAID disks).

    d. Monitors (if priced separately from the PC).

    e. Printers.

    f. Scanners.

    g. Network hardware such as routers.

    h. Development servers.

2. System software.

    a. Server operating system.

    b. PC operating systems.

    c. Communications software.

3. Application software (the product you are buying).

    a. Price of the application product (the unique product you are buying, such as an accounting system or a document management system).

    b. Price to customize it per requirements in RFP.

    c. Price for development servers (may be at a reduced price but limited in its functionality).

4. Consumables (printer cartridges, backup tapes, and so on).

Management Section

1. Project implementation and management services (includes supplier personnel who are on-site).

2. Integration of unique hardware or software.

3. Development or customization of the application.

4. Installation.

5. Acceptance testing.

6. Maintenance.

7. Training.

8. Documentation.

9. Project staffing.

10. Facilities upgrades.

✍ Require pricing to be at the lowest component level to facilitate evaluation.

Breaking the pricing down into its component parts makes it easier to see where the differences are among the proposals received. If suppliers were allowed to provide just a lump sum price (which they would like to do), it would be very difficult to see if you were being undercharged for hardware but overcharged for integration services (compared with other suppliers and your own estimates). You would not be able to figure out that a server from one supplier was priced at $6,000, while another supplier priced the same server at $12,000. Another area to review is the hourly charge for labor or software customization. This hourly rate can vary greatly depending on your geographical location, where the work is being done, and the particular company.

Hardware

Hardware is straightforward. Suppliers are required to list each piece of hardware being purchased and the quantities proposed for each item. The pricing evaluator must be able to cross-check the quantities in the pricing section with the quantities in the supplier's technical proposal section. Often, a supplier will make a last-minute change in the technical section that may not be reflected in the pricing section. If a discrepancy occurs, the supplier will have to provide an addendum to the proposal reflecting the correct amounts.

✍ Suppliers should specify components and quantities for parts purchased by your company.

However, a very different situation exists if your company is purchasing all or part of the hardware. Often, a company will already have a contract with a hardware supplier and will receive more favorable pricing than the project supplier would receive. In that case the RFP should instruct suppliers that although they will not be purchasing the hardware, they must still propose the specifications and quantities required for each hardware component. Your company can then go to your own hardware suppliers with the correct specifications and quantities for the hardware and find out the costs needed to complete the proposal pricing.

This equipment list can either be in the technical section or part of the pricing section. Typically, suppliers develop spreadsheets of all the equipment components, which could be placed in the pricing section along with the other equipment, but not priced.

> ACME will purchase all required hardware components; however, suppliers are responsible for specifying each hardware component required to satisfy the requirements of this RFP. Specifications are to be detailed enough to allow ACME's hardware supplier to provide the equipment. Any component that is unique and cannot be substituted by a generally available component shall be specified by brand name and model number. Otherwise, ACME will assume that all equipment specified is commercially available through standard sources.

However, suppliers may differ in their estimates for the hardware quantities and specifications, which means that you will have to do some additional homework to make sure all suppliers have the correct total pricing associated with their proposal. For example:

1. Suppliers' quantities may differ. One supplier may require two workstations, whereas a second supplier requires only one. You will have to price both ways to compare each supplier.

2. Suppliers' specified hardware may be different. One supplier may require a server with four processors and one gigabyte of memory; another may require a two-processor server with 512 megabytes of memory. Again, you will have to price for each equipment specification.

In order to make sure these differences are taken into account, you must create a hardware pricing spreadsheet and have your hardware supplier cost out each component that the suppliers propose. Only after this exercise is complete can you truly compare the differences in final pricing.

System Software

System software is considered to be standard, commercially available software—often referred to as " commercial off-the-shelf" software (COTS)—that operates on a variety of hardware platforms. Examples of system software are the computer operating systems: Microsoft's Windows, UNIX, LINUX, and various communications software such as Ethernet software or Internet or Intranet software. Each supplier may propose different system software.

Pricing differences will emerge for system software depending on the quantity of hardware proposed and whether the software license is included with the hardware. For example, for most PCs the operating system is bundled into the hardware price. But server hardware does not necessarily come bundled with the operating system, so you may be able to purchase the operating system of your choice.

One area to review carefully is who is responsible for the annual software license fees. If an application product (see the following paragraph) requires a full version of a database program in order to operate, the database program cost and license fees may or may not be bundled into the application software fees. Ensure that you fully understand this aspect of the pricing proposal.

Also review the long-term costs associated with different operating systems and/or other system software products. For example, the operating costs for Linux may be different from those for Windows operating system over a five-year period. Remember that operating costs include supplier support, your internal support needs for the operating system and support for the end-user in the form of a help desk. While one operating system may appear to be less expensive, it may cost more over a period of time.

This comparison applies not only to software costs but to each and every component that is being proposed, whether hardware or software.

Application Software

Application software generally refers to the software being purchased to perform the work requested in the RFP. Application software may be, for example, the accounting software program, the electronic document management software, the workflow software, the manufacturing process control software, the Intranet search engine, the content management software, the Intranet portal software, or the database software. The application software typically sits on top of the operating system software and does not run by itself.

There are two important aspects to the application software. The first is that suppliers will propose different software products to meet your requirements. For example, for a database application, suppliers may propose database products such as Oracle, IBM's DB2, Sybase, or Microsoft's SQL Server. These products will differ somewhat in functionality and price. Ensure that your evaluation concentrates on the primary functions required of the software and that those requirements are reviewed against the price.

Second, the software application will have to be customized to meet the specific requirements of your RFP; hardly ever will a software product perform the required functions out of the box. This means that in addition to the primary cost of the application software, there is a secondary customization cost, more generally stated as the development cost, which can be substantial depending on the situation. It is not unheard of for the development costs to be more than the actual software costs.

For example, workflow application software provides a company with the ability to specify electronically each step in a business application such as claims processing at an insurance company. But each company will have different claims-processing steps involving different tasks and different people. The workflow software would therefore need to accommodate these differences. This development work is typically done using the tools that are part of the software and/or writing new software code that is then integrated with the original software application.

> ✍ Application software performs the work.

> ☑ Establishing a "fair" development price is a complex matter and requires some detective work on your part. In most cases the prices are not directly comparable because the competing suppliers may be approaching the problem from different angles.
>
> Be aware of "lowball" pricing because a supplier (1) may be desperate to get your (or any) business and may go out of business or (2) may be intending to increase the size of the contract later. In either case, you lose.
>
> Ensure that all prices are within a given range and that suppliers are not fudging their responses so that you are not sure what you are getting. See "Validating Prices" later in this chapter.

 Development costs can be substantial.

The cost of the development effort can therefore be a substantial part of the overall price, in some cases exceeding the price of the application software and in some projects exceeding all other costs. The development price can vary greatly depending on the supplier and the location of the development work. A large variation in development pricing among suppliers should be closely reviewed to determine the reason for the discrepancy. If it is found that one supplier is charging $500 per hour for programming while another is charging $150 per hour, you may want to try to negotiate the higher price as being excessive relative to other suppliers' proposals, your geographic areas, and average industry rates—if these are available. You should also be aware of any proposal that appears to be a "lowball" price.

Also, remember that a larger software project may require a development environment to be established. This environment should be consistent with your own development environment and allow you to test new versions or revisions of the software or to prototype and build new applications before moving those applications to the production environment. Since the application software must be running on a machine that is independent of the production environment, many software suppliers will provide a development server license at a reduced cost or at no cost. However, severe restrictions are usually placed on the development license to ensure that software is not used for profit.

Pricing for the application software may include prices for the following items:

1. The application software package.
2. Yearly license fees.
3. The development/customization effort.
4. The development server software (not the application server).
5. Yearly license fees for the development server.

As you can see, there are many costs associated with the business application. But if you have done your requirements analysis correctly, these hidden costs should be exposed in the RFP and there should be no surprises.

Because development and customization are involved, you must ensure that pricing for the project management section is consistent with the development of the application. Pricing the development effort includes the following:

1. Requirements definition and agreement.
2. Time to develop and customize the application.
   a. Number of programmers.
   b. Hours by task.
3. Testing of the application.
4. Integration of finished application with other software.
5. Any documentation for the custom-developed application.

Generally speaking, as the number of people required to perform the work increases, there is a corresponding increase in administrative services and general overhead. These items should also be provided on a line-item basis in the pricing section.

Custom Software Development

Your project may involve developing software specifically for your application. In this instance, there may be no off-the-shelf software that is suitable for your application, and suppliers will custom-build the entire application based on the requirements in the RFP.

If your RFP includes a fixed-priced contract, the RFP itself will have to provide the suppliers with enough information to propose a fixed price that they are comfortable with. Since they are locked into that price once they bid, the suppliers run a considerable risk if the requirements have been misjudged, misstated, or misinterpreted. Although it is the supplier who is at risk, it must be realized that the project itself will be at risk if the supplier cannot complete the project due to miscalculation.

In his book *Effective Requirements Practices* Ralph Young argues that the concept of "partnering" is an effective means of dealing with the inevitable discrepancies that will arise in a project and may threaten its well-being. He writes, "Partnering is a structured process designed to create an atmosphere of commitment, cooperation, and collegial problem solving among organizations and individuals that work together on a project. Partnering uses mutually developed vision statements, common goals, guiding principles, issue resolution procedures, and evaluation methods to help ensure project success."[1]

Therefore, the pricing for this type of project must include the breakdown of the development time, resources, and other components such as project management, development meetings, issue resolution meetings, and testing. While similar in nature to customizing an existing application to meet a project's requirements, developing an application from scratch is much more complex, and this must be reflected in the pricing of such an effort.

---

1. Ralph R. Young. *Effective Requirements Practices*. Boston, MA: Addison-Wesley, 2001.

Consumables

Consumables are items used in a project that either need to be replaced periodically, such as a printer cartridge, or supplemented over the life of the project, such as backup tapes. For very large projects, consumables can play an important role, and their cost should be considered over a five-year period.

At a minimum, have the suppliers list those items that are considered consumables and estimate the number required per year.

Project Implementation and Management Services

Costs associated with the overall project management, development of software and hardware, and the integration of these components into a working solution must be presented in this section.

This section applies to larger projects in which you expect the supplier to be on your site to install the product. Even if one person can complete the installation in two days, you should request that this step be separately priced, unless installation is free of charge. This is an area in which suppliers typically try to bury their installation charges into the price of the product or some other cost area. You may get around all of this by requesting that suppliers provide their hourly or daily charge for each member of the installation team.

✎ Due to shrinking profit margins, most suppliers cannot afford to support an installation at no charge.

The supplier's pricing should cover the following:

1. The cost of the overall project plan.
2. The numbers and types of people who will be on the project team and their daily rates.
3. Anticipated incidental expenses.
4. Estimated travel and expenses.

If your project is going to be implemented over several phases, you should request that the supplier provide a schedule listing the costs for each phase of work. Each phase should have the same work items listed. If your project is going to be lengthy, try to lock in prices for the duration of the project.

Maintenance and Support

Maintenance and support are priced according to the requirements in the RFP and the supplier's standard maintenance pricing. When you purchase a software product, for example, a maintenance fee generally covers the supplier's help desk support, technical support for problem troubleshooting and isolation, product revisions, bug fixes, and upgrades.

When setting the requirements for maintenance and support, be careful to note the supplier's standard support hours and which time zones they cover. If you are requesting coverage outside these hours, you will most likely be charged a premium rate.

Also note that some suppliers have different levels of support programs, such as "gold," "silver," and "bronze." Gold, the most expensive, offers more services and longer coverage periods than bronze. Check to make sure that the supplier has placed you in the proper category and not given you the gold service plan when all you need is the bronze.

Training

> ACME requires that the supplier provide comprehensive training for administrative, technical/operational, help desk personnel, and users as outlined below. The supplier shall provide a list of all proposed training, indicating the source, a brief description of the content, the intended audience, the maximum number of students permitted in a given session, the location of the training session, and the proposed method and format of the training. A list of all prerequisites for all courses shall be provided.

The training section will depend on the type of product you are buying. If the product is for services, you would not require training and this section would be omitted. If the product is to be installed at your location and people need to operate it, training would become part of your RFP.

Training is generally broken down into three types:

1. Training involving the people who will administer and maintain the system, whether it is a computer system, a mechanical system, or some other type of equipment that needs to be maintained. This is often called administrative or operator training. An administrator may, for example, add or delete users to the system, print and review the daily log-on and usage reports, or restart the system as needed.

2. Training involving the customization and development of the application, which is different from the administration of the product. This type of class teaches how the product can be customized or changed to meet the individual needs of the company; it is typically attended by programmers and/or system development personnel. A programmer may be needed if, for example, you wish to add a new data field to the database, or to add a new feature previously not required.

3. Training for the users who will actually use the product on a day-to-day basis.

When reviewing the prices for each of the types of training above, remember to include travel if the training is at the supplier's location. Often, the administrator training and the programmer training last from three to five days and are generally held at a supplier's location.

 You may question having your programmers go to a customization and development training class if the supplier is developing the product. It is possible that in the future you may wish to tweak the product environment or add new components to the product. If you are going to do the work in-house, your staff will need to have this type of training.

User training can become quite complex if there are large numbers of users and the locations are geographically dispersed. Suppliers may not provide training at your site, and users may have to go to the supplier's local office for training. There are four typical options for user training:

1. Supplier offers training at the supplier's facility.
2. Supplier can train at your facility in a large, computer-equipped classroom.
3. Supplier can train small groups of users at your facility at a local workstation or temporary classroom set up with computers.
4. Supplier can train at a local, computer-equipped conference or training center.

Depending on your project and the number of users to be trained, the cost of the training may not be the issue. Sending 100 people to a remote site for training, for example, would incur tremendous travel expenses. Think these issues through during the requirements phase when writing the training section for the RFP. When reviewing the pricing, remember also to calculate travel as part of the expense.

Documentation

Documentation refers to the product literature and manuals that are provided with the product. In most cases, the supplier provides one copy and you are expected to pay for any additional copies required. Ensure that you specify how many copies of the documentation are needed. You may also request that documentation be provided both in hard copy and on CD-ROM, or in hard copy and some other form of electronic media such as HTML as part of the product help menu.

Review the prices for documentation carefully, as many suppliers will supply one hard copy with the system and charge for each additional copy. If the documentation is available on CD-ROM or electronically, you may not require additional copies.

Other Costs Not Specifically Requested

If the project is large and you may not have covered all of the requirements or potential cost areas, you may want to include a section for the supplier to annotate and price any item that needs to be separately spelled out for your benefit. This section will also help suppliers to categorize costs and prevent them from "bundling" a cost into some other area. You may word it like this:

> Suppliers shall list and price any item that is part of their solution—whether hardware, software, or management-related—that has not been specified in the requirements but is needed in order to complete the supplier's product list.

This step also ensures that a supplier cannot come back during negotiations and try to add items because they were not specified in the RFP.

Organizing the Pricing Section

It is advisable to provide suppliers with a physical layout for their pricing proposals. This is typically done as part of the general instructions to suppliers for organizing their proposals. However, if the pricing section is more complex, you may request more specific types of information.

If you have a complex project that requires hardware, software, installation services, and project management, you may want to outline each of the major pricing sections and provide guidance for the supplier on what content is expected in each section. You may caution suppliers against providing a single price without adequate detail as follows:

> ACME requires all prices to be broken down into categories and subcategories. Each of the individual price components shall be a line item in the pricing tables.
>
> Section XX – Pricing Section
>
> XX.1   Introduction
>
> XX.2   Hardware Requirements

In the example below, the instruction under Project Management is to provide all costs in a spreadsheet form. The last sentence provides additional guidance and warns suppliers not to place all of their costs in the first stage of a multiphase project. For example, if the project will consist of three phases and the project manager is to cost $90,000, $30,000 should be allocated to each of the three phases, not $90,000 in the first phase. Suppliers often try to recoup costs as early as possible in a project, and it is necessary to guide them away from this practice.

Project Management

Costs associated with project management, facilities management, staffing, and other related costs shall be separately identified and presented in this section using the spreadsheet example provided. These costs should include all labor, travel, lodging, per diem, car rental, and so on required to complete each phase of the project. Expenses shall be billed at cost. Costs should be listed in the project phase in which they will occur: suppliers shall not preload continuing costs into the first phase.

Tables 6-1 and 6-2 show suppliers how to lay out their pricing using a spreadsheet. Depending on your skills and the project, you may consider providing suppliers with an electronic version of the spreadsheet that will be used for pricing. In this example, the RFP instructions state that the tables are provided as examples only and that suppliers are expected to provide pricing in tables similar to those examples.

The first table requires suppliers to summarize their pricing so that evaluators can quickly compare pricing totals with those of other suppliers. The second table requires suppliers to provide as much detail about the individual components as possible, which allows evaluators to see differences in individual areas readily.

Table 6.1   Summary-Level Pricing Description

Product Description	Price	Annual Maintenance	Annual License
System hardware			
System software			
Application software (product)			
Application development			
Project management/integration			
Training			
Documentation			
Miscellaneous (detail provided below)			
Shipping			
Taxes			
Total			
Example only, supplier to complete.			

Table 6.2   Detail-Level Pricing Descriptions

Product Description	Qty	Unit Cost	Extended Cost	Annual Maintenance	Annual License
Hardware					
Application server					
Data server					
Communication server					
User workstation					
Standard printer					
Color printer					
Subtotal					

continued

Table 6.2   Detail-Level Pricing Descriptions (continued)

Product Description	Qty	Unit Cost	Extended Cost	Annual Maintenance	Annual License
Software					
System software					
Servers					
Workstations					
Application software					
Subtotal					
Project Management					
Development/integration					
Staffing					
Travel					
Training class – admin					
Training class – tech					
Training class – user					
Standard documentation					
Custom documentation					
Subtotal					
Grand total					
Example only, supplier to complete.					

Validating Prices

☙ How do you know that a supplier's pricing is reasonable?

The RFP team should make every effort to substantiate prices for products and services in order to ensure that those prices are considered fair and reasonable. Prices for products should be stable across the country, but prices for services—development, programming, project management—can vary according to a region.

Pricing can be validated using one or more of the following:

- ❑ comparison against other product and service proposals submitted
- ❑ comparison with prior contracts for similar products when available
- ❑ comparison with published prices and surveys found in supplier sites or professional association documents
- ❑ budget established with an industry consultant or research group such as IDC or Gartner Group
- ❑ internal time and resource estimates for development areas such as application software
- ❑ local "street" prices for programming services

If you do validate pricing and find that suppliers vary significantly in similar areas, you may consider reviewing this section in more depth to determine why such a wide variation exists.

If you can demonstrate that a supplier's prices are not in line with your estimates and other local pricing, the supplier may be more agreeable to reducing those prices to stay in the competitive range. Most suppliers respond positively if you have clearly done some homework and can show them that they are out of line, as opposed to simply asking for a 25 percent discount. A good sales representative will use your work to show his or her management that pricing needs to be adjusted, not just discounted.

Other Pricing Notes

The final price may not provide enough information to evaluate a proposal. There are generally a number of other factors to consider, depending on the type of project that is being undertaken.

Recurring costs. Recurring costs are for items that will continue to incur expense over the life of the project. For example, tapes used to perform backups will be a continuing cost over the life of the project. Other such costs include software licensing fees, maintenance, training (as people come and go), increased facilities costs, additional personnel costs as a system grows, and consumables. These costs can be substantial and may actually differentiate competitors in a final review of the life-cycle cost of the system.

Nonrecurring costs. Nonrecurring costs are onetime project expenses such as the cost of equipment, development by the supplier, and so on. Onetime costs are generally expected to be undertaken at the beginning of the project to enable the project to be fully realized. It is possible that at least one supplier will require you to have or purchase additional equipment, hardware, or software in order for the product to work. This would be an additional nonrecurring cost that other suppliers may not require. For example, you may prefer a supplier's computer training program to live standup instruction. But you may have to purchase computers or a DVD player and equip a training room for this to work, or purchase a DVD player for each user workstation. Ensure that suppliers provide you with a list of related equipment for specialized needs.

Life-cycle pricing. In evaluating the recurring and nonrecurring costs, it is useful to understand the concept of project life-cycle pricing. In this analysis, the recurring costs are projected over the expected life cycle of the project to arrive at the total price of a project over five or ten years. This pricing model is also called a "total cost of ownership." In a large and complex procurement, one supplier might win based on technical merit and initial price, whereas another supplier would win based on a five-year life-cycle pricing model.

Price variations. When pricing varies by more than 25 percent in either direction, the RFP requirements should be reviewed to determine where the discrepancies lie. If you have established what you consider to be a realistic budget, say $750,000, and you receive five bids that range from $300,000 all the way up to $2 million, there is too large a discrepancy between the highest and lowest prices and your budget. This indicates either that your budget is not valid or that the RFP requirements were too open, allowing suppliers to interpret requirements freely and resulting in the wide cost variation. Remember that pricing reflects work and equipment, and a variation in price from $300,000 to $2,000,000 reflects a great deal of work and equipment. Rarely do suppliers simply overcharge or double their prices.

If you encounter this type of wide price differential, it probably means that you will have to rescind the current RFP, restudy your requirements vis-à-vis the suppliers' proposals, and rerelease the RFP. You may consider inviting the high and low supplier in to help you understand why they differed so much in their interpretation of the requirements.

For the estimated budget of $750,000, the bids should come in around 25 percent of the budget, as shown here:

$550,000

$625,000

$700,000

$825,000

$1,000,000

Given that the figures above are the non-negotiated list prices, the spread is reasonably close to the target of 25 percent variation; during negotiations, final prices are likely to be lower for the highest two suppliers.

Discounts. Suppliers may offer discounts from the list price of the product and may give the discount for a variety of reasons. Discounts may be received during contract negotiations, based on the skill of your contracts person, or the supplier may provide a list price and discount in the price proposal. If the supplier discounts without being asked, you may want to consider why. Suppliers who discount heavily without being asked may be trying to get the business at any price because they are in financial trouble.

Be wary of suppliers bearing discounts.

In that case, chances are you will be saddled with a product for which the supplier has either gone out of business or the business has been sold to a competitor. In either case, the product you purchased will suffer, as it will not be updated and supported (supplier out of business), or it will be changed to a new version and the old version will not be updated or supported (product sold to another supplier).

Another reason for the discount may be that the supplier is a startup and is still seeking a pricing watermark. In such a case the list price was probably very high based on the company's need to generate cash and what management thought the market would bear. If this is so, be sure to negotiate a price that is within the targeted market range and your budget. However, ensure that the supplier is financially stable enough to last through the startup period. A company may discount prices to get as much business as possible in order to make the books look good prior to being sold. In the event that this is the case but the supplier is in fact not sold, the company would most likely not be able to sustain itself financially and would place itself on the market again or simply close its doors.

Whether the maintenance price for the software is based on the original published price or on the discounted price may also be an issue. For example, a supplier may set its annual maintenance fees at 20 percent of the list selling price. Software with a list price of $500,000 will thus have an annual maintenance price of $100,000. But if the software is discounted 25 percent to $375,000, will the maintenance fee be $100,000 or $75,000? This point should be negotiated with the supplier. Otherwise, the supplier may assume that the maintenance fee is still based on the original list price. You may also try to negotiate the maintenance fee down to a lower percentage based on other proposals and industry average percentages.

✎ Suppliers will not always follow your instructions.

The reality of supplier pricing. While we assume that most suppliers try to follow directions and are open about their pricing, that is not always the case. Many suppliers will not follow your directions, will persist in lumping prices together to confuse you, or will simply not be good at math. It is easy to disqualify these suppliers, but there is always one supplier whose products are attractive and whom you would like to keep in the competition.

In the case of suppliers whose pricing section needs work, it is best to evaluate them technically, see if they make the shortlist based on technical merit, and then let them know that their pricing section is either incomplete or in adequate. This is best done in a formal letter that tells them what additional work they need to do if they still want to be considered. It is advisable to do this in writing so that you will have an audit trail of your efforts that can be produced if it is ever needed. The letter should advise these suppliers to follow the pricing instructions exactly if they wish their proposals to be considered.

If suppliers still cannot meet the pricing section requirements, it is advisable to drop them from further consideration.

Payment terms. The pricing section should also request that suppliers provide their payment terms as part of their proposal. While a supplier would like to receive 100 percent of the payment upon signing the contract, this practice is not generally acceptable. Most suppliers will propose some type of milestone payment schedule, such as 25 percent on contract signing, 25 percent on equipment delivery and installation, 25 percent on passing an initial acceptance test, and 25 percent when you have formally accepted the system.

It is reasonable to pay some percentage up front, but it should be understood by the supplier that a certain percentage of the payment will be withheld until the system is accepted into production. For example, a final acceptance test may run for 30 days and perhaps longer if the system has problems and the acceptance test is extended. The balanced owed should be enough to prevent the supplier from not completing the acceptance test.

Warranty period. Suppliers should also be required to describe their warranty period and how it is calculated if a part fails or the system fails during the warranty. The end of the warranty period means the start of maintenance payments. For example, if the maintenance fee for a $1 million software system is 20 percent, you would like to delay that charge as long as possible. Typically, there are two areas of contention between buyer and supplier:

1. When does the warranty period start? Suppliers would like it to start when the equipment has been delivered. Buyers would like it to start when the system has been finally accepted. The difference between these two opinions can be six months.

2. What happens when the system fails or a major piece of hardware has been replaced while under warranty? Is the warranty extended to cover the new piece of equipment?

The maintenance contract. There may be some hidden costs to you depending on the type of maintenance contract proposed by the supplier. The supplier may propose a minimum contract for support—from 8 A.M. to 5 P.M. EST— even though you are on the West Coast. Effectively, you waste three hours of morning support and then lose three hours of support in the afternoon. If you pay for support calls outside the principal period of maintenance (PPM), you will face additional costs that have not been planned for. The supplier may have other support plans with extended PPM hours that are more suitable and potentially less costly.

Contracts and License Agreements Section

Generally, most RFPs request that suppliers include a copy of their purchase contract, software license agreement, and maintenance agreement in the pricing section. While this is not a hard and fast rule, in most companies the procurement group handles both the pricing and the contracts aspects of a proposal, so it is more convenient to place the two together physically in the same volume.

Most commercial companies also rely on their purchasing staff to review
the contract terms and conditions (T&Cs) and the pricing. Purchasing
depends on the technical review team to make a technical decision and to
sort out the suppliers on the shortlist, but purchasing negotiates the price
and the contract.

This section provides suppliers with basic guidance on how to respond to
contracts and agreements. Types of contracts can include the following:

- purchase agreement
- maintenance contract
- warranty period
- software license agreement
- performance bonds
- payment bonds
- nondisclosure agreements

The following section is not meant to be a tutorial on contracting and contracts
or to provide legal advice, but rather to provide an overview and discussion
of two basic contract types that are typically the foundation for a pricing
section. To ensure that the RFP and the contract type are not at odds with
each other, it is important to include contracts personnel on the RFP team.

The pricing section is closely associated with the type of contract under
which the project will operate. Contracts specify not only the terms and
conditions of the project but also how and when the supplier will be paid.
Payment terms must be spelled out in the RFP, since they may affect
whether bidders choose to respond to the RFP and if so, how they will price
their proposals.

Fixed-Price Contract

Most commercial RFPs for products and services require what may be
termed a fixed-price proposal from bidders. This means that the RFP

requirements have sufficiently detailed technical information for suppliers to feel comfortable in developing a fixed price for the project. If you decide to accept such a proposal, the supplier is bound to the price provided in the proposal.

During the final proposal review and negotiations, you and the supplier may discover that a requirement needs to be modified, omitted, or added. Any changes to the original proposal must be preceded by a change in the RFP, and both you and the supplier must accept the revised RFP and proposal.

Time and Materials (T&M)

If the RFP requirements are not clearly stated or are confusing, suppliers are faced with either not bidding or bidding high to cover any contingencies that may occur. A supplier will hesitate to bid on a project if the requirements are so broad that it is impossible to determine the exact products and work that are needed. Under a fixed-price bid, a supplier is bound to the price and must absorb any work performed over and above the contracted amount.

The opposite of a fixed price is a time and materials (T&M) price in which the bidders provide an hourly rate and estimate the amount of time and materials required. A T&M contract is open-ended, because the bidders do not have a firm estimate for the amount of work that is needed to complete the job and are allowed to start work based on an estimate.

It is possible to "cap" a T&M contract by asking suppliers to establish a "not to exceed" price as part of their estimate and contract. Otherwise, a T&M contract provides suppliers with an open project and an open price.

If you are contemplating a T&M contract, ensure that your project management requirements specify project review points and progress assessments so that you can adequately monitor the project. You may also consider tying payments to deliverables, thus preventing the supplier from simply billing you every 30 days while providing the supplier with an incentive to get the work done as quickly as possible.

Associated Contract Considerations

Of the two contract types listed, and there are many variations of the two, a fixed price is less problematic for well-defined projects. A fixed-price contact also provides the supplier with the proper incentive to bring the project in on time and on budget. If the project is completed ahead of schedule, the supplier may realize some additional profit in labor savings.

Evaluation of Pricing

There are several schools of thought on how to evaluate proposal pricing. One school suggests that pricing should not be considered until the technical evaluations are complete and a shortlist of suppliers has been designated. Only once the shortlist is established are the pricing sections opened and evaluated. If the shortlisted suppliers are fairly equal on the technical level, but one of them has a lower price, then that company is awarded the contract.

This method is used for several reasons. The first is that meeting the technical requirements is generally considered more important than the price, and it is assumed that prices will fall into the estimated budget ballpark with a nominal variation (assuming that the team has done the requisite homework and therefore that pricing ranges should normalize). The second reason is that if pricing is considered prior to the technical evaluation, exceptionally low or high pricing may influence evaluators, thus making the evaluation of technical requirements more subjective than objective.

The second school of thought is that pricing should be reviewed as part of the technical requirements and that whichever supplier meets the technical qualifications and has the lowest price is the winner. There is no need to establish a value index that compares which supplier provides the most value per dollar.

Conclusion

While all sections of a proposal are important, it is the pricing section that pulls all of the parts together and gives you an itemized view of what you are buying and what it will cost. It is, in essence, a summarized version of the proposal, boiled down to parts and prices.

The pricing section will most likely be the deciding factor among the short-listed proposals, and in the event of a tie, it will be the tiebreaker, even if the lowest price does not win. If you are able to build a spreadsheet of all the prices that reflects the major product areas such as hardware, software, management, maintenance, and so on, you will quickly be able to see variations in pricing between suppliers and perhaps what your estimated budget was projected to be.

Once you have selected the shortlist of suppliers, you may want to analyze the pricing further by developing three- or five-year cost-of-ownership models (include new hires if needed, training, annual maintenance charges and license fees, facilities upgrade costs, depreciation, and so on). You may also want to consider the depreciation of hardware and software development and how that affects the overall price, or compare a proposal based on continuing services with one based on a purchase.

Analysis of the pricing will also prepare you to negotiate the final price and the contract more effectively. It is often possible to obtain a price concession if you can show suppliers exactly where their prices are not in the normal range or that they have overestimated a particular area in their proposal.

Finally, if you have done your homework on application and business requirements, thoroughly studied the potential suppliers, and adequately understood your company's role in introducing new technology, there should be no surprises in the prices submitted by suppliers. The pricing section can only mirror the quality of work done in the technical and management sections.

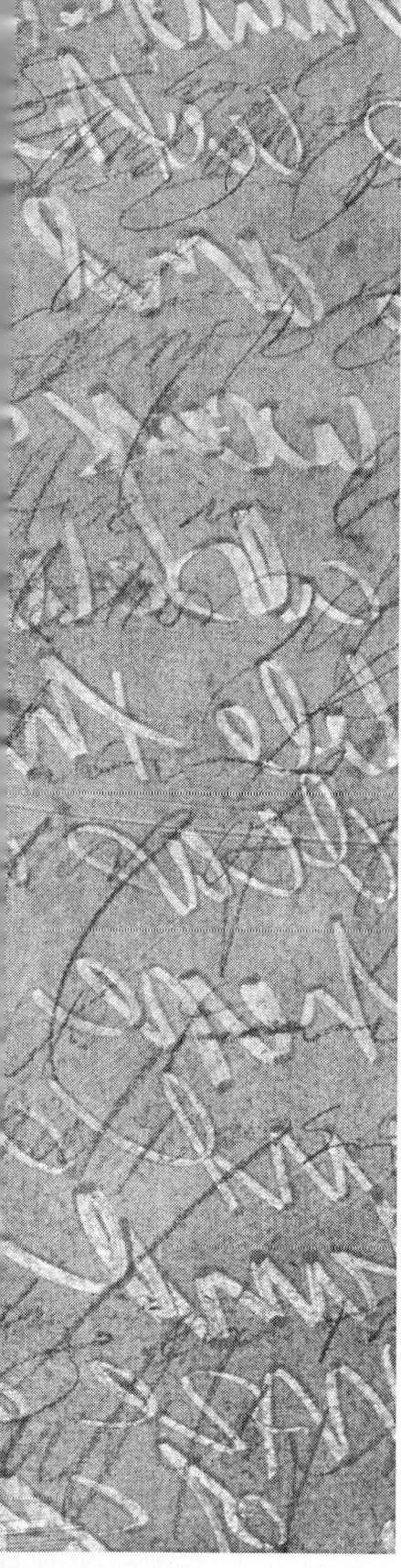

7

Evaluation Guidelines

Introduction

ACME Bank will select the successful bidder through a formal evaluation process. Consideration will be given to products and advantages that are clearly described in suppliers' proposals, confirmed through presentations and demonstrations, and verified by information from reference sources.

All proposals will be initially reviewed to ensure compliance with the RFP. The initial review will encompass administrative and mandatory requirements, and if proposals are not administratively compliant, they may be dropped from further consideration. If proposals do not meet the mandatory requirements, they will be dropped from further consideration.

Evaluating proposals is a way of assessing a supplier's response to requirements contained in the RFP. Typically, the RFP team will have a list of the requirements and other concerns and issues that suppliers should have addressed in their proposals. The evaluation, in essence compares the requested items with the responses.

There are two basic considerations when evaluating requirements. First, much as we would like them to be, requirements are not always clear-cut and easily measurable. For something to be measureable, there has to be a known answer or standard against which it is measured. If we require a computer to have two CPUs, we can easily measure compliance with that requirement. Second, as evaluators, we may not understand the response well enough to know if the proposed product truly answers the requirement. What if a supplier states that his or her single CPU has more power than two regular CPUs?

In a perfect RFP world, all requirements would be easily evaluated against recognized standards, and all supplier responses would be as clear and unambiguous as the corresponding requirement. But in reality many of the requirements found in RFPs are not easily measured, not subject to strictly binary answers, and may comply to varying degrees.

These types of questions are bound to come up during evaluation. The key is to keep them to a minimum by making requirements as objectively measurable as possible and working out beforehand how to handle those that are more subjective in nature. As part of the RFP planning and writing process, time should be devoted to discussing how proposals will be evaluated and how formal the evaluation process will be.

The evaluation process, and the project itself, may be driven by a number of factors. One factor may be pricing, that is, lowest price wins. Another may be value, that is, you are more concerned with the value (or functionality) of the product and price is only a secondary consideration.

You should evaluate on price alone if the RFP is generally for a situation in which you are simply buying a quantity of the product or goods. You may have many different "requirements" for this product but when you evaluate them, the suppliers will either have met the requirements or not. If not, they should be eliminated from further competition. If you employ this selection strategy, price becomes the deciding factor, as it is assumed that the finalists have all met the requirements and are equally qualified to provide the product or price.

This type of evaluation method is used when you have the exact requirements, allow no deviation by suppliers, and consider *price the single determining factor*. You may use this type of evaluation strategy when purchasing known and identified products such as PCs, printers, scanners, or white paint by the gallon. However, such projects in fact constitute more of a request for quotation (RFQ) than an RFP as defined in this book. An RFP is by definition used when price is not the sole consideration and vendors must interpret requirements to provide a solution. (See also the discussion on price evaluation in Chapter 6.)

The second type of evaluation method, which is more in line with an RFP effort, allows you to evaluate proposals for their value and not on price alone. If value is to be taken into account, the scoring system must allow for a requirement to be met based on a predefined ranking scale, for example:

1. Meets requirement and has other desirable attributes.
2. Meets requirement.
3. Does not meet requirement.

For complex and technical RFPs, you will most likely be concerned about the value of a supplier's solution and therefore will probably have a scoring system for your requirements evaluation. The rest of this chapter discusses how to build the evaluation section of your RFP and score proposals.

The Evaluation Team

One of the first decisions you should make when writing an RFP is who will be part of the evaluation team. The number of people on the team depends somewhat on how large and complex the RFP is and how much time will be devoted to the evaluation. In general, some subset of the team that wrote the RFP becomes the evaluation team. You may also include technical or subject matter specialists to evaluate particular requirements and the corresponding response. The specialists may be used to evaluate a particular section, or they may be available to review selected responses and answer questions from the evaluation team.

The core evaluation team, which also wrote the RFP, will be primarily responsible for the evaluation criteria and the actual evaluation. However, some companies believe that having the RFP team also evaluate the proposal

The RFP team is generally the core evaluation team.

is allowing the fox to guard the chicken coop and, therefore, that the evaluation criteria and evaluation team should be composed of people from another department and/or be supplemented with consultants. While this argument has merit, it also may be unrealistic for most companies because of the drain on time and resources. It remains a good idea, however, and if possible you may try to include outside people on the evaluation team.

If you wish to give some consideration for outside evaluators, you may choose to include people from other, but similar business departments, other members of the information technology (IT) group (if this is a technical product RFP), people from the project management group, purchasing, contracting, and legal. However, keep in mind that outside people *must* have the time to acquaint themselves with the technology, the RFP, and the potential suppliers in order to understand what they are evaluating. Although people can read proposals "cold" and make relevant comments, it is more likely that they will not understand the requirements and misinterpret the responses, causing additional delay to the evaluation.

The RFP evaluation team must also be available to travel, if there are site visits, must have the time to record evaluations and justify responses, and must have the time to participate in the evaluation meetings. Evaluation of proposals is time consuming and can thoroughly disrupt normal schedules.

The following are examples of areas for evaluation for a typical computer project:

1. Technical requirements.
2. Management requirements.
3. Price.
4. References.
5. Qualifications/similar projects.
6. Site visits/oral presentations.
7. Product tests or demonstrations.

8. Overall completeness of the proposal and adherence to administrative requirements.

Evaluation Considerations

While the primary evaluation criteria should be written as part of the RFP process and finalized prior to distributing the RFP, there are also other ongoing considerations leading up to receiving proposals and after the "formal" reading of proposals is completed.

Evaluation Criteria in the RFP

An important consideration when developing an RFP and conducting the evaluation process is deciding how much of the evaluation criteria to share with suppliers. Most RFPs let suppliers know that their proposals will be evaluated against a predefined set of requirements and that the evaluation process will be as objective as possible. But exactly how many of these do you give away to the suppliers?

One school of thought is that few, if any, evaluation criteria should be provided in the RFP, to prevent suppliers from tailoring their proposals solely to those criteria and not giving equal thought to other areas that might not be listed among them. Proposals, it is argued, would be somewhat lopsided, with suppliers trying to satisfy mostly what they believed to be the most critical or most heavily weighted requirements.

Another school of thought says that suppliers should be provided with as many evaluation criteria as possible without being given the exact point values for each requirement. This information provides the suppliers with a roadmap that helps them to spend their resources in the most appropriate places. An example of a simple scoring detail is provided in Table 7.1.

The evaluation criteria can influence how suppliers respond to your RFP. If they see that price is the primary criterion for winning, they will most

How much of the evaluation criteria is shared with suppliers?

Table 7.1   Basic Scoring Detail

Description	Points
Administrative requirements	100
Technical requirements	100
Management requirements	100
Price	100
Presentation and demonstration	100
Total	**500**

likely concentrate on keeping their prices at the lowest possible level. If price is not the primary criterion, suppliers will most likely concentrate on selling you the technical solution.

Some RFPs break down the major sections into their actual requirements and the point values associated with them. This provides the supplier with an exact roadmap of how their proposals will be evaluated and allows them to concentrate on the most important requirements. A brief example is shown in Table 7.2.

While both schools of thought have their advantages, the best policy lies somewhere in the middle and in your own company history and custom. Suppliers should know that their proposals will undergo an objective

Table 7.2   Detailed Scoring Exzmple

Requirement	Points
Network printer	10
Network scanner	25
User workstation	10
System server	50

evaluation, but they should not necessarily have the detailed evaluation criteria. It is legitimate to allow the suppliers to spend their resources in the most appropriate areas, but not to the detriment of other requirements.

It is also possible to provide the supplier with some of the "hot buttons" that will be given additional consideration. These hot buttons generally revolve around the business goals and objectives for the project. For example, you may state that this project is highly time-sensitive and that proposals with the most aggressive, but believable, schedules will be given additional consideration. Another example may be that additional consideration will be given to solutions that allow the system to be easily and quickly customized to meet the ever-changing needs of a customer base. These "hints," if you will, are directed more at the business issues behind the project and are broad enough to apply generally, but not specifically, to a proposed solution. Other, similar clues include the following:

❏ Improve customer service.

❏ Reduce response time.

❏ Increase productivity.

❏ Reduce operational costs.

❏ Improve access to information.

If one of the hot buttons is quick implementation, a supplier may opt to use off-the-shelf software instead of building the software application. A second supplier may make exactly the opposite decision, knowing that the programming resources need to be doubled in order to meet the deadline.

The business reasons for the procurement are important and must be reflected in your RFP. These business reasons are also referred to as the "goals and objectives" or "critical success factors" for the project. It is certainly possible to reiterate goals and objectives or critical success factors as part of the evaluation section to reinforce the idea that suppliers are solving a business problem, not just selling equipment.

> ✐ Include your business goals and objectives in the evaluation criteria.

Beginning the Evaluation Process

Before receiving actual proposals, you should be clear about who will be on the evaluation team and what is expected of them. While most of the team will be taking a breather from their RFP duties while proposals are being written, the team should be kept informed of the RFP's progress and such things as supplier questions, supplier dropouts, or other issues that may arise during this period. Keeping the team connected will be especially critical if a supplier's question causes a change in the RFP schedule or precipitates a change or addition to the technical or management section.

Once proposals are received, the team should be assembled as a group and the evaluation criteria reviewed. This allows team members to ask questions and to get back up to speed on the finer points of the project.

During this meeting, the evaluation ground rules should be laid out, with special emphasis on the schedule. While proposals were being written, most of the team returned to their normal work and may not be immediately ready to give their full attention to evaluations.

✎ Review the evaluation criteria with the team to ensure that all questions are raised and answered.

If you have evaluation forms or spreadsheets, ensure that each team member understands how to use the forms and how to evaluate the mandatory requirements.

If there are questions about how a requirement should be evaluated or if several team members share a misconception about some issue, request a group meeting to air these questions. Chances are that others had the same questions but didn't voice them.

As reviewed in the next sections, it may be possible to eliminate several proposals immediately based on obvious administrative or technical deficiencies. These proposals should not be given to the group, as evaluating them would not be a productive use of their time. The RFP team leader can do initial administrative reviews and eliminate proposals if needed.

Once the evaluation team has the proposals to be reviewed and the evaluation matrix, team members generally review proposals at their own work area and make the necessary time to meet the schedule. General meetings are convened to discuss the reviews and either to move suppliers forward or eliminate them from further consideration.

Requests for Clarification

In reading proposals and trying to understand why or why not a supplier responded in a certain way, it may be necessary to ask the supplier a question. Such questions should be collected from the team and sent to the suppliers periodically. There is no need to group these questions, as they will be directed to individual suppliers and will be specifically about a supplier's response.

Suppliers' proposals are not always clear, and you may have to question a supplier.

Suppliers should be given an appropriate amount of time to respond, but suppliers should know that being late or not responding may be grounds for disqualification. Since it may be necessary to receive a supplier's response before any further evaluation can take place, time is of the essence.

The team member who wrote the question should be responsible for determining whether it has been adequately answered. If the answer clarifies information in the proposal, this clarification should be noted in a memo and passed to other team members. Responses from suppliers should *answer or clarify only* and not try to add new information or substantially change information already provided.

Other Considerations for the Evaluation Team

1. Develop and maintain an online or physical library of the RFP and associated documents. The library should include the final RFP, all correspondence with suppliers prior to the RFP, all supplier questions asked during the RFP and your answers, and supplier collateral materials such as brochures, booklets, and so on. Make sure the evaluation team is aware of the library and has access to it.

2. A copy of the evaluation matrix or spreadsheet, if one is developed, should be distributed to the team with enough time to discuss and review how to use the evaluation matrix. If the spreadsheet is computerized, it should be posted in the RFP library.

3. A detailed calendar of the evaluation and award schedule has to be written and distributed to all team members. It is quite possible to lose one's sense of time when evaluating proposals, scheduling demostrations, and planning for site visits. The calendar be available online and kept current.

4. Once a shortlist of suppliers has been determined, it may trigger other events such as a supplier demonstration, a supplier presentation, a visit to the supplier's factory, and visits to suppliers' reference sites. The team leader needs to be responsible for initiating and scheduling these events. Scheduling different RFP team members with the reference's personnel can be difficult—get started early.

5. If there is a reference visit, whether local or not, you must decide who will participate in the visit—perhaps users from the business area, a technical representative, and the project manager. These are typically one-day visits lasting several hours.

6. For reference site visits it is always good to have an agenda of items to cover with the people at the reference site. The agenda may include routine questions such as, "Did the supplier install on time?" but additional questions may arise from the supplier demostration or presentation. Therefore, consider the agenda a "live" document to which the evaluators contribute.

7. Who decides on the evaluation weight factors and importance of a particular section? It is generally the case that one aspect of the project has priority, and this point must be decided as part of the overall evaluation criteria. For example, the weighted factor may be whether a supplier can meet the time frame for installation, assuming that the hardware or software solution is equal among suppliers.

8. Consider having negative values for weights for those items that you do not want to see in a supplier. For example, you may penalize a

supplier for not having any applications in your business area, making the weight a negative 2 (−2).

9. Arrange meetings after each evaluation phase. These meetings are necessary to move suppliers forward or eliminate them from further review.

10. Ensure that the team notes any "good ideas" found in proposals. Even though the proposal may lose, the idea may be good. Often, suppliers will have insights that are valid regardless of the supplier or product. These insights may point out missing requirements or suggest a different way of approaching a problem. Have these ideas and insights recorded and kept as part of the evaluation. When it is time to begin the project, discuss them with the winning supplier and make changes or corrections where needed.

Anatomy of an Evaluation Section

Evaluating proposals is hard work. It requires a dedicated close reading of the proposals in the competitive range, attention to detail in order to grasp subtle differences between two or more proposals, and an understanding of how those differences will affect your project. In addition to all of that, you must be prepared to defend your reviews, whether good or bad, and challenge others on your team about their reviews.

This process, of course, requires a certain amount of organization on your part, but more important, on the part of the RFP team when the project was initially started. The evaluation of proposals can only be as good and as objective as the documentation of the requirements and budget considerations against which the suppliers are being judged.

> ACME Insurance is interested in obtaining a complete solution to the stated requirements in this RFP. Proposals that meet the proposal instructions and requirements will be given a thorough and objective review. Proposals that are late, do not comply with proposal instructions, or take exceptions to mandatory requirements will be eliminated without further consideration.

Make suppliers aware that the evaluation will be objective.

The evaluation section should contain an introduction assurring suppliers that their proposals will be given a fair review. Many suppliers believe that the RFP process is flawed and a supplier has already been selected. While no words may suffice to eliminate that doubt completely, a well-documented evaluation section will give suppliers reason to believe that their proposals will be fairly evaluated.

Evaluate proposals objectively, but be prepared to consider subjective or personal criteria in the final analysis. Give evaluators the freedom to note items such as the following:

❑ the professionalism and presentation of the proposal

❑ the demeanor, capability, and professionalism of the supplier's personnel

❑ the perceived commitment of the supplier to the project and the long-term relationship that will be necessary for a successful project

Technical Evaluation

The technical evaluation should be based on the requirements of the RFP. If the RFP is to purchase an Intranet search engine, for example, the technical requirements may require that the search engine be able to search by the following methods:

1. Standard single-word or multiple-key-word search.
2. Advanced search using standard Boolean query terms.
3. Natural language search using phrases.
4. Proximity searching.

This requirement may have a total point value of 100, with each of the four subrequirements having a value of 25 points. The next requirement, using metatags, gets a point value of 100, giving the total search requirement a value of 200 points. Following is an example of how the requirements are listed in an evaluation spreadsheet.

Note that suppliers can be given partial points for their responses so that, for example, in natural language searches a supplier may be given only 15 points because the search has to be enclosed with quotation marks and is therefore not truly natural language.

If possible, the technical requirements should be broken down to their lowest level, as shown in Table 7.3. That is, break the "search methods" down into four types of searches instead of just a paragraph stating, "Supplier must list and review the different methods of searching. . . ."

Also note that there is a bonus point value in which suppliers may be awarded additional points for exceeding the basic requirements. For example, a supplier may also be able to search based on inputting or pasting a complete paragraph or page into the search area. This, if deemed worthwhile but not "great," may give the supplier an additional 5 points out of 10. Awarding bonus points is purely optional and not necessary.

✎ Evaluation criteria should reflect the lowest requirement level.

Table 7.3   Breakdown of Requirements and Point Values

RFP Reference		Point Value	Total points
2.5	Search requirements	200	
2.5.1	Search methods		
2.5.1.1	Standard key word search	25	25
2.5.1.2	Standard Boolean search	25	20
2.5.1.3	Natural language search	25	15
2.5.1.4	Proximity search	25	25
2.5.2	Use of metatags	100	100
	Bonus points for additional search methods	10	0

Management Evaluation

Evaluating the management section, like the technical section, depends entirely on how well the requirements were documented and how important the management part of the project is compared with the technical portion. In addition to stating specific mandatory requirements such as providing a project plan or demonstrating an understanding of the project goals, these requirements must somehow be measured and evaluated.

If we return to our project plan example, it is not enough to submit a simple project plan, if requested; the plan must be meaningful. Or, if you ask for the resume of the project manager, how do you objectively compare four or more people, all with great experience? Following are some typical areas to evaluate in the project management section:

- ❑ project plan
- ❑ understanding of project goals
- ❑ staffing and resumes
- ❑ capacity to perform project
- ❑ experience and past performance
- ❑ support capabilities

Here are some specific requirements:

- ❑ Start and finish within the specified time.
- ❑ The company must have specific experience in your project area.
- ❑ The project manager must have experience directly related to your application area.
- ❑ The company must have a support location in your time zone, or have a physical location within a two-hour drive of your business.

The spreadsheet in Table 7.4 provides an example of the evaluation criteria for the management section.

Table 7.4   Example Project Management Criteria

RFP Reference		Point Value	Total Points
3.2	Project management	200	
3.2.1	Project plan		
3.2.1.1	Project plan completeness	25	
3.2.1.2	Start on planned schedule	25	
3.2.1.3	Resumes of key personnel	25	
3.2.1.4	Training	25	
3.2.1.5	Documentation	25	
3.2.2	Site prep and facilities installation plan	75	
	Bonus points for project management	10	

Price Evaluation

As discussed previously, price is typically reviewed after suppliers' proposals have been technically qualified. For suppliers still in the competition, pricing can become a deciding factor. When pricing is opened and reviewed, there may be a wide range of prices that vary greatly (above and below) from your budget and what may be considered the competitive range.

However, simply looking at the prices does not tell the whole story, and it is therefore advisable to put all suppliers' prices into a spreadsheet that allows you to look at the prices in different ways.

Reviewing the spreadsheet in Table 7.5, the Total column shows us that there are four out of six viable competitors (suppliers 2 and 6 appear to be out of the competitive range), but if we look at the seven-year maintenance column we can also eliminate supplier 5. Supplier 5 is deceptive; it's an outsourcing company, so the initial costs are very low, but the ongoing maintenance and support costs are among the highest of the group, and over time they are substantially higher than others.

Table 7.5 Example Pricing Spreeadsheet

	Software	Hardware	Dev	Impl	Maint	Support	Training	Total (1 year)	3 year Maint/Sup	5 year Maint/Sup	7 year Maint/Sup
Vendor 1	675,000	175,000	0	20,000	121,500	0	5,000	996,500	364,500	607,500	850,500
Vendor 2	3,000,000	225,000	20,000	0	540,000	0	7,200	3,792,200	1,620,000	2,700,000	3,780,000
Vendor 3	702,800	150,000	0	339,300	140,560	0	5,000	1,337,660	421,680	702,800	983,920
Vendor 4	695,000	142,000	0	153,600	165,000	135,000	16,000	1,306,600	900,000	1,500,000	1,155,000
Vendor 5	0	125,000	395,000	0	309,000	95,000	5,000	929,000	1,212,000	2,020,000	2,828,000
Vendor 6	120,205	0	0	0	21,000	0	0	141,205	63,000	105,000	147,000

Supplier 6 is so low that one should suspect the supplier either of purposely low-balling the bid or of proposing products that are not equal to other products being proposed. However, don't discount the apparent lowball bid. You might reexamine the technical evaluation and compare it with that for the other suppliers. A very low bid may be submitted because a supplier has taken a different approach in terms of equipment or services, but the proposal can still be technically compliant.

Of course, this simple spreadsheet does not contain variables such as staffing, which would add cost to suppliers 1, 2, 3, 4, and 6 but not 5, or the depreciation of hardware and development software; but it gives you a starting place to begin your evaluation and to see where each supplier sits in relation to the next.

When a supplier's pricing is far above or below the budget estimate, but the proposal is technically competitive, you may want to do some additional research to understand why this discrepancy exists.

Oral Presentations and Demonstrations

Oral presentations and demonstrations are usually reserved for the suppliers who are on the shortlist. These presentations and demonstrations are generally scored simply, with the suppliers gaining points for how well they perform. The scoring will usually be somewhat subjective, as the supplier is asked to give a presentation with minimal guidelines. It is possible to provide suppliers with guidelines for their presentations and require that they cover certain areas.

Point values for presentations and demonstrations can be as simple or complex as you need them to be. In many cases, the presentation and demotration are scored "pass" or "fail" without a point value being assigned. However, you may assign more "weight" to the presentation and demotration and score individual components as they are presented or demonstrated. It is difficult to score presentations objectively, as they are generally more free-form and the supplier takes the initiative in preparing the presentation.

The demonstration may be more directed, and you may specify that certain properties of the product must be shown as a condition of the demonstration. These mandatory items can be assigned point values that add up to the total point value of the demonstration.

Part of the value in these presentations is that the RFP team is (or should be) much "smarter" about the products and suppliers at this point in the process, and their questions about the products should therefore be much more focused. The performances of the remaining candidates at this point can be the deciding factor between two closely matched suppliers. It is quite possible that a supplier with a slightly lower technical score will be preferred to another because that company presents a superior image and a better potential working relationship than the slightly better qualified competition.

It should be remembered that in many cases, the supplier becomes part of the company team during the project and may continue to be part of your working culture after the project's initial implementation.

The Evaluation Process

Introduction

Now that we have covered the what and how of an evaluation, in the following paragraphs we review the basic steps involved in reviewing proposals. The central idea of this section is to help you eliminate as many noncompliant and incompetent proposals as early as possible, giving you more time to spend on proposals that deserve your attention.

Preliminary Evaluation

All proposals will undergo a preliminary evaluation to determine if basic administrative and technical requirements have been met. Proposals may be eliminated from further consideration for such deficiencies as being late, incomplete, or inadequately prepared.

The preliminary evaluation step is an absolute necessity. Faced with ten (or more) 150-page proposals to read, you must eliminate any that are grossly noncompliant so that you do not waste time reading them. There is a reasonable chance that if you receive ten proposals, at least two of them will be eliminated immediately for noncompliance. The team leader and a selected assistant can accomplish this first round of preliminary evaluations. An example of a preliminary evaluation checklist can be found in Appendix J. This checklist can be included with the RFP, and you can request that suppliers complete the checklist and include it with their cover letters. The checklist should list the important administrative and contractual requirements, but not the technical or management requirements.

The preliminary evaluation should ascertain that all potential suppliers are able to do the following:

- ❑ Understand the basic issues and problems as presented in the RFP.
- ❑ Comply with the administrative requirements of the RFP.
- ❑ Satisfy mandatory technical requirements.
- ❑ Demonstrate sufficient qualifications and experience, including customer references and resumes of key personnel.
- ❑ Meet demonstration requirements (if needed).
- ❑ Include a project management plan.
- ❑ Price the proposal fairly, relative to other proposals received.

Typical reasons for rejection during preliminary review include the following:

- ❑ The proposal is received late with no request for extension or last-minute explanation based on *force majeure*.
- ❑ Requested materials such as annual reports, references, or an electronic version of the proposal are missing.
- ❑ The proposal is sloppy, poorly prepared, and does not not follow the requested proposal structure.
- ❑ Exceptions are taken to major requirements or responses to requirements are missing without explanation.

❑ Pricing is unreasonably high or low compared with other proposals and your budget and expectations.

❑ Efforts are made to influence the RFP team by circumventing team members and talking directly with upper management.

While it may be difficult to eliminate a supplier who possibly has a good solution, if a supplier is guilty of any of the above sins (or worse), it is a good indication of trouble to come, should that supplier progress and possibly win the award. Cut your losses early and devote time to more deserving suppliers.

✎ Notify disqualified suppliers as soon as possible.

It is in your best interest to notify disqualified suppliers right away and add that they may contact you for a debriefing after the contract has been awarded. The purpose in eliminating suppliers early is to gain time and to be able to focus on those proposals that warrant your attention, namely, those proposals that have a reasonable chance of winning. By notifying suppliers right away, you will stop them from asking questions and otherwise continuing to absorb valuable time. The notification should be in writing, and the completed letter should be stored in the project database.

Second Round of Evaluations

✎ The second round is not the final round.

Proposals that survive the preliminary evaluation are now given a more thorough review. Depending on the length of the proposals and the number of suppliers left in the competition, it may be wise to try to eliminate more candidates based on a further reading of the proposals. In many cases, you will find that suppliers are not thorough, have not responded to requirements, or have taken exception to requirements and have tried to offer non-compliant solutions instead. If the weight of problems adds up for a supplier, disqualify that supplier at this point.

The second round of evaluations should include all of the team members, but they should be instructed simply to read proposals for obvious errors and omissions that would allow them to eliminate the proposal from further consideration. Advise them not to spend too much time at this stage, as this is a "quick and dirty" reading.

When all team members have completed the second round, a meeting is held to discuss and review the results. Members will share their evaluation sheets, and once these are tabulated, it will be possible to eliminate suppliers who do not make the second cut.

Detailed Evaluations

The purpose of the first two rounds of evaluations is to eliminate as many proposals as possible. If, for example you started with ten proposals, you may have been able to eliminate three initially and two during the second round of evaluations, reducing the remaining number of proposals to five.

These five are now given in-depth consideration, as all are potential winners. This group is not yet considered the shortlist, but after this third round of evaluations further eliminates suppliers, the last two or three constitute the shortlisted suppliers. Ideally, the shortlist comprises two suppliers. The reason for getting down to the shortlist is that you want to spend time on demonstrations, presentations, and site visits only from those suppliers who are viable winner.

✎ The supplier shortlist is established during the third round of evaluations.

The evaluation team should proceed with a detailed evaluation of all the remaining serious contenders. This evaluation involves reading the proposals very closely while filling in the evaluation sheets. If evaluators have questions for suppliers, these should be asked as quickly as possible once the proposal has been read.

This step is designed to yield the shortlist of suppliers, but it may be that only one supplier will still be qualified at this point. In that case, the shortlist consists of only one supplier, and the evaluation team should proceed with activities planned for the next stage.

The Shortlist

The shortlist normally comprises the remaining two or three suppliers. These suppliers have been evaluated and rated, and they are close together in the scoring. At this point, they are close enough that a clear decision is not possible, so the evaluation continues with presentations, demonstrations, reference checks, and site visits.

Typically, reference checks are scheduled with the referenced account and can take place at any time. Before these telephone conference calls, the team should put together a list of important questions to complement a general discussion of the project at the reference site. If possible, allow the person to speak freely about his or her project and interject questions as needed. Also, you may want to record the telephone call for future reference; alternatively, ensure that good notes of the important points are kept.

The presentation and demonstration can take place at the same time, depending on how extensive the demonstration is going to be. The presentation should review the high points of the supplier's solution, examine the major business reasons their product should be considered, and then, if appropriate, move into a more technical discussion of the solution and proposed management plan. (Pricing is not generally a discussion topic during the presentation and demonstration.)

Developing the Scoring Methodology

Evaluation of proposals is not a straightforward exercise. By its very nature, a proposal is a presentation of an idea, based on some specifications and requirements, but still a *proposal* of an idea. Remember that an RFP is written when you want several suppliers to propose their individual and unique solutions. As much as we would like to, it is not always possible to score proposals objectively, and the answers are not always clearly right or wrong. If you have written an RFP with functional requirements, you have asked suppliers to design and propose what in their opinion is the right solution. You will have to interpret the solution, possibly make some assumptions and adjustments, and hope that it will actually work once purchased.

Scoring methods can range from simple adjectives to complex numerical ratings. Some form of numerical score is preferable to using adjectives such as "excellent," "good," and "poor," because numerical ratings allow ranges of compliance to be established. For example, a scoring system with numbers from 0 to 3 (0 = noncompliant) allows evaluators to view compliance with any one requirement within a range of compliance, not as a simple binary "compliant or not compliant" or "yes/no" scoring system. The following is an example:

> ✎ Numerical scoring allows for degrees of responsiveness.

    0 = does not meet requirements

    1 = marginally meets requirements

    2 = fully meets requirements

    3 = exceeds requirements

A second common reason for developing scoring criteria is that a supplier may not meet a requirement or may exceed the requirement as stated. For example, if the requirement is for a printer with a speed of 20 pages per minute (20 ppm) and a supplier bids two 10 ppm printers, will this disqualify the supplier? Conversely, if a supplier bids a 34 ppm printer, will credit for exceeding the requirements be awarded (given that there are no pricing consequences)?

A third reason for developing numerical ratings is that scoring some requirements will be a matter of the evaluators' interpretation and the suppliers' credibility. This type of requirement does not ask for a simple yes or no answer; as it might require a reasonably long and detailed response. For example, if a software development plan was required, evaluation points would be given for the credibility of the plan and response, not for whether a plan was provided. Similarly, suppliers' maintenance and training responses will necessitate some interpretation by the evaluators to reflect different methods and programs offered by suppliers. Below are examples of evaluation criteria that are hard to evaluate objectively:

❑ project management plan

❑ excellence of design

- ❏ understanding of requirements
- ❏ degree of risk in the project
- ❏ project manager's resume

It is important to develop an internal sense of those requirements that are easy to measure objectively and those, like the preceding list, that are inherently subjective and hard to measure. Distribute this information to the evaluation committee before the formal evaluation of proposals begins, and advise them that their evaluation of these types of requirements will be somewhat subjective and often to individual interpretation. Be prepared to discuss the subjective requirements during your meetings, and try to reach agreement on each supplier's response to these requirements.

On the other hand, these subjective requirements spark some of the most interesting debate among team members, and this debate often leads to a deeper understanding not just of the supplier's proposal, but of the underlying requirement and the project itself. So don't be too cautious or conservative when evaluating these types of requirements, but don't let them bring the evaluation to a halt.

On a larger scale, proposals will be allocated scores for different sections. The sections may or may not be equal in weight, depending on what is important. These are typical major sections scored in an evaluation:

- ❏ administrative requirements
- ❏ technical requirements
- ❏ management requirements
- ❏ pricing
- ❏ oral presentation and demonstration

A section can be "skewed" or weighted by several methods. The most typical method is to assign each section a different number of total points. For example, the technical section might have a total of 200 points, whereas the management section might have 100 points. Once the major sections have been identified, it is possible to subdivide each section into its component parts and assign numerical values to those components.

How do you know which sections are most important? For example, suppose you have an office full of computer workstations that need to be replaced because they are old and slow. The distributor from whom you purchased them no longer carries that brand, so when the machines need servicing, they have to go back to the manufacturer, who happens to be downsizing at the moment and is not servicing your needs adequately.

When writing the RFP for replacement workstations, the RFP team may agree that since current workstation technology is very stable, it is not merely a question of buying "better, faster, cheaper" machines; rather, the key factors are supplier stability and the supplier's ability to service products locally. Therefore, this RFP may be "light" on the technical requirements but very detailed on such things as the supplier's long-term financial stability, the supplier's management team, local depot parts and repair locations, and the ability to diagnose and repair workstations on site.

In this example the management and maintenance requirements, references, and a factory visit may far outweigh the technical requirements in terms of evaluation points and weights. This type of reasoning will help you to decide where to place the emphasis when developing the evaluation points for your RFP.

Figures 7.1 and 7.2 are examples of proposal evaluation matrices. Figure 7.1 is for a straightforward evaluation with no weighting involved except giving individual sections more or fewer points. Figure 7.2 is the same, except that a column has been inserted to show that certain requirement areas have been given more weight.

Figure 7.1   Evaluation Matrix
without Weighting

	Requirement	Point Value	Supplier 1	Supplier 2	Supplier 3	Supplier 4
1	Hardware solution	200	200	175	190	180
2	Software solution	200	150	175	200	150
3	System design	400	350	325	375	300
4	Maintenance	25	25	20	25	20
5	Training	25	15	25	25	10
6	Documentation	25	25	15	25	15
7	Support	25	25	25	25	25
8	Project plan	100	90	90	95	75
	Total	1000	880	850	960	775
	Supplier ranking		2	3	1	4

Figure 7.2   Evaluation Matrix
with Weighting

	Requirement	Point Value	Weight Value	Supplier 1	Supplier 2	Supplier 3	Supplier 4
1	Hardware solution	200	0	200	175	190	180
2	Software solution	200	0	150	175	200	150
3	System design	400	.25	437.50	406.25	468.75	375
4	Maintenance	25	0	25	20	25	20
5	Training	25	0	15	25	25	10
6	Documentation	25	0	25	15	25	15
7	Support	25	.25	31.25	25	18.75	25
8	Project plan	100	.35	121.50	121.50	128.25	101.25
	Total		1000	1005.25	962.75	1080.75	876.25
	Supplier ranking			2	3	1	4

Evaluation Report

✐ Collect all your information into an evaluation report.

Once all of the proposals have been evaluated, from the first one to be disqualified to the selection of the winner, you may consider writing a report summarizing all of the proposals and their evaluation results. This is also a chance for you and your team to review the final selection against the runners-up and ensure that you can (1) defend your final selection and (2) justify the elimination of other suppliers. This report, when completed, may be used as a basis for a supplier selection presentation to management.

The report can vary in its format and the amount of detail provided, but it should be structured as follows:

1. Executive summary.
   a. Review purpose of the RFP project.
   b. Primary business goals and objectives—business case.
   c. Primary technical goals and objectives.
   d. Provide a brief review of the RFP steps.
   e. Review any potential business constraints or issues associated with the selection.
   f. Recommendation with summary detail.
2. Summarize the RFP team and their individual participation and contributions to the effort.
3. Evaluation methodology.
   a. Technical.
   b. Management.
   c. Price.
4. Review the suppliers in the competition and explain why they were not chosen for the project.
   a. Highlights of the early proposals eliminated.
   b. Highlights of the proposals on the shortlist.
   c. Discuss any "substantial" trade-offs between final candidates.
5. Review winning supplier.
   a. Technical risks.
   b. Management risks.
   c. Contract risks.
6. Review project start plan, giving initial tasks and dates.

When complete, this report should be filed (if on paper) with the associated project documents; the electronic version, and the presentation if produced, should be filed with the other RFP project documents. It may be necessary at some point to revisit these documents if there are changes in management, the budget, or the system architecture—or if your winning supplier fails (which has been known to happen!).

Conclusion

Evaluating proposals and awarding a contract is the link between a successful RFP effort and a (future) successful project. Choosing the wrong supplier or approaching the evaluation phase carelessly will have a direct, and most likely adverse, impact on the project. The evaluation should ensure that the RFP was not biased and that the suppliers who responded were given a fair and objective review.

Chapter 4 "RFP Technical Requirements Section," emphasized writing requirements that were real and measurable, in addition to the following:

1. Requirements must be for real products or solutions.
2. Requirements must be unambiguous.
3. Requirements must not be subjective (or such requirements must be limited).
4. Requirements must be objectively measurable.
5. Requirements must be complete.

These five points are the guidelines for writing clear requirements that are then converted into evaluation criteria and point values.

The other main consideration is whether evaluators fully understand suppliers' responses to the requirements. Ensure that the detailed technical aspects of a response are understood and not just taken for granted or shrugged off as "too technical for me." If you need more information or don't understand some aspect of a response, ask the supplier to be clearer or to rewrite the response from a different angle.

Years ago, there was a saying, "You can't be fired for buying IBM." The subtext of this was, of course, that even if other suppliers had better products and lower prices, if they didn't work out, you were up a creek without a paddle because only IBM could be counted on to "make it right." IBM was a safe decision. Getting a totally objective evaluation will be difficult due to personal biases, company politics ("We've always done it this way. . ."), and human failings ("I didn't have time to read all the proposals"). The best way to ensure an objective evaluation is to define the requirements clearly, ensure that they are broken down into easily evaluated components, and discuss in detail during the evaluation review meetings any requirement that can be subjectively evaluated.

The result of a competitive RFP is that a good mix of suppliers will have submitted proposals that were competitive and offered the evaluation team a real choice.

Appendix A

Administrative Information

The information and examples that follow are to be used for writing the initial administrative requirements section of your RFP. The purpose of this section is to provide suppliers with a framework for their responses so that all proposals received have the same information and structure. This "sameness" facilitates the proposal evaluation process immensely.

Not all of the ideas presented below will be applicable to your RFP. Feel free to delete, modify, and add material that would help clarify your RFP. Also keep in mind that the instructions should be fair in their demands and that suppliers should not be required to shoulder unnecessary expenses as part of their proposal efforts.

Section 1: Administrative Information

1 Administrative Information

ACME Corporation (AC) is issuing this request for proposal (RFP) for the purchasing and implementation of a corporate enterprise content management system and Intranet knowledge management tools. This section provides the RFP administrative information and guidelines for suppliers.

1.1 RFP Schedule

The following table lists the activities relevant to the RFP process. AC reserves the right to change these dates and will notify suppliers in such a case.

Table A.1   RFP Schedule

Activity	Time	Date
RFP released		12/1/200x
Notice of intent to bid due	5:00 PM	12/1/200x
Supplier conference questions due	5:00 PM	12/1/200x
Suppliers' conference	9:00 – 11:00 AM	12/1/200x
Facility tour	1:00 – 4:00 PM	12/1/200x
RFP questions deadline	5:00 PM	12/1/200x
Proposals due	5:00 PM	12/1/200x
Questions to suppliers due	5:00 PM	12/1/200x
Evaluations complete		12/1/200x
Reference site calls		12/1/200x
Reference site visits		12/1/200x
Live test demostration start		12/1/200x
Live test demostration ends		12/1/200x
Contract negotiations complete		12/1/200x

1.2 Contact Information

Please use the following name and address for all correspondence with AC concerning this RFP. Suppliers who solicit information about this RFP either directly or indirectly from other sources will be disqualified.

All correspondence should be directed to

> Bud Porter, IT Manager
> ACME Corporation
> Hwy 101, Suite 101
> Mill Valley, CA 94941
> Voice 415-555-1212
> Fax 415-555-1313
> bud@ACME.com

1.3 Intent to Bid

Supplier must sign and return the Intent to Bid to the address specified in Section 1.2 no later than 5:00 P.M. Pacific Daylight Time on the date identified in the RFP schedule. The notice of intent to bid is part of this RFP package.

Submission of this notice constitutes the supplier's acceptance of the RFP schedule, procedures, evaluation criteria, and other administrative instructions of this RFP. Suppliers who do not return this notice will be disqualified from further participation in this RFP.

1.4 Submission of Proposals

Proposals are due December 1, 200x at 5:00 P.M. Bids must be sealed and not delivered in open packages or binders. Additional proposal materials such as books, CDs, and other materials should be packaged separately but should be received with proposals. Proposals should be marked as follows and sent to

> **Intranet Project RFP 21-A62**
> Bud Porter, IT Manager
> ACME Corporation
> Hwy 101, Suite 101
> Mill Valley, CA 94941

1.5 Questions

Submit questions in writing by mail, e-mail, or fax to the address listed below. *No telephone questions will be accepted or considered.* Suppliers should refer to the specific RFP paragraph number and page and should quote the passage being questioned. AC will respond to questions promptly and will send answers to suppliers as a group. In doing so, AC will delete supplier names from the text of questions and answers being sent. Refer to the RFP schedule for the deadline date.

> Bud Porter, IT Manager
> ACME Corporation

Hwy 101, Suite 101
Mill Valley, CA 94941
Voice 415-555-1212
Fax 415-555-1313
bud@ACME.com

1.6 Supplier Pre-Proposal Conference

AC will hold a suppliers' conference. The purpose of the conference is to allow each supplier to review the RFP with the AC project team and to answer questions. Questions may be submitted prior to the conference. The answers to such questions will be given in writing and distributed to attendees.

AC will also provide a demonstration of its current Intranet application during the conference.

Suppliers are requested to limit attendance to two people from each company. Attendance is not a requirement of responding to the RFP, but it is recommended, as there will be no tape or transcript of the conference.

Refer to the RFP schedule for the date. The conference will be held at

ACME Corporation
Hwy 101, Suite 101
Mill Valley, CA 94941

Suppliers will be directed to the main conference room from the reception desk.

1.7 ACME Corporate Facilities Tour

AC will conduct a tour of the current facilities for interested suppliers. Please refer to the RFP schedule for the date and time.

1.8 Supplier Reference Library

An online reference library has been established for your use. This library contains additional information about AC, our standards, infrastructure, and various studies that we have accumulated as part of this project. Information in the library is for your use and review.

Also included in the library is a representative subset of the current Intranet that is made available to you for reference and searching. The content on this site is not classified but should not be made available to anyone outside the proposal team members.

1.9 Nondisclosure Agreement

AC requires all suppliers responding to this RFP to sign and return a nondisclosure agreement (NDA). Suppliers may not disclose this RFP to any person not directly involved in the proposal effort and may not disclose this RFP to any other supplier or company without permission from AC. NDA forms are in Attachment XYZ.

1.10   No Referrals

Suppliers may not refer or pass on this RFP to another supplier without prior approval from AC.

1.11 No Press Releases or Public Disclosure

Suppliers may not release any information about this RFP. The winning supplier may not issue a press release until it has been reviewed and approved by AC.

1.12 Oral Presentations

Suppliers who are on the shortlist will be required to give an oral presentation of their proposal to the RFP team and AC management personnel. This presentation should concentrate on the business aspects of the proposal and should not be a technical review of the solution. Appropriate visual and written materials are expected, but the format is left to the discretion of the supplier. Suppliers may not have more than two people attend the presentation. Presentations may not exceed three hours. Appropriate handouts should be prepared and distributed. There will be no more than fifteen AC people at the presentation.

1.13 Demonstrations

AC may require a product demonstration for those suppliers on the shortlist. The demonstration must use the same products being proposed and provide enough functionality to simulate the basic functions being proposed. Suppliers will be provided with advance notice of the demonstration date and are responsible for their own demonstration equipment. AC will provide a demonstration script.

1.14 Live Test Demonstration (LTD) (Optional, as an LTD is more rigorous than a simple demonstration)

AC expects to select several finalists to participate in a live test demonstration (LTD) process. The LTD will be conducted at AC facilities in Mill Valley, California, and will be a test of suppliers' capabilities. The LTD test is described in this RFP. The LTD will be a part of the evaluation criteria for supplier selection.

Failure to participate in the LTD will eliminate a supplier from further consideration for this project. AC is not responsible for any costs incurred by the supplier in preparation of the LTD.

1.15 Award Notification

AC expects to make a first cut of suppliers and develop a shortlist of finalists. Suppliers who are not finalists will be notified in writing at the same time as finalists are notified they are on the shortlist.

After a final selection is made, the winning supplier will be invited to negotiate a contract with AC; remaining suppliers will be notified in writing of their selection status.

1.16 Ownership of Materials

All materials submitted in response to this RFP become the property of AC. Proposals and supporting materials will not be returned to suppliers.

1.17 Rejection of Proposals

AC reserves the right to reject any or all proposals. One copy of each proposal will be kept on file for six months; all other copies will be destroyed, along with any collateral materials sent with the proposal.

1.18 Proposal Costs

AC is not responsible for any costs incurred by the supplier in the preparation of the proposal, the site visit, or the live test demonstration.

1.19 Errors in Proposal

AC is not liable for errors in supplier proposals. A supplier may correct an error in his or her proposal with AC approval. Changes after the submission date may be made only to correct an error in an existing part of a proposal. New material may not be submitted. No oral, telephone, or faxed modifications or corrections will be accepted.

1.20 Evaluation Criteria

AC is interested in obtaining a complete solution to the requirements contained in this RFP. Proposals that meet the proposal instructions and requirements will be given a thorough and objective review. Proposals that are late, do not comply with proposal instructions, or take exceptions to mandatory requirements will be eliminated without further consideration.

AC will evaluate proposals using a number of factors as outlined in the next paragraphs. A more complete description of the evaluation criteria can be found in Section X.X.

1.20.1 Technical Solution

Primary consideration will be given to meeting the mandatory functional requirements as listed in this RFP. Proposals will be evaluated according to the following criteria:

1. Fulfillment of the requirements as stated in this RFP.
2. Understanding of the work to be performed.
3. Technical approach and methodology to accomplish the work.
4. Completeness and competence in addressing the scope of work.
5. Solutions that allow AC to develop applications within the framework of the Intranet.

1.20.2 Project Management

AC also believes that effective project management is essential for successful project implementation. Suppliers will be evaluated on the completeness and responsiveness of their project management plans and the project team assigned.

As part of the project management plan, suppliers must demonstrate adequate experience in developing and implementing similar corporate Intranet projects. AC's confidence in the supplier's ability to meet deadlines and successfully manage similar projects will be a primary consideration.

Special consideration will be given to suppliers who propose a detailed project plan with sufficient breakdown of tasks and steps to demonstrate a complete understanding of the project.

1.20.3 Pricing

AC will consider pricing as part of the evaluation criteria. It is not essential to bid the lowest price to win; however, large pricing differentials among suppliers will be carefully examined. Price will be used as a final indicator for determining the winner when all other criteria have been normalized.

1.20.4 References and Demonstrations

Supplier references, site visits, and the LTD will be evaluation factors. Suppliers may not refuse to participate in either the site visits or the LTD.

1.21 Proposal Format

Suppliers are requested to adhere to the following proposal format, which provides a section layout for the proposal and pricing section.

Volume 1: Technical Proposal

    Transmittal Letter

Section 1	Executive Summary
Section 2	Technical Section
Section 3	Management Section
Section 4	Supplier Section
Appendix A	Supplemental and Collateral Material

Volume 2: Price Proposal

Should be separately bound. Volume 2 must also be submitted in Microsoft Excel format.

Transmittal letter. A transmittal letter must accompany all proposals. A corporate officer or person who is authorized to represent your company must sign this letter. The letter of transmittal *must* meet the following requirements:

1. Identify the submitting organization.
2. Identify the name and title of the person authorized by the organization to obligate the organization contractually.
3. Identify the name, title, and telephone number of the person authorized to negotiate the contract on behalf of the organization.
4. Identify the names, titles, and telephone numbers of persons to be contacted for clarification.
5. Explicitly indicate acceptance of the requirements in this RFP.

6. Bear the signature of the person authorized to obligate the organization contractually.

7. Acknowledge receipt of any and all amendments to this RFP.

1.22 Submission of Proposals

Proposals shall be submitted in writing and in MS Word format. AC prefers Microsoft Word for the electronic submission. Electronic copies may be submitted on diskette, ZIP disk, or CD-ROM, but not File Transfer Protocol (FTP). AC will not accept any faxed proposals or oral submissions.

Please refer to the RFP schedule for the due date and location.

1.23 Alternative Proposals

AC will not accept any alternative proposals in response to this RFP. AC has taken great care to ensure that requirements are functionally stated and expects suppliers to respond to those requirements with standard products.

1.24 Late Submission

Proposals submitted after the closing date will not be accepted. AC is not responsible for late delivery or proposals lost in delivery. Suppliers must notify AC if there is an extenuating circumstance that may prevent on-time delivery. Refer to the RFP schedule for the due date.

1.25 Number of Proposals

Suppliers shall provide five copies of each volume. Each volume must be clearly marked and packaged separately. One copy of the electronic version is sufficient. Only one copy of any collateral materials need be submitted if there is additional material.

1.26 Proposal Preparation

Proposals should be prepared simply and economically without emphasis on the presentation of the proposal. Expensive bindings, color photographs, and excessive promotional materials, such as videos, are neither desired nor needed. Suppliers may submit brochures if requested but should not include materials not requested.

AC prefers to receive proposals in appropriately sized three-ring binders with index tabs to separate sections.

1.27 Confidential or Proprietary Information

AC has no obligation to share proposal material with any other party and will respect any documents or materials that suppliers have clearly marked "Confidential" or "Proprietary." However, only those pages that contain the proprietary information should be so designated, not the complete proposal. AC is not obligated to maintain the confidentiality of any information that was known prior to receipt of a proposal, or becomes publicly known through no fault of AC, or is received without obligation of confidentiality from a third party.

1.28 RFP Amendments

AC reserves the right to amend this RFP at any time prior to the closing date. Amendments will be issued only to suppliers who are going to complete a proposal. Suppliers must sign and return an amendment acknowledgement form. No other amendments, verbal or otherwise, will be acknowledged by AC.

1.29 Primary Supplier

AC expects to negotiate and contract with only one "prime supplier." AC will not accept any proposals that reflect an equal teaming arrangement or from suppliers who are cobidding on this RFP. The prime supplier will be responsible for the management of all subcontractors. AC will not accept any invoices from subcontractors or become part of any negotiations between a prime supplier and a subcontractor.

1.30 Complete Solutions

AC will accept only complete solutions from a prime supplier. Suppliers may not bid on only one item or selected items from the RFP.

1.31 Offer Expiration Date

Proposals in response to this RFP will be valid for 120 days from the proposal due date. AC reserves the right to ask for an extension of time if needed.

1.32 Post-Award Debriefing

AC will upon request offer to debrief suppliers who were disqualified or did not win the contract. This request for debriefing will be accommodated only after the final contract has been awarded. Suppliers may either make appointments for a conference at AC or be debriefed via a telephone conference.

1.33 Designation of Requirements

To prevent any confusion over identifying technical and management requirements in this RFP, the following definition is offered: The word *shall* is used to designate a mandatory requirement. Suppliers must respond to all mandatory requirements presented in this RFP. Failure to respond to a mandatory requirement may be cause to disqualify your proposal.

Appendix B

Supplier Information

This section asks you to provide information about your company to us. Please adhere to the following format in responding.

Qualifications and Experience

To warrant consideration for this contract, suppliers and all major subcontractor(s) must submit financial information, including an annual report or audited balance sheets and income statements. For the purposes of this section, "audited" shall mean that a certified public accountant has reviewed the financial reports and has expressed an opinion regarding the fairness of the information reviewed. A major subcontractor will have at least 25 percent participation in the contract measured by dollar amount.

Company Information

1. Full legal company name.
2. Year business started.
3. State of incorporation or headquarters.
4. Are you a United States corporation?
5. Tax identification number.
6. Brief company history.
7. Does another company own you? If so, provide the corporate structure.
8. Do you own other companies? If so, provide the corporate structure.
9. Location of company headquarters.
10. Current number of people employed.
11. Current number of sales locations.
12. Current number of service locations.

13. Are you a public or private corporation?

14. Stock symbol, if publicly traded.

15. Is your company currently involved in any litigation in which an adverse decision might result in a material change in the company's financial position or future viability?

16. Audited company financial data for the last three years (use appendices).

17. Most recent annual report, if public (use appendices).

Current Customer Base and User Groups

18. Total number of customers using the products being proposed for this RFP.

19. Information about any user groups sponsored by your company, or independent groups that are based on your product or company. The list must include location, contact information, and approximate number of members in the group.

Business and Market Focus

20. What is your business focus? What percentage of revenue comes from this focus versus other products or services?

21. In which vertical markets or specific business applications do you specialize?

22. In which vertical market do you have the most customers?

23. In which national or international standards committees do you participate?

24. In which national or international industry consortiums (such as the World Wide Web Consortium) do you participate?

25. How many times and when have you updated your software in the past three years?

26. How many software releases have been delayed in the last three years?

27. Describe the process you have established for your customers to influence product development.

28. How many customer suggestions have you implemented in the past three years?

29. Is there a user group for your products? If so, please provide contact information for the user group.

Company Research and Development

Please provide information about your research and development (R&D) activities as follows:

30. Do you have an R&D group?

31. If so, how many people participate in this group?

32. What percentage of revenue is devoted to R&D?

Supplier References and Site Visit Information

Suppliers and subcontractors shall provide a list of three installations where the supplier's systems are installed in which the work is similar in size, application, and scope to the projects described herein. We will contact these companies and will ask them about your technical capabilities, project management skills, and ongoing support after installation. One of the three reference accounts may be chosen for a site visit by our evaluation team.

To warrant consideration for this contract, suppliers and subcontractor(s) must successfully pass reference checks. Subcontractors with more than 25 percent participation in the project by dollar amount shall provide references. If less than 25 percent, suppliers shall list all subcontractors who participate in the project.

The reference account information must be given in the format listed below.

1. Customer/account name.

2. Street address.

3. City/state/zip code.

4. Contact name/title.

5. Contact telephone number.

6. Contact e-mail address.

7. Summary of project.

8. System description.

9. Description of software installed.

10. Description of hardware installed.

11. Hardware platform.

12. Software platform.

13. Number of users.

14. Date system implementation started.

15. Date system was approved for production.

16. Approximate cost.

17. Details of any products or functionality added to the project after the initial project was completed.

Appendix C

Proposal Preparation Instructions

One of the primary issues concerning RFPs is how to compare the responses in suppliers' proposals with the requirements of the RFP. Suppliers are for the most part earnest in their proposal efforts *but are likely to fall short if left on their own when organizing a proposal.* Sales representatives and sales organizations are not typically organized around producing written documentation and proposals. Even though writing proposals is a necessity, it is rare for a company to have a proposal support group.

Therefore, it is in your best interests to provide suppliers with a roadmap for writing their proposals that requires them to respond in a consistent manner. The instructions provide an outline of the proposal and request suppliers to follow the outline when writing their proposals.

Use this example as a baseline to write your own proposal formatting instructions. Your sections may be different and you may want to expand further the individual sections that follow.

1.1 Introduction

This section of the RFP provides specific instructions regarding the correct format and content of proposals. Proposals shall include all data and information required by this RFP. Failure to conform to the instructions may be grounds for disqualification.

Proposals shall address and track the specific information requested in numerical sequence according to these instructions and shall be consistent with the requirements of this RFP. In preparing the proposal, suppliers should emphasize brief, complete, and factual data in the areas that are set forth in the RFP. Phrases such as "yes," "will comply," "standard procedures will be employed," "industry standards are followed," or, "well-known techniques will be used," will be considered insufficient and grounds for rejection of the proposal. Content and quality of the responses are more important than quantity.

1.2 Physical Presentation of Proposals

1.2.1 Binding

Proposals shall be submitted in three-ring presentation-style binders no more than 2 inches wide. In the event that a proposal exceeds this width, it shall be conveniently separated into multiple binders. If the proposal is divided into multiple binders, a cover sheet shall clearly identify the supplier's identity and proposal section as part of each subsection.

1.2.2 Page Size and Printing

Pages shall be 8½ x 11 inches in size and shall be printed using 1½ line spacing with a minimum of 12-point type. Paper printed on both sides shall be counted as two pages. Photographic reduction of printed material shall not be used to increase the volume of material. A 1-inch minimum margin shall be used on all pages for top, bottom, and sides.

Drawings, charts, graphs, tables, and photographs shall be no larger than foldout size, (8½ x 17 inches), shall fold entirely within the standard page size, and may not include any material on the back. Foldout text pages will not be allowed.

Drawings larger than 8½ x 17 must be rolled, placed in a tube, and delivered along with the proposal. A blank call-out page shall direct the reader to this separately provided illustration, and the illustration must include a figure number, figure title, and cross-reference to the relevant page number in the text of the proposal.

1.2.3 Indexing

The supplier shall include a master table of contents for the overall proposal, which shall identify major paragraphs by section, number, title, and page number. See the following example.

Section 1. Executive Summary

1.1 Introduction	1-1
1.2 Technical Solution	1-5
1.2.1 Overview	1-6
1.2.2 Assumptions	1-7

1.3 Format of Sections

Proposals must be submitted in the format prescribed below. Each section shall be numbered and tabbed with the name of the section on the tab as shown:

```
 _____/  SECTION 1          _____
            |  Executive Summary   |
```

Cover Page

Complete Table of Contents

Transmittal Letter

Section 1–Executive Summary

Section 2–Technical Section

Section 3–Management Section

Section 4–Supplier Corporate Information

Section 5–Supplier Reference Information

Section 6–Additional Information

Section 7–Pricing Section

If appendices are incorporated into your proposal, they shall be numbered and tabbed as follows:

> Appendix A–Sales Contract
>
> Appendix B–Sample Training Program

Instructions for each section are provided below. These instructions are mandatory, and suppliers failing to comply may have their overall evaluation score reduced or their proposal disqualified.

Transmittal Letter

The supplier shall prepare a brief transmittal letter on business stationery with a company logo. An individual authorized to bind the company to all statements in the proposal, including services and pricing, must sign the letter in ink. The letter must accompany the original proposal and each copy.

The transmittal letter should provide all of the following:

1. The supplier's legal company name and addresses for the office submitting the proposal as well as the address of the company's legal headquarters.
2. A statement that the person signing this proposal is authorized to make decisions on the configuration proposed and the prices quoted.
3. The name, title, and telephone number of the person authorized to negotiate the contract on behalf of the organization.
4. The names, titles, and telephone numbers of persons to be contacted for clarification of the proposal if needed.
5. Acknowledgment that the conditions governing this RFP, as stated in the administrative requirements section, have been read and accepted.
6. Acknowledgment of the receipt of any amendments to this RFP (indicate "none" if no amendments were received).
7. Additional information as deemed appropriate.

Section 1—Executive Summary

The executive summary shall serve to familiarize ACME Corporation (AC) executives and evaluators with the key elements and unique features of your proposal by briefly describing what you are proposing and how you intend to accomplish the work. This section must be written with the executive in mind and should not be overly technical but rather concentrate on the business reasons for selecting your proposal.

The executive summary shall contain the following:

1. A summary of your approach to the project, including the main points of all sections. Material presented in this section shall not be considered as meeting any technical requirement. Try to maintain a "features/benefits" style of writing and include the business reasons that make your proposal attractive and different.

2. A master milestone schedule of all major efforts to be undertaken in the program. Dates shall begin as listed in Section X.X of this RFP. The schedule should be a high level summary of the detailed schedule.

3. A list of exceptions taken to this RFP and the reason these exceptions were taken. If an alternative solution or product is being proposed, it should be briefly described.

4. A list of problematic areas that are cause for concern, such as unrealistic deadlines, incompatible technologies, or overly tight specifications. Any request to delete, change, or relax a requirement must be fully supported in this section. Suppliers will not be evaluated on this paragraph and cannot lose evaluation points by listing areas of concern. These concerns will be addressed with the successful supplier prior to the contract negotiation.

5. A discussion of the price proposal. Suppliers shall submit firm, fixed pricing for this contract. If assumptions have been made on behalf of AC to facilitate pricing or if special pricing is being offered, including discounts or products bundled to represent a value purchase, suppliers shall describe these special pricing arrangements. If there

are other special offers that AC is not aware of but may qualify for, suppliers should describe the offer and the time frame for purchasing that service or product.

(Note: If you require pricing to be submitted under separate cover, request suppliers not to include the pricing information in the executive summary.)

Section 2–Technical Section

The technical proposal shall consist of complete responses to all requirements listed in the technical section. Responses shall follow the outline of the technical section and refer to each paragraph that is being addressed.

Suppliers are encouraged to answer all requirements without reference to manuals, data sheets, product brochures, or other supporting material. When necessary, suppliers may support answers by reference to other material, but answers should be understandable without reading the supporting material. Answers such as "See Appendix A, Technical Manual" will be marked as nonresponsive. Any supporting material cited in an answer must be referenced by appendix, name of document, and page(s) to be reviewed.

Section 3–Management Section

In this section the supplier shall provide information organized into the following sections.

Project management. Suppliers shall present their company's approach and ability to control and integrate the system proposed. Specifically, they shall describe their company's organizational structure, listing all key personnel functions. More consideration will be given to suppliers who can list personnel by name, placement in the project structure, title, qualifications, and experience.

Maintenance. Suppliers shall provide a detailed description of all maintenance activities, typical daily or monthly support activities, and principal period of maintenance, together with an organizational chart of their headquarters support operation, the proposed support organization for this project, and the escalation procedures for reporting problems. Suppliers shall follow the requirements as listed in the maintenance section.

Education and training. Suppliers shall provide a detailed description of all education and training required for this project. This section shall include an introduction that justifies the training programs described, explains the basic approach taken, provides an organization chart of the headquarters education operation and an organization chart for this project, and describes the benefits for AC.

Section 4–Supplier Corporate Information

Suppliers shall provide a brief description of the overall organization of their company, including headquarters organization, divisions, and operations. This description shall note how long the company has been in operation and whether it is the subsidiary of a parent company or is itself the parent company of other subsidiaries.

Suppliers shall provide a description of their major facilities, unique or special manufacturing equipment, and any other facilities that will provide support for this program.

Suppliers shall also include subcontracting information in this section if subcontractors are being employed. Subcontractors shall be named and their role in the project briefly described.

Section 5–Supplier Reference Information

Suppliers shall include a minimum of three related contracts awarded within the last three years. The supplier shall provide a synopsis of each contract and discuss its relevance to this project and proposal.

Section 6–Additional Information

Suppliers may submit additional information that is relevant but was not requested in the RFP. This information should clarify or enhance the proposal or provide information about areas in the RFP that are deficient and need to be corrected.

Section 7–Pricing Section

Suppliers are to provide firm, fixed-price proposals for this project, including all prices for hardware, software, installation, training, and project management as listed below.

The pricing proposal should list these items in the same order. Suppliers are encouraged to provide explanations where needed for clarification. If a price is based on an assumption made by the supplier, the assumption should be explained in this section, or there should be a reference to an explanation in the supplier's technical proposal.

These instructions are intended to assist suppliers in submitting pricing data. Compliance with these instructions is mandatory. Failure to comply will result in disqualification of the proposal.

Bidders are cautioned against submitting a single price without adequate detail. AC requires all costs to be broken down into categories and subcategories. Each of the individual cost components must be a line item in each of the cost tables. A pricing table, as shown in Table C.1, should be provided with information on the following:

- ❑ product application software
- ❑ hardware
- ❑ software
- ❑ maintenance
- ❑ training
- ❑ documentation
- ❑ project management
- ❑ travel expenses

Table C.1   Sample Pricing Table

Product Description	Qty	Unit Cost	Extended Cost	Annual Maintenance	Annual License
Hardware					
Application server					
Data server					
Communication server					
Subtotal					
Software					
System software					
Servers					
Application software					
Subtotal					
Project Management					
Development/integration					
Staffing					
Travel					
Training class – admin					
Training class – tech					
Training class – user					
Standard documentation					
Subtotal					
Grand total					
Example only; supplier to complete.					

Appendix D

Budget Planning and Investment Analysis

Introduction

It is a rare exception when a project is authorized without a budget. The problem that the RFP team typically faces is how to establish the budget initially and how to ensure that it remains credible once it is established. It is possible simply to poll vendors and ask the cost of their equipment, but it is generally not that easy because you also need to understand the installation charges and the ongoing maintenance costs before you can determine whether the return on investment analysis will be positive enough to make your project attractive to your management.

Companies typically compare a capital acquisition project against all of the projects vying for company funding. In addition to being compared against each other, the projects may also meet or exceed what a company will make on its capital if the capital is left in current investment programs.

The following brief review of the cost justification process is meant only as a general guideline. Each company should follow its own process and guidelines.

Many projects are funded because of the savings they can generate. If the project investment costs can be repaid through capital savings, then the project is a good candidate to receive funding. However, depending on the project itself and whether equipment is being purchased, the "payback" time is generally required to be within two years—faster is considered better. The payback time might be only one of the criteria for capital acquisitions; other financial indicators such as net present value (NPV) and return on investment (ROI) might also be considered.

Prior to beginning work, the project leader should work with the company's financial group, typically the chief financial officer (CFO), to understand what information is needed and how projects are evaluated from a financial point of view. The project leader should also be in agreement with the CFO concerning what is being measured and how that measure is calculated.

All of the work compiled for the cost justification can be used later to develop a credible project budget and technical requirements section, assuming the cost justification is positive and the project moves forward. Other sections of the study can be sanitized and used as background information in the RFP appendices.

Cost justifications typically fall into two primary categories. The first is hard dollar savings, whereby the new project allows a company to realize actual cost reductions in its operating budget. For example, after a project is complete, the department payroll might be reduced from $2 million per year to $1 million per year. This $1 million reduction represents actual savings to the company. Hard dollar savings may be identified in the following areas:

- reduction in personnel
- business operating costs (photocopying, postal mailing, telephone, fewer support personnel such as human resources [HR], information technology [IT])
- reduction in facilities costs (by selling a building or averting costs by not renewing a lease)
- reduction in computer system costs (fewer computers, more efficient computers, less IT overhead)

The second type of cost justification yields soft dollar savings, whereby benefits are realized but cannot easily be translated into verifiable dollar amounts. For example, a new customer support system may improve your customer service without reducing overall operating costs for the department. Soft dollar savings may be identified in the following areas:

- improved customer service
- increased competitive advantage

❑ better and faster access to information

❑ faster internal communications

While hard dollar savings are preferred because you can calculate the system's payback time, soft dollar savings can also be persuasive. How many angry customers can you tolerate, how do unhappy employees affect the company spirit, and how do you not justify a system that will give you a competitive advantage? (But it may take 12 to 18 months before you realize whether it actually works or not.)

An example of a soft dollar presentation may go something like this:

> Each person using our corporate Intranet takes approximately two minutes to locate the information that he or she is looking for. Out of 10,000 employees, approximately 3,500 use the Intranet *once* each day. The average cost per hour for each employee is calculated at $45 per hour, or $0.75 per minute. The cost of locating information manually is
>
> > 0.75/hr*2 min = 1.50*3,500 = $5,250 per day
> >
> > $5,250/day*252 work days = $1,323,000 per year
>
> Based on our information from testing an Intranet search engine, we believe that we can save each user one minute of search time, resulting in a savings of $661,500 per year ($1,323,000/2 = $661,500). The Intranet search engine being considered costs $400,000 for the software and implementation. Adding one person to our IT department costs $60,000 a year, and associated implementation costs total an additional $140,000. The total first-year cost of implementing the search engine is $600,000, thus resulting in a payback time of just 12 months. Annual savings thereafter are about $600,000 taking into account the additional personnel cost of $60,000.

As you can see, this argument all sounds very good, and the numbers look impressive—especially, goes the sales pitch, if you think that many people will use the Intranet more than once per day and that as they find the Intranet easier to use and navigate, more users will take advantage of it.

However, to put things into perspective, does saving one user one minute in an eight-hour day (480 minutes) even remotely provide any gains in efficiency?

Can one person effectively use that one minute to do other work? This type of soft dollar savings argument is made every day to corporate management and is often used successfully to win approval to purchase products.

Cost Justification Analysis (CJA) Process

The CJA process is a method of gathering data from current operational processes and comparing that data against a proposed system's processes and costs. The projected differences are viewed over a period of time, and the result shows whether your new system is a good investment.

For example, think of the improvements companies have made because of one simple tool: the spreadsheet. In years past it took hundreds of hours and several people, including a special typist and specialized typewriter, to create a complex company spreadsheet. Today, similar work may take only a few hours and actually yield better and more accurate results. Hence, you not only save time and resources, you get a better finished product. This is the holy grail of cost justifications.

The cost-benefit analysis needs to be accomplished with as much accuracy as possible. It is the financial foundation upon which your project is built, and it will become the basis for the long-term evaluation of the project.

Figure D.1 is a diagram of the basic CJA process. It starts with analyzing current operations to determine what work functions are performed and ends with the derived cost-benefit analysis.

Current Operations
The baseline for all of the CJA work hinges on establishing an accurate accounting of current operations. These costs include

- number of personnel
- salary and benefits

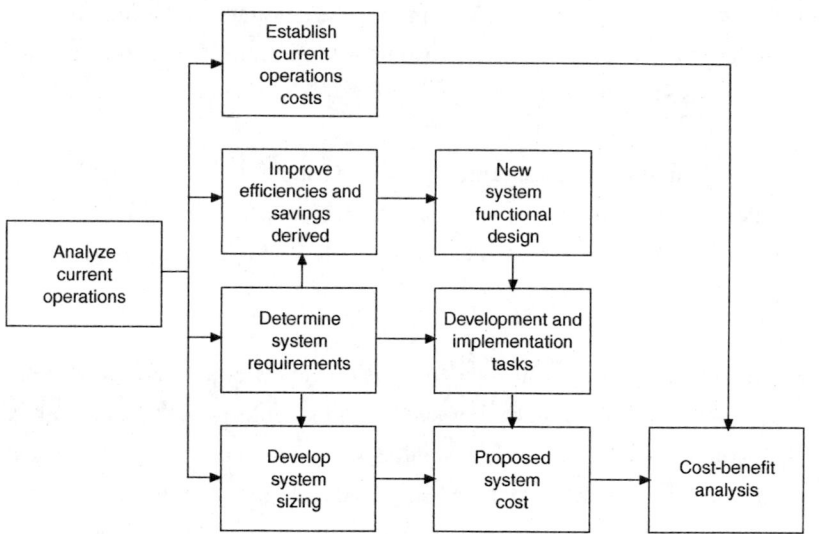

Figure D.1   Cost Justification Analysis

- ❏ facilities rentals and maintenance
- ❏ resources (mainframe computer usage)
- ❏ other miscellaneous identifiable costs that will be associated with the work that is going to be improved upon

Once the costs of running a department have been determined, the CJA task is to document and understand each step in the work process that is going to be the subject of the study.

Let's use an insurance claims-processing group as a model for our study. In a typical claims process, the claim may be received via mail, courier, or fax and may even be posted to a database automatically. Once a claim is received, it has to be processed, that is, it is not automatically paid but is reviewed by certain people who may approve or question the claim and the amount.

One of the key elements in understanding current operations is interviewing the people who perform the work. For each person who works with the claim, two basic types of information need to be established: (1) each step in the work they do to resolve a claim; (2) the amount of time required to complete each step; and (3) what resources (mainframe) and what consumables are used in the process.

Table D.1 shows the current time spent on a function compared with the projected time spent doing the same work with a faster, better, and cheaper system. For example, a customer service clerk might have duties as outlined in the table.

For this clerk, we would then try to envision how the reengineered system would affect his or her work. For task 1, for example, some filing organization would still be needed, but a significant amount could be accomplished by the new system. We may then estimate that 40 percent of task 1 can be automated, reducing the percentage of time spent on that task from 25 percent to 15 percent. For task 2, we might estimate that the new system will reduce both the number of calls (claims are paid faster) and the amount of time spent answering requests. Therefore, we can reduce task 2 by 60 percent. This process needs to be repeated for each task.

The end result of this study is that if there were eight clerks in the current operations, their working time would be reduced by 50 percent. This result

Table D.1   Current versus Projected Time Spent on Tasks

Tasks	Current percentage of time spent on task	Projected percentage of time spent on task
Organize new claims and file	25%	15%
Respond to customer questions	25%	10%
Photocopy and pass information to adjusters	40%	15%
General support	10%	10%
Total	**100**	**50**

can be viewed in one of two ways. On the one hand, if the new system was implemented, it would enable only four clerks to handle the present volume of work, so the number of clerks could be reduced by 50 percent. On the other hand, for companies undergoing high growth, the new system would allow the current number of clerks to handle approximately 50 percent more work before additional clerks need to be hired (an "aversion cost" item).

Being able to calculate the gains and efficiencies requires a thorough understanding of the new system and the potential ability to reengineer a process. Some steps in a process may never be eliminated, for political or marketing reasons, whereas other steps can be totally eliminated. For example, a company could have an automated voice response system for all calls but choose to continue employing someone to answer the phone and put the call into the voice response system if the person being called is not available.

Strawman System Architecture: System Sizing

Once the basic work has been documented and the reengineering possibilities are becoming evident, the next step is to begin to establish the components of the new system. This is typically called strawman architecture, because it allows you to identify and list all of the system hardware, software, and application software needed for the new system. From this strawman, you will also begin to build your "estimated" budget for the project.

The system architecture is dependent on the information that results from the first step. The basic number of workstations and other components can be derived from the reengineered processes and workflows—in the preceding insurance example we can reduce the clerical count from eight to four. As a result, we can correspondingly reduce all system expenses for such things as computer workstations, software, perhaps even the size of the server if significant processing reductions are being made.

This type of thinking will allow the team to develop the equipment list and system software accurately. Once this list is compiled, pricing estimates can be assigned to the equipment.

Equipment Pricing

Pricing is a straightforward exercise that involves working with established vendors or asking selected vendors to provide system pricing. Several vendors should be polled and an average price developed. For example, data servers, workstations, scanners, and printers all have multiple sources.

It will be harder to obtain an average price for the system software, since software vendors' pricing has a wider range than that of hardware vendors. However, by contacting potential vendors and using the information from the operations analysis, the application software supplier should be able to provide pricing. Again, these prices should be averaged if possible and the average price used in the model.

Estimating the amount of development time required to build the application will be the most difficult step in this pricing effort. Although software vendors and system integrators typically provide this service, the project team can elect to assume this role. If the development is to be done in-house, additional costs such as training may need to be calculated. *This component of the cost model should not be ignored, because it can equal or surpass the cost of the equipment.*

System implementation involves facilities costs, hardware and software, and the software application. Training, documentation, maintenance and support, and projected long-term costs for consumable supplies must also be included.

Financial Indicators

Once all of the above information has been developed and estimated, all of the numbers can be totaled and a financial analysis performed. The three most commonly used indicators for capital acquisition projects are payback period, NPV, and ROI.

Payback Period

The payback period is the time required to recoup the initial investment in the system. For example, if the system cost is $500,000 and the system provides a financial benefit of $250,000 per year, the system would have a payback of two years. From a financial point of view, the sooner the payback, the greater the value of the project. Projects are not decided on this indicator alone, however, because payback does not take into account the time value of the investment.

NPV

NPV is expressed in dollars as the difference between the present value of cash inflows (savings) over the life of the project (typically three or five years are used, depending on the type of project) and the initial investment. The general rule is that if the NPV is positive, the investment is sound. (But remember, other competing projects may have a better NPV and ROI than your project.)

ROI

ROI is a formula that calculates a percentage equal to an interest rate. Generally, the ROI of the project is compared with the company's required internal rate of return on its capital. The general rule is that if the ROI is equal to or greater than the internal cost of money, then the project is sound.

Your CFO might also ask to see the projected cash flow, the average annual savings, or other internal measurements that are normally used to evaluate a project.

After the CJA has been completed, it is possible to develop and test a number of possibilities. For example, what if the justification turned out negative? Using the work performed, the project team should be able to pinpoint the area(s) that were not providing a positive return and project what would be needed to change the situation for those deficient areas and make the overall project positive.

In addition to providing a sound financial foundation for the project, the CJA model provides two essential numbers needed to proceed to the next phase of the project, which is to develop and write an RFP.

The first essential number is the project budget. This CJA study gives an overall estimated budget for the project. As a bonus, if the budget is too high, you have all the information needed to study where project costs can be reduced. Alternatively, you also have all the materials to convince your CFO that even though the projected budget is too high, the project pays for itself and should therefore be approved.

The second essential number is the estimated cost of individual materials (hardware and software) and time (development and implementation) for the project. Thus, when you are reviewing vendor pricing proposals, do so with an established set of figures so that you can judge whether the prices are out of line. If they are, the project team should be able to identify where the discrepancies are and question the vendor about those specific areas.

CJA Summary

The three areas of budget analysis and cost justification, process reengineering, and equipment identification are important steps to be considered when developing the requirements for a system RFP. All three are somewhat intertwined and need to be considered together. The work done during the CJA will help the team understand whether simple or complex reengineering will be financially sound. Reengineering and conversion must be accomplished to some degree, but how far should the project team go, and on what basis should they make a decision? Carrying out the CJA will help the team understand these issues and develop a sound and defensible position.

These interrelated issues depend on many variables that might not be intuitively obvious to the project team, such as the company's financial position, the team's experience, the project's complexity, and the technology.

Given these variables, there should be consideration for the accuracy of the project analysis. For example, the CJA may be considered to be accurate within 20 percent. Therefore, a certain amount of risk is involved in going ahead with the project.

Once the detailed analysis has been accomplished and you are certain that you have worked at a level of detail that will satisfy your management team, the data can be manipulated and a number of "what if" scenarios can be prepared. For example, what if the development software costs are off by a factor of 35 percent? How will that affect the investment? What if hardware prices and quantities are underestimated? How much incremental change can the model stand before the investment turns negative? What will it take to turn a negative analysis into a positive one?

Beyond ROI; Measuring Project Results

Part of the life cycle for a system project should be the continual measurement of gains and efficiencies achieved. In many cases, a reengineering project will be approved based on some anticipated gains in business efficiency, and these gains provide the ROI that pays for the system costs. If the project began by analyzing the potential benefits of reengineering a business process, then at some point after installation those gains should be measurable.

If the project is based on a positive CJA, then the groundwork for the post-implementation study is already laid, and the tools for measuring results are already available. If the project is not based on a CJA, it may be difficult to measure gains, since there is no benchmark against which to measure.

The easy answer is to review the new system against the original cost justification and the projected savings. Was the 35,000 square feet of floor space recovered? Were 20 FTEs (full-time equivalents) released or reassigned as predicted? Is paper usage down from 500,000 sheets per month to 10,000? Are business processes completed faster, for example, is a claim resolved in three working days instead of 15? Can you process a contract in one day instead of three days? Have you received fewer customer complaints since the new system was brought on board? Have you started to influence the rate of customer attrition?

The answers to these questions are relatively easy to determine and will provide at least an indication that the newly installed system is working as expected. However, what if your system purchase is not based on retrieving floor space, or cutting printing costs, or eliminating FTEs? What if your system purchase is based purely on soft dollar benefits such as improving customer service or providing new work processes that were not previously used? What if the new system is not based on previous processes?

Intangible benefits are difficult to prove or disprove and even harder to measure. How do you know that employee morale has improved as a result of the new system and is responsible for an 8 percent decrease in employee absenteeism? How do you measure customer satisfaction in dollars, and more important, how do you attribute the increase (or decrease) to the new processes and systems?

Measurement of the life-cycle benefits of a system must be factored into the overall CJA.

The results of installing a new system may not become evident for at least a year and possibly longer. If a complete overhaul of the business is undertaken, the changes will cause short-term increases in problems, which may cause a temporary spike in the work for a department. If the measurements are conducted before the "electronic dust" has settled, the conclusions will be false.

For example, if the current company benefits system is replaced, the new system's "customers" may respond with increased questions about benefits (they were reminded about a question previously forgotten), confusion about new forms and procedures, or simple inquisitiveness about the change.

This increased activity should not be regarded as a general rise in questions (work) from 100 per day to 150 per day. The increase is temporary due to the change itself, and once the new processes begin to work, the number of daily questions should drop based on the better procedures and systems now in place. If the number of questions does not drop or goes up, the new system should be reviewed to determine why, but at least the benchmark now tells you where you are starting from.

A second example of intangible benefits would be gains realized due to increased customer satisfaction. This type of gain or loss might be calculable only after years of continual monitoring, and in any event must be based on a previous understanding of customer satisfaction. For example, customer turnover may have been previously established at 30 percent per year by reviewing the company's records for the past five years. Turnover may have been traced in part to poor customer services such as lack of, delayed, or inadequate response. It may require as much as two years or more before the new customer turnover percentage can be analyzed due to annual contract renewals and other factors. And it might take several years before it can be established that customer turnover has been reduced as a result of the new system.

As noted, measurement of results should be planned for as part of the original project. A proper baseline must be established; the original figures should be maintained and kept available for several years, and the appropriate resources must be dedicated to maintaining the information needed for a new analysis. A side benefit to revisiting the cost-benefit analysis is that mid-course corrections may be made based on new data, leading to further process improvement.

Conclusion

This brief explanation of CJA should have provided you with an overview of the process itself and the resulting benefits. We suggest that before starting your analysis, you consult with your financial department and explain what you are going to do and what is the intended result. Your CFO may have additional ROI indicators that should be considered at the conclusion of the study. Certain other information will be required from the financial staff, such as your company's cost of money, depreciation method, and depreciation time.

If you are undertaking a project that is based on long-term improvements, be prepared to assign someone to ensure that measurements are conducted at the proper intervals and their results considered in some meaningful way.

The work accomplished will provide you with an insight into your company's operations that perhaps few managers will share. Based on this knowledge, and the benefits that can be achieved through new technology or systems, the detailed data behind the numbers will become a solid foundation for your system request.

Appendix E

Nondisclosure Agreement

The nondisclosure agreement (NDA) that follows is an example only and should not be used in its current version. If you require an NDA to accompany your RFP, request one from your legal department. NDAs can be of varying types and may have different wording and clauses depending on your industry, company, and location.

The NDA in this example is a mutual NDA, that is, one that allows you to share confidential information with the vendor and the vendor to share confidential information with you under the terms of this agreement. A second type of NDA allows the information to be shared only in one direction.

Nondisclosure Agreement

This Mutual Nondisclosure Agreement (the "Agreement") is entered into as of this ___ day of _____, 200X by and between _____, a California corporation (the "Company"), and _____ ("XXX").

1. <u>Definition of Recipient.</u> For purposes of this Agreement, the term "Recipient" shall mean the Company with respect to Confidential Information (as defined below) supplied hereunder by XXX and XXX as to Confidential Information supplied hereunder by the Company.

2. <u>Purpose.</u> The Company and XXX wish to explore a possible business relationship pursuant to which each party may disclose its Confidential Information to the other party. This Agreement is intended to bind Recipient and prevent it from disclosing the Confidential Information of the other party as herein provided or from using the Confidential

Company _____   1 of 7   Vendor _____

Information for purposes other than evaluation of the business relationship described in Section 4(b) below.

3. Definition. "Confidential Information" means any information, technical data, or know-how, including, without limitation, that which relates to research, products, services, customers, markets, developments, inventions, processes, designs, drawings, engineering, marketing, or finances of the disclosing party, which Confidential Information, to the extent practical, shall be disclosed in documentary or tangible form marked "Confidential." In the case of disclosures in nondocumentary form made orally or by visual inspection, the disclosing party shall have the right, or if requested by Recipient, the obligation to confirm in writing within sixty (60) days after the disclosure is made, the fact that such information is confidential and protected hereunder. The amount and type of Confidential Information to be disclosed is completely within the sole discretion of each party. Confidential Information does not include information, technical data or know-how which (i) at the time of disclosure, is available to the general public; or (ii) at a later date, becomes available to the general public through no fault of Recipient and then only after such later date; or (iii) Recipient can demonstrate by Recipient's files and records was in its possession before receipt; or (iv) is disclosed to Recipient without restriction on disclosure by a third party who had the lawful right to disclose such information; or (v) is disclosed by Recipient with the prior written approval of the disclosing party; or (vi) is disclosed pursuant to a court order or is otherwise required by law to be disclosed; provided that Recipient has notified the disclosing party immediately upon learning of the possibility of any such court order or legal requirement and has given the disclosing party a reasonable opportunity (and cooperate with disclosing party) to contest or limit the scope of such required disclosure (including application for a protective order). Information shall not be deemed to be available to the general public for the purposes of the above

Company _____   2 of 7   Vendor _____

exclusions from the definition of Confidential Information (x) merely because it is embraced by more general information in the prior possession of Recipient or of others, or (y) merely because it is expressed in public literature in general terms not specifically in accordance with the Confidential Information.

4. <u>Nondisclosure and Nonuse of Confidential Information.</u>

   (a) Recipient agrees not to disclose the Confidential Information disclosed to it by the other party to third parties or to Recipient's employees except employees who are required to have the Confidential Information in order to carry out the contemplated purposes described in paragraph 4(b) below. Each party has had or will have employees to whom Confidential Information of the other party is disclosed sign a nondisclosure agreement, prior to such disclosure, in content substantially similar to this Agreement and will notify the other party in writing of the names of the persons who have signed such agreements promptly after such agreements are signed. Each party agrees that it will take all reasonable steps to protect the secrecy of and avoid disclosure or use of Confidential Information of the other party in order to prevent it from falling into the public domain or the possession of unauthorized persons which shall include the highest degree of care that Recipient utilizes to protect its own Confidential Information of similar nature. Recipient shall require each of its employees to whom Confidential Information is disclosed to hold such Confidential Information in confidence and not to disclose or, except in accordance with the terms hereof, use such Confidential Information. Each party agrees to notify the other party in writing of any misuse or misappropriation of such Confidential Information of the other party which may come to its attention.

   (b) Recipient further agrees not to use the Confidential Information provided to it by the other party for any purposes other than to

Company _____   3 of 7   Vendor _____

evaluate the possibility of entering into a business relationship with the other party regarding

_____.

5. <u>Return of Materials</u>. Any materials or documents which have been furnished to Recipient by the disclosing party shall be promptly returned, accompanied by all copies of such documentation and a certificate from an officer of the Recipient stating that the Recipient has fully complied with this Section 5, within five (5) days after receipt by Recipient of a written notice from the disclosing party requesting the return of the disclosing party's Confidential Information.

6. <u>No Warranty</u>. All information is provided "AS IS" and without any warranty, express, implied or otherwise, including but not limited to, any warranties regarding its accuracy, performance or noninfringement of third party rights, or its merchantability or fitness for a particular purpose. In no event shall the disclosing party be liable to Recipient for direct, special, incidental, consequential, or punitive damages of any kind, including lost profits, by reason of any use by the Recipient of any Confidential Information.

7. <u>No Rights Granted</u>. Nothing in this Agreement is intended to grant any rights under any patent, trade secret, or copyright of the disclosing party to Recipient, nor shall this Agreement grant Recipient any rights in or to the disclosing party's Confidential Information, except the limited right to review such Confidential Information solely for the purpose of determining whether to enter into the proposed business relationship between the parties.

8. <u>Continuing Obligation</u>. Whether or not the business relationship described in paragraph 4(b) is consummated, unless otherwise mutually

Company _____ 4 of 7 Vendor _____

agreed in writing, Recipient's nondisclosure and nonuse obligations hereunder with respect to each item of Confidential Information shall terminate _____ (__) years from the date of the receipt thereof by Recipient.

9. <u>Governing Law and Jurisdiction</u>. This Agreement shall be governed by and construed under the laws of the State of California. The federal and state courts within the State of California shall have exclusive jurisdiction to adjudicate any dispute arising out of this Agreement. XXX hereby consents to jurisdiction and venue in the state and federal courts sitting in the State of California, and to accept service of process by United States certified or registered mail, return receipt requested, or by any other methods authorized by California law.

10. <u>Remedies</u>. Each party agrees that its obligations hereunder are necessary and reasonable in order to protect the other party and the other party's business, and expressly agrees that monetary damages would be inadequate to compensate the other party for any breach of any covenant or agreement set forth herein. Accordingly, each party agrees and acknowledges that any such violation or threatened violation will cause irreparable injury to the other party and that, in addition to any other remedies that may be available, in law, in equity or otherwise, the other party shall be entitled to obtain injunctive relief against the breach or threatened breach of this Agreement or the continuation of any such breach, without the necessity of proving actual damages.

11. <u>Attorneys' Fees</u>. If either party brings an action to enforce the provisions of this Agreement, the prevailing party (including a party who agrees to dismiss an action upon payment of sums allegedly due, or who obtains substantially the relief sought) shall be entitled to attorneys' fees and court costs.

Company _____   5 of 7   Vendor _____

12. <u>Miscellaneous</u>. This Agreement shall be binding upon and for the benefit of the undersigned parties, their successors and assigns, provided Confidential Information of the disclosing party may not be assigned or transferred, by operation of law or otherwise, without the prior written consent of the disclosing party. Failure to enforce any provision of this Agreement shall not constitute a waiver of any term hereof. Nothing contained in this Agreement shall be deemed to obligate either party to negotiate the terms of the proposed business relationship in good faith or otherwise.

13. <u>Publicity</u>. Both parties agree that Recipient will not, without the prior written consent of the disclosing party, disclose to any person the fact that the Confidential Information of the disclosing party has been made available to it, that discussions or negotiations are taking place concerning the possible business relationship, or any of the terms, conditions, or other facts with respect thereto (including the status thereof), unless such disclosure is required or advisable under law and then only with as much prior written notice to the disclosing party as is practicable under the circumstances.

14. <u>No Waiver</u>. No waiver of a breach of any provision of this Agreement shall constitute a waiver of any prior, concurrent or subsequent breach of the same or any other provision hereof, and no waiver shall be effective unless granted in writing and signed by an authorized representative of the waiving party.

15. <u>Partial Invalidity</u>. If any provision of this Agreement is held by a court of competent jurisdiction to be illegal, invalid, or unenforceable, the other provisions shall remain in full force and effect, and the illegal, invalid, or unenforceable provision shall be deemed replaced by a legal, valid, and enforceable provision that most nearly reflects the intent of the parties in entering into this Agreement.

Company _____   6 of 7   Vendor _____

16. <u>Interpretation</u>. Section headings are used in this Agreement for convenience of reference only and shall not affect the meaning of any provision of this Agreement. This Agreement is in the English language only, which language shall be controlling in all respects, and all versions hereof in any other language shall be for accommodation only and shall not be binding upon the parties hereto. All communications and notices to be made or given pursuant to this Agreement shall be in the English language, and all dollar amounts referenced herein or payable pursuant hereto refer to and shall be made in United States dollars.

17. <u>Entire Agreement</u>. This Agreement contains the entire agreement of the parties with respect to the subject matter hereof and supersedes all prior and contemporaneous communications, understandings, and agreements. This Agreement shall not be amended other than in writing signed by the Company and XXX.

COMPANY: XXX:

_____   _____

By: _____   By: _____

Title: _____   Title: _____

Appendix F

Proprietary Notice

Proprietary and Confidential Information Notice

This RFP contains proprietary and confidential information of (YOUR NAME), which is provided for the sole purpose of permitting the recipient to respond to the RFP submitted herewith. In consideration of receipt of this RFP, the recipient agrees to maintain such information in confidence and not to reproduce or otherwise disclose this information to any person outside the group directly responsible for responding to its contents. There is no obligation to maintain the confidentiality of any information that was known to the recipient prior to receipt of such information from (YOUR NAME), or becomes publicly known through no fault of the recipient, or is received without obligation of confidentiality from a third party owing no obligation of confidentiality to (YOUR NAME).

Appendix G

Notice of Intent to Bid

Intent to Bid

RFP Title _____

Vendors must complete and return this form within the time specified in the
RFP schedule in the administrative section. Vendors who do not return this
form will be disqualified from further participation. The undersigned
authorized person has read all RFP instructions and requirements and will
submit a proposal in compliance with those instructions. Return this form
to the name and address listed in the administrative section.

Will you be responding to this RFP?   Yes   No

Company Name: _____

Name: _____ Title: _____

Address: _____

_____

_____

_____

Telephone: _____ Fax: _____

E-mail: _____ Web site: _____

If not responding, reason for not doing so: _____

_____

I will attend the bidders' conference: Yes   No

Names of personnel attending:

1. _____

2. _____

Signature: _____

Date: _____

Appendix H

Questions and Answers

Questions and Answers for the ACME Intranet Project

Question Set #1, April 15, 20xx

This is the first set of questions being answered. Vendors are reminded that April 30, 20xx is the final deadline for questions.

Question 1:

Is this project officially funded, and what is the funded amount?

Answer:

This project has an established budget, which will not be revealed.

Question 2:

Will you list all of the vendors who were present at the vendors' conference?

Answer:

No

Question 3:

In reviewing the live test demonstration requirements, it appears that ACME will provide the data server and the connection to the Internet. Please confirm.

Answer:

ACME will provide a data server and Internet connection. Please review paragraph 4.3.11.

Question 4:

How many people will be logged into the system simultaneously?

Answer:

ACME has 10,000 employees; we estimate that at any given time during normal business hours 1,000 employees will be logged in and using the system. Our research shows that the average employee stays online for approximately eight minutes.

Appendix I

Compliance Matrix

Suppliers shall create a compliance matrix and list all requirements
responded to as shown in the example below. "Meets" indicates that you
fully meet the requirement, "Partially Meets" indicates that you meet the
requirement but not fully, and "Does Not Meet" indicates that you do not
meet any part of the requirements. You may use the comment column, if
necessary, for additional information.

Table I.1   Supplier's Compliance Matrix

Requirement	Meets	Partially Meets	Does Not Meet	Comment
5.1 General requirements	X			
5.1.1 Overview	X			
5.1.2 Application development	X			
.				
.				
.				
5.3.1 Workstation	X			
5.3.1 #1		X		
5.3.1 #2	X			
5.3.1 #3	X			
5.3.1 #4			X	
.				
.				
.				

Appendix J

Preliminary Evaluation Checklist

Vendor's name: _____

Item	Yes	No	Description
1			Notice of intent to bid received
2			Proposal received on time
3			Proposal in accordance with RFP preparation instructions
4			Proper number of paper copies received
5			Electronic copy received and format checked
6			Proposal valid for 90 days
7			No major exceptions taken
8			Annual report included
9			Copy of equipment manual included
10			Vendor agreeable to performing live test demonstration
11			Four references provided
12			Vendor agreeable to factory visit and meeting with senior management
13			Vendor confirmed as prime contractor
14			Vendor agreeable to production schedule
15			Vendor agreeable to uptime and performance schedules

Appendix K

RFP Reverse Planning Calendar

Item	Start Date	End Date	Activity Description
1	July 20		Start project.
2	July 17		Sign contract.
3	July 6	July 16	Negotiate contract.
4	July 6		Select a winning proposal/vendor.
	July 5		Make management presentation for selection.
	June 29	July 3	Review all reference notes and evaluation notes and write a final selection report.
5	June 26	June 27	Conduct factory tour.
6	June 22	June 24	Hold vendors' demonstrations.
7	June 18	June 20	Conduct reference site visit.
8	June 16		Make reference calls.
9	June 15		Select the shortlist; do a close reading of proposals.
10	June 14		Wrap up any final vendor questions for shortlist.
11	June 13		Hold second evaluation meeting and eliminate more vendors.
1	June 9	June 12	Read second-round proposals; fill in evaluation form.
	June 8	June 8	Hold first evaluation meeting and eliminate vendors.
	June 2	June 7	Read first round of proposals.
	June 1	June 1	Eliminate first proposals.
	May 30		**Proposals Due**. Receive proposals and check them for completeness.
	May 15		Question cutoff.
	April 27		Vendors' conference.

continued

Item	Start Date	End Date	Activity Description
	April 20		**RFP Sent**
	April 18		Post final RFP to Web site.
	April 18	April 19	Print RFP, bind, and prepare for sending.
	April 15	April 17	Final QA on RFP and make any corrections.
	April 15		Complete RFP.
	April 9	April 14	Complete RFP evaluation criteria.
	April 6	April 9	Complete RFP draft and conduct first review.
	Mar 6	April 5	Start writing RFP.
	Mar 6	Mar 6	Allocate writing assignments.
	Mar 5	Mar 5	Start RFP.
	Mar 4	Mar 4	Have project approved by management.
	Mar 1	Mar 3	Establish project budget.
	Feb 8	Feb 28	Vendor's reviewed and team education.
	Feb 6	Feb 8	Approve requirements.
	Feb 1	Feb 5	Report on requirements.
	Jan 3	Jan 30	Complete requirements analysis.
	Jan 2		Start project.

Index